HOW TO
HAVE YOUR
HIT
P SONG
UBLISHED

"Jay Warner has written a book that finally explains to my writers and artists the answers about publishing I have never been able to come up with."

—BILL HALVERSON
Producer/engineer of Crosby, Stills & Nash

"Finally, a practical book on the publishing business of today. Jay Warner doesn't miss a trick."

—AL De LORY
Two-time Grammy winner and producer of Glen Campbell's "By The Time I Get To Phoenix."

"The best legitimate guide for songwriters and background scorers. I recommend it highly."

—VIC MIZZY
Vice President Songwriters Guild of America

"Instead of just another book for the music shelf, Jay Warner's book is one to keep handy on the desk. He has done a great service to every member of the music community."

—ARTHUR HAMILTON
Vice President, ASCAP

"All the 'savy' that starting songwriters need to help find their way."

—JOHANNA VAGODA
Attorney for Stevie Wonder

"An indispensable guide for songwriters looking for a step-by-step approach to successfully market their songs. Should be required reading for all songwriters."

—FLIP BLACK
Vice President, American Song Festival

"This is THE book—make that the BIBLE—for songwriters and publishers! Great book—I liked it so much I'm keeping Jay's copy."

—BILL CUOMO
Co-writer of the #1 Steve Perry Hit "Oh Sherrie"

HOW TO HAVE YOUR
HIT
SONG
PUBLISHED

Jay Warner

HAL LEONARD BOOKS

Library of Congress Cataloging-in-Publication Data

Warner, Jay.
    How to have your hit song published.

    Includes indexes.
        1. Popular music--1981-   --Writing and publishing.
    I. Title.
MT67.W26 1988   784.5'0028   87-37830
ISBN O-88188-779-X

DEDICATION

To Mom, Dad, Jonathan and Jackie

ACKNOWLEDGEMENTS

My sincerest thanks and appreciation to those who took time to let me enter their lives, cling to their encouragement and partake of their knowledge and experience so that my own life could reach such a high degree of fulfillment.

All organizations within the recording industry, especially ASCAP and BMI, have my sincere gratitude.

And, this book could not have been written if it hadn't been for what I learned from all of you: Steve Bedell, Wes Farrell, Sidney Seidenberg, Floyd Lieberman, Billy Meschel, Fred Frank, Stan Kahan, Charles Koppelman, David Chackler, Joe Isgro, Danny Davis, Rick James, Wally Schuster, Irwin Schuster, Ralph Murphy, Artie Wayne, Chas Peate, Paul Vance, Vince Rotkamp, Bernie Lawrence, Irwin Pincus, John Gluck, Jim Kemper, Stan Glogower, Jerry Wagner, Lucky Carle, Stu Silfin, Al Altman, Ira Howard, Mario Rossi, Joe Renzetti, Tony Camillo, Bert DeCoteaux, John and Joel Dorn, Irwin Segelstein, Denny Diante, Kelli Ross, Glen and Nicki Wesen, Ronny Schiff, Joe Smit, Ariana Attie (my invaluable assistant), Ina Meibach, Frank Unruh, and especially Jackie.

A Word About "Gender"...

It's always difficult to address the question of gender in a book without resorting to the use of "he/she" whenever gender is referenced. Since both men and women are involved in the various areas of the music industry, I've alternated between using "he" and "she" throughout this book to circumvent that problem.

ABOUT THE AUTHOR

JAY WARNER was born and brought up in Brooklyn, New York. He started playing piano when he was seven, and guitar in his late teens. His classical lessons came to an abrupt end when, at the age of fifteen, his mother caught him playing jazz riffs to *"The Moolight Sonata."*

He began his career in the music business in the early '60s as a singer with a street corner group, The Carolons. Their little known recording of *"Let It Please Be You"* on the Mellomood label was the beginning of Jay's diversified career.

In the mid-1960s, he wrote and recorded with the rock group The Love Six and the well-known New York folk group The Travelers. His introduction to the business end of the music business came in 1970 when he joined the firm Record On Film Company. Having spent the previous four years knocking on doors to interest publishers in his songs, Jay had a working knowledge of what publishing was about. While there, he handled publishing companies' activities and learned administration, in addition to working on music for promotional films.

From there, Jay began to wear a multitude of hats. He went into independent production, producing and writing commercials such as Coca Cola and Cold Power for Sherman and Kahan Associates and also managed artist Ersel Hickey of *"Bluebirds Over The Mountain"* fame. Through all these activities, he continued to write songs with various people including Joe Shapiro, who wrote *"Round and Round"* for Perry Como and *"Treasure of Love"* for Clyde Mc Phatter, John

Gluck, who wrote *"It's My Party"* for Leslie Gore and *"Trouble Is My Middle Name"* for Bobby Vinton, and with Dave Appell (producer for Tony Orlando and Dawn).

In 1972, his publishing, management and film promotion experience brought him in contact with Sidney Seidenberg, President of SAS Incorporated, the management firm for Gladys Knight and the Pips and B.B. King, among others. Jay joined the company as assistant to the president and again handled administrative duties for the publishing companies which consisted of the Tallyrand (Jeff Barry and Ellie Greenwich), Gladys Knight and the Pips' and Gene McDaniels' catalogs.

By mid-1973, he realized his desire was to be totally involved in publishing, so he joined the Wes Farrell Organization in New York as a professional manager. Three and a half years later he rose to the position of vice-president of the Wes Farrell Organization Music Group and was relocated in the company's main office in Southern California.

In September of 1977, he was offered the position of vice-president at the newly formed Entertainment Company and began by organizing and running their West Coast base of operations.

1979 began on an up-note with Jay's election to the ASCAP advisory board. He was also a recipient of the American Song Festival's "Ears Of The Year Award." Then, in 1980, Jay received the award again for an unprecedented second time!

1980 also heralded another change in Jay's life. He became the founder and president of The Creative Music Group, the publishing arm of the worldwide K-Tel International organization. While at K-Tel, he was one of the first publishers in America to set up an in-house division devoted full time to the pursuit of music coordinating for films and music administration for such films as "Halloween," "Fade To Black," "The Deer Hunter," and "Falling In Love." Under Warner's leadership, The Creative Music Group became the first independent music publishing company to administer the music rights for an entire major film company when Creative Music Group took on the Avco Embassy Pictures catalog.

In 1983, Jay decided to put his experience to the test by forming his own publishing company, the Jay Warner Music Group. From the outset it was a chart-topping success, with the acquisition of writer/artists like Rick James, the Mary Jane Girls, Lakeside, Larry Graham of Graham Central Station, and Van Redding, who has played and written with both the Commodores and Confunkshun. Continuing his involvement with film, he coordinated the music and/or administered music for such films as "Inchon" starring Sir Lawrence Olivier, "Jimmy The Kid" with Gary Coleman, "Evita Peron," and "The Mac" with Richard Pryor. In the year and one half of its existence, Jay's company racked up fourteen chart singles and seven chart LPs. One of his companies was named the number two independent publisher for 1983 by Billboard Magazine right behind perennial leader Jobete Music.

In mid-1984, Warner merged his company with the Private I Music Group and became president of the combined music publishing companies, where he successfully oversees the company's operations to this day.

Through his years as a publisher, Jay has worked with many diverse writers and catalogs including: Barry Manilow, Bruce Springsteen, Rick James, Jimmy Webb, Johnny Rivers, Carol Bayer Sager, The Rascals, Ellie Greenwich, REO Speedwagon, Bob Gaudio (writer of most of the Four Season's hits), Ben Weisman (writer of fifty-seven Elvis Presley songs), Levine and Brown (writers of most of the Tony Orlando and Dawn hits), Jim Weatherly ("Midnight Train To Georgia" and other Gladys Knight hits), Scott and Dire ("Who Do You Think You Are" by the Heywoods), Kenny Nolan ("My Eyes Adored You"), Bruce Roberts ("Enough Is Enough" for Barbara Streisand and Donna Summer), Alan Gordon ("Happy Together"), and many others. He has published songs recorded by artists ranging from Streisand and Elvis to Springsteen and Whitney Houston.

Jay is fulfilling a dream of building a creative music publishing environment for writer/artists and writer/producers to work in. The time and caring that he puts forth for people is additionally evident in his business philosophy that the promotion of the songwriter is as important as promotion of the song. It is doubly-evident from Jay's effort in writing this book that he wishes to share all of his publishing experience with you, to pave the way for a smoother entrance into the music business and to help your songs become hits!

CONTENTS

A General History of Publishing in America

The birth of music publishing was a direct outgrowth of the invention of the printing press, along with its moveable type. Prior to this, the only means of transferring music so that people could play and replay it was by means of handwritten notation. Now, instead of hand printing, many copies of a work could be printed, distributed and sold. Therefore, the first music publishers were actually music printers. America's music publishing history goes back over 300 years to a time when Harvard University received the first printing press shipped over from England. Soon after the press was set up, the first book published in the colonies was printed. It was no more than a pocket-sized edition of singing psalms entitled "The Bay Psalm Book," but it was the beginning of continuous music publication started in this country in the 1640s.

Popular music was generally published first in England, where in 1650, John Playford, a London publisher, began the task of compiling a collection of popular songs exclusively for resale. In the U.S., however, most music books and sheet music had been imported from England for well over a hundred years. It was not until 1752 that the earliest American publication containing music printed from type was issued. The title was "Kern Altar Unt Neva" by Christopher Soma of Germantown, Pennsylvania.

In 1674, none other than Paul Revere engraved Josiah Flag's "Collection Of The Best Psalm Tunes," and rumor has it that his publication was printed on the first paper manufactured in America. William Billings of Boston became the first publisher to print a songbook of original music by an American-born writer in the year 1774.

Ironically, because the first U.S. Congress protected intellectual properties but neglected to protect music in its copyright law of 1789, most music publishers copyrighted musical creations as books. Up to this time, American publishers were men of dual careers: printers, engravers, composers, and teachers. However, during the 1790s, a number of professional music publishers from Europe flocked to the cities of New York, Boston, and Philadelphia to set up their own companies. So many, in fact, that by the early 1820s more than 10,000 popular songs were printed in the U.S., although most were European compositions.

The first American success was entitled "The Minstrel's Return From The War" by John Hill Hewitt in 1827. Ironically, the author lost a great deal of royalty income when a relative of his, who was his publisher, failed to properly copyright the song. This must have been of even greater frustration to Mr. Hewitt when one considers that his father, James Hewitt, was one of the country's first publishers.

By the 1830s, New York publishers inspired what was to be the next entertainment format. The black-faced minstrel show spawned a wide variety of songs that were quickly printed as sheet music.

In the 1850s, another trend developed as more and more homes became their own entertainment centers with the acquisition of the family piano. For the first time, the public on a large scale, rather than the entertainers, became the market for the publisher's songs.

When the nation's calm was broken by the Civil War, instead of retreating or going into hibernation, the music publishing business actually grew. Over 10,000 songs were published during the war in both the North and the South.

After the end of the Civil War, two factors emerged to bring music publishing even closer to the American people. The first was that the new technologies' improved printing presses, cheaper paper, lithography, and less expensive transportation made large-scale distribution of sheet music possible. Secondly, this same transportation explosion helped the newest entertainment phenomenon, vaudeville, rise up out of the saloons of New York and spread across the country. These vaudevillians were the pioneers of touring, often going out for almost a year and performing in fifty to 100 cities each tour. Before they left, however, they would stop at various publishing houses to supplement or even rebuild their repertoires.

The next foot up for the publishing business came in the form of the 1891 copyright law, which finally recognized that reciprocal, international protection for copyrights was necessary. After incorporating such protections in the law, the American music publisher received international credibility for the first time, as well as the ability of being able to deal in the international marketplace with some degree of fiscal protection.

By the end of the nineteenth century, New York City became the music publishing capital of America. Firms like F.A. Mills, E.B. Marks, Francis, Day and Hunter, the Witmark Brothers, Leo Feist, and Shapiro-Bernstein and Company became the founding fathers of the modern music publishing business with a newer approach to publishing than their predecessors. They went out seeking people to perform their songs. No one realized it in the early 1900s, but the publishers' aggressive pursuit of anyone who could publicly perform a song became "songplugging" and the person doing it has been forever immortalized in history as the "songplugger." Apparently the publishers' new found aggressiveness began to pay off (to the obvious delight of songwriters) as over 100 songs sold a million or more copies each of sheet music in the years from 1900 to 1910.

During this time, vaudeville became bigger and bigger while the music publishing community moved uptown to the area of 28th Street and Broadway. Tin Pan Alley, as it was coined, became the center of music publishing, and therefore the center of the American music scene. Each company had small rooms with talented pianists sitting at upright pianos playing songs from the company's catalog for performers. These people were actually the first "professional managers," and many (depending on their position in the company) got to choose the material they would play, as opposed to having the owner tell them what to "plug."

It is appropriate at this time to mention that song publishers in the early twentieth century were almost always the actual printers of the sheet music they sold. Hence, the splintering of the printers from publishers in the '50s created a printer who printed sheet music and folios exclusively, thus giving birth to the print music publishers. The true separation between song and print publishers was not complete until recordings and airplay performances reduced the song publisher's print income to a small fraction of its former yield. For example, in 1910 as much as 90% of a publisher's income could have come from sheet music, but by 1950, it could have been as little as 10%.

It is interesting to note that although records were around early in the 1890s (starting with cylinders and then thick one-sided 78 rpm Edison discs), recording was a medium of secondary importance for many years and therefore of less interest to publishers. The primary exploitation of songs was still live performance. Most recordings made were by already established and successful performers. Therefore, most of their songs were hits before they recorded them (an almost unimaginable possibility today), and, in many cases, these hits were not recorded until months or years after their peak of success.

Even though there were numerous million-selling records in the early days of the twentieth century, music publishers would not direct their promotional attention to records until the advent of nationwide radio. By 1926, network radio could make a song instantly known across the country. At first, publishers, who were used to months and months of building a song's popularity, were faced with overnight reactions and six-to-eight-week cycles of popularity, thus creating a need for more and more songs. Song pluggers were now faced with a new challenge as radio performers (such as big bands and their singers) began to replace vaudeville, and popularity charts were born from the instant competition between songs that radio provided.

Adding to the technological explosion was the advent of talking pictures in 1927. Songs became a tremendous asset to films, and publishers immediately realized the potential for building hits from their use in films. For the first time, publishers were creating songs specifically for an exploitation medium, since performers were hired to sing their songs in films, whereas in the past, songs were created and then had to be placed with a performer.

All was not sunshine and roses however, as the Depression of 1929 ruined the sale of sheet music, and greatly damaged the sale of records, which heavily reduced record royalties. The saving grace for songwriters and publishers through the 1930s was radio. The entertainment medium that was drastically reducing the sale of sheet music, even before the Depression, was creating a whole new and much larger area of income through performance airplay as monitored by ASCAP (the first, and at that time, the only licensing society).

The economic turnaround after World War II coupled with advancing wartime technology made new changes and challenges for publishers again. Changes came from the country's new economy with its higher wages, making almost every American a potential buyer of the latest record players. What had held back the growth of the 78 rpm record over the previous forty years was the size of its grooves. Because they were so large, you could only get one song on a side. The microgroove invention of 1948 changed all that by reducing the size of the grooves, allowing up to six songs on a side of a single disc. Along with this technology came the first format choice in the form of the 45 rpm "single" record.

All of this created a challenge for publishers to provide more music to a music-hungry nation. Publishers at this time devised three general strategies to cope with this problem. First, they began plugging songs directly to record company A&R people and recording artists. They realized the secondary promotional aspects of records from the '20s had grown into the primary promotional aspects that could easily dwarf the past exposure of music. Coupled with radio (the natural user of recordings), the publisher found two equally strong media for income—record sale royalties (mechanicals) and radio airplay royalties (performance). Secondly, publishers realized that to maintain a consistent quality supply of music to the record companies, they would have to go out and aggressively find writers rather than just waiting for them to walk in the door. Third, they began the process of becoming the first talent scouts as they went out to discover new artists to sing their songs and bring them to record companies. Wherever they found an artist who wrote some or all of his or her own music, they would sign him or her up and promote the artist.

This was also the beginning of national recognition for music that was formerly ethnic or regional, such as rhythm and blues and country music. Publishers were quick to recognize the possibilities for a broader audience of this music and jumped to the forefront of exposing it. With the advent of the disc jockey, continuous music on radio became commonplace, and most of that music was new music by new artists. By the mid-fifties, TV became another user of music, and publishing became increasingly complex with the diversity of formats available to publishers and songwriters for the exploitation of their songs.

Today music publishers have to deal with a multitude of uses and formats never before equalled in the history of music. Examples are radio, network TV, syndicated TV, public broadcasting (PBS), theatrical films, restaurants, night clubs, made-for-TV films, made-for-cable films, LPs, EPs, videocassettes, video discs, CDs, DAT systems, CDIs, 8-tracks, cassette singles, 45 rpm singles, 12" singles, dance mix recordings, club mix singles, cassette LPs, and whatever is coming in the future. The print music business started hundreds of years ago and has matured into the modern music publisher whose job it is to protect, collect, and exploit the nation's heritage of music for the benefit of songwriters and song publishers everywhere.

What is Publication?

THE COPYRIGHT LAW of the United States provides for copyright in musical compositions. This includes original compositions made up of melody alone or words (lyric) and music combined. It also includes the arrangements and other new versions of earlier compositions if new copyrightable work has been added. The term "musical compositions" now includes song poems or other works consisting of words with no music. With this definition as your guideline, you can more easily understand and prepare yourself for such things as *owner rights* and *duration of copyrights, how to copyright a musical composition,* and *how to register claims.*

"Publication" generally means the sale, placing on sale, or distribution of copies, or phonorecords of a work to the public. Public performance, such as TV or stage, is not a publication, no matter how large the viewing audience. *Under the new law, the sale of recordings is now considered publication.* Limited distribution of so-called professional record copies to publishers, disc-jockeys, artists, managers, etc., ordinarily would not constitute publication. However, the dividing line between a preliminary distribution and actual publication may sometimes be difficult to determine. The copyright law states that a Notice of Copyright should be placed on publicly distributed copies of the work. This may be confusing, since a phonorecord is not considered such a copy. This is because a Notice of Copyright on the actual music is different from the Notice of Copyright on the overall recording. Therefore, a Notice of Copyright for the song does not have to be printed on recordings. Instead, a Notice of Copyright in sound recordings is printed on the label. The Notice for recordings will carry the ©, year, date, and company name (example: © 1988 A & M Records). The author should affix notice of copyright to copies of his song that are to be circulated beyond his control to show that his interests in the work are protected. For example, an unpublished work should say ©, year, date and your name (© 1988, John Doe). If the song is published and you retain the publishing rights (see Chapter 11) the notice might read: © 1988 John Doe Music Company or any other name you choose as your music publishing company name. It's also worth noting that publication of your song via recordings has no bearing on the copyright protection of your song.

Many steps are taken from the beginning of writing and copyright stages of a song, up to the stage where the song becomes a record and reaches the national charts. What is important for the writer is the following of correct copyright and business procedures for the protection of his work. This protection is further augmented by copyright protection given to the writer by the publisher upon the publisher's acquisition of the song. At the time a song or a record justifies to a publisher its merits based on popularity and record sales, the publisher may choose to print and sell sheet music. On the next page, the chart shows the various processes a song goes through before it reaches publication.

CHART SHOWING FINISHED SONG TO RELEASED RECORD

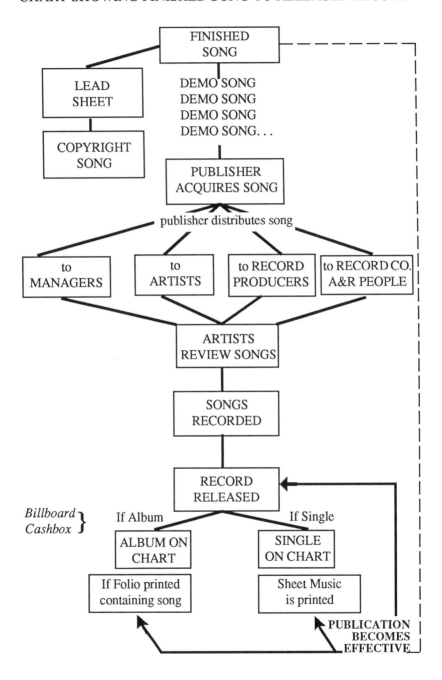

Copyrights, Copyrighting and You

THE COPYRIGHT OFFICE defines copyright as the "right to copy." The term has come to mean that body of exclusive rights granted by statute to authors for protection of their writings. It includes (1) the exclusive right to make and publish copies of a copyrighted work, (2) to make other versions of the work, and with certain limitation, (3) to make recordings of the work and/or to perform the work in public. Publishers, or writers who become publishers, own the copyrights to musical compositions they acquire.

The first Copyright Act dates back to 1790 and said in part: "to Promote the Progress of science and useful arts, by securing for limited times, to inventors and authors the exclusive right to their respective writings and discoveries." The Copyright Act of 1790 was only for protection against the copying of printed matter. The performing right was granted in 1897 and mechanical reproduction rights (records) was added in 1909. The protection under the copyright law extends to all areas of music use (see Ch. 6, The New Copyright Laws).

The musical composition should be written in some legible form of notation for deposit at the copyright office. If the composition includes words, they should be written beneath the notes to which they are sung. A lead sheet is acceptable for an unpublished work. A phonorecord such as a disc, cassette, tape recording or other reproduction of a sound recording is also considered a copy of the musical composition recorded on it, and is now acceptable as a deposit copy for copyright registration of the musical composition. For information about the registration of copyright claims and sound recordings as works in themselves you should request *Circular R56* from the Library of Congress.

The Copyright Office registers claims to copyrights and issues certificates of registration, but it does not issue or grant copyrights. Statutory Copyright protection is the protection afforded by the Federal Law when certain requirements are met. There are two ways to secure statutory copyright in a musical composition. (1) Register it in the Copyright Office in unpublished form or (2) publish the work with a statutory notice of copyright affixed to each copy.

To obtain copyright registration for an unpublished musical composition, send the following material together to the Copyright Office, Library of Congress, Washington, D.C. 20559.

1) Application Form PAU. This form is provided by the Copyright Office and may be obtained free upon request. It should be properly completed and signed.

2) Send one complete copy of the musical composition. Do not send your only copy because manuscripts and records are not returned.

3) The registration fee is ten dollars ($10.00). Make the check payable to the Register of Copyrights. It is important to note that song lyrics without music are now registerable for copyright in unpublished form as of 1/78 Copyright Law.

After registration, the Copyright Office issues a certificate as evidence that the claim has been registered. When a certificate has been issued, no further action in the Copyright Office is necessary until the work has been published, recorded, or substantially revised.

Is registration necessary? Copyright registration for an unpublished musical composition is not required in order to protect your work. Unpublished works are now protected by the new Federal Law against unauthorized use as opposed to the previous Common Law protection of the various states.

On the other hand, registration in the Copyright Office for an unpublished musical composition has certain advantages, and may sometimes be important, especially if a sound recording is to be made.

Even if the work has already been registered for copyright in unpublished form, the following two steps should be taken to preserve copyright protection in the published composition:

1) Produce copies with Copyright notice. Produce the work in copies by printing or other means of reproduction. Make sure that every copy contains a copyright notice in the correct form and position. Place the copies on sale, sell or publicly distribute them. Register the copyright claim.

2) Promptly after publication, send the following material together to the Copyright Office, with Application Form PA: Send two complete copies of the best edition of the work, as first published with notice of copyright, one complete copy if the work is first published outside of the United States. Also include ten dollars payable to the Register of Copyrights.

In order to secure and maintain copyright protection of a published composition it is essential that all published copies contain the required Statutory Copyright Notice. The person entitled to the copyright may place the copyright notice on his work without obtaining permission from the Copyright Office. The notice must contain these three elements:

1) The word "Copyright" or the symbol ©. Use of the symbol © may result in securing copyright in some countries outside the U.S. jurisdiction under the provisions of the Universal Copyright Convention.

2) The year date of publication.

3) The name of the Copyright owner must also be added.

The year date of publication is ordinarily the year in which copies of the work are first placed on sale, sold, or publicly distributed by the copyright proprietor or under his authority. However, if the work has been previously registered for copyright in unpublished form, the notice should contain the year and date of registration for the unpublished version. Or, if there is new copyrightable matter in the published version, it is advisable to include both the year of registration as an unpublished work and also the year of publication.

The three elements must be legible and must appear together. For example: © 1988 John Doe. The notice must appear on the title page or first page of music. The 1909 law said: *"If the work is published without the notice, the copyright is lost and cannot be restored!"* But the new law states that the copyright notice must appear, as before, on copies of the work. However, omission of the notice now will *not* immediately result in the loss of copyright. The new law allows for a grace period in which to correct such omissions (see Ch. 6).

Musical compositions by U.S. citizens can be copyrighted in many foreign countries, but the methods for securing copyright differ. The United States and about sixty other countries are adherents to the Universal Copyright Convention, which came into force on September 16, 1955. Basically, the UCC requires a participating country to give the same protection to foreign works, which meet the Convention requirements, as it gives to its own domestic works. The UCC affords protection automatically to unpublished works without notice, registration or other formalities. A published musical composition by a U.S. citizen may obtain protection in other UCC countries, as well as the United States, *if* all published copies bear a particular form of copyright notice from the date of their first publication. This notice consists of the symbol © accompanied by the name of the copyright holder and the year and date of publication. For example: © 1988 John Doe. This notice should be placed on the title page or first page of music. Following publication, the claim to U.S. copyright should be registered in the Copyright Office in the usual manner. No foreign registration is necessary. (See chart on the Conventions on Page 18.)

WORLD COPYRIGHT CONVENTIONS
In General

United States copyright relations with other countries are based on bilateral treaties, Presidential proclamations regarding copyright protection for nationals of other countries, and various international conventions to which the United States has acceded. Currently, the United States is a member of the Universal Copyright Convention (¶ 11,250 and ¶ 11,335), the Buenos Aires Convention (¶ 11,365), the Phonogram Convention (¶ 11,385), and the Mexico City Convention. The United States also has bilateral treaty agreements with many countries, including some of those that are also signatories to the international conventions; while the conventions have largely superseded many of these agreements, convention memberships do not necessarily abrogate bilateral agreements. In addition, the President is authorized to extend, by proclamation, copyright protection to nationals of foreign countries that extend copyright protection to United States nationals on the same basis as to their own nationals.

The copyright relations of the United States with specific countries are charted in Copyright Office Circular R38a at ¶ 15,027.

Berne Convention

The Berne Convention was first formalized in 1886 and has been revised five times since that date—in Berlin in 1908, in Rome in 1928, in Brussels in 1948 (¶ 11,512), in Stockholm in 1967 (¶ 11,483), and in Paris in 1971 (¶ 11,400). Because of these revisions, it is difficult to speak in general terms of "the Berne Convention" since it is necessary to know to which version reference is being made. Each version applies only to those countries that have signed it. The U.S. is not currently a member of Berne. (NOTE: At the time this book went to press, the U.S. was expected to join Berne, and therefore the paragraphs contained herein referencing Berne would include the U.S. writers and publishers.)

Generally, the basis of Berne is "national treatment," in that an author obtaining a copyright in a country signatory to Berne is given protection in the other countries on the same basis as an author of the nation whose protection is sought—there is no discrimination against the works of foreign authors. The prerequisite for protection is first publication (or simultaneous publication under the later revisions) in a member nation, and protection extends to "literary and artistic works," which is defined in the Convention.

The term of copyright protection granted by Berne is generally the life of the author plus 50 years. Since the Rome revision, Berne has also protected the "moral rights" of authors to control the use of their works to prevent distortions, mutilations, or other derogatory actions in relation to the works, that might damage the author's reputation or honor.

The Berlin and later versions of Berne provide protection without the necessity of complying with any formalities.

The "Back Door" to Berne Protection

The Berlin (1908) and later revisions of Berne provided protection not only in case of first publication, but also in case of simultaneous publication, in a Berne nation by nationals of nonmember states. Since the U.S. is not currently a member of the Berne Convention, this "back door" to Berne has been used by many United States authors to obtain protection for their works under Berne. At the same time publication is made in the United States, they publish the work in a Berne nation. It is important to note, however, that the definition of "simultaneous publication" differs between Berne versions. Under the Rome (1928) version, simultaneous publication must take place on the same day in both countries, while under the Brussels (1948) and later versions of the convention, publication is simultaneous if made in the two countries within 30 days of each other. Thus, persons seeking Berne protection via the "back door" must take care to know with which version of Berne they are dealing.

Buenos Aires Convention

The Buenos Aires Convention (¶ 11,365), which was signed in 1910, is understood to be in effect as between the United States, Brazil, Colombia, Costa Rica, the Dominican Republic, Ecuador, Guatamala, Haiti, Honduras, Nicaragua, Panama, Paraguay, Peru, and Uraguay (.06). The Convention protects "literary and artistic works," which include books, writings, pamphlets of all kinds, dramatic or dramaticomusical works, choreographic and musical compositions with or without words, drawings, paintings, sculpture, engravings, photographic works, astronomical or geographical globes, plans, sketches or plastic works relating to geography, geology or topography, architecture or any other science; and all productions that can be published by any means of impression or reproduction.

When a copyright is acknowledged in one state of the Convention, in conformity with that state's laws, the copyright will be reciprocally recognized in the other signatory states, without the necessity of complying with any other formality, provided that the work carried a statement reserving the property right—the familiar "All Rights Reserved" line. Each signatory country grants to the authors and their assigns the rights granted by their respective laws; however, the term of protection cannot exceed the term granted in the country of origin. The country of origin of a work is that of its first publication in the Americas; if a work is published simultaneously in several signatory countries, the country of origin is considered the country that fixes the shortest period of protection.

.06 Copyright Office Circular 38c, 15, 028.

Universal Copyright Convention

The Universal Copyright Convention, dated at Geneva, September 6, 1952, was ratified by the United States in 1954, and came into force for the United States on September 16, 1955 (¶ 11,335). The U.S. is a signatory to both the 1952 Geneva UCC and the 1971 Paris version of the UCC. The current list of countries adhering to either version of the UCC appears in Copyright Office Circular R38a, at ¶ 15,027.

The UCC provides for the protection of the rights of authors and other copyright proprietors in literary, scientific, and artistic works, including writings, musical, dramatic, and cinematographic works, and paintings, engravings, and sculpture. Published works of nationals of each contracting state and works first published in that state enjoy in each other contracting state the same protection as that other state accords to works of its nationals first published in its own territory. Unpublished works of nationals of each contracting state enjoy the same protection in other contracting states as the other states accord to unpublished works of their own nationals.

Any formalities required under the domestic law of a contracting state as a condition of copyright are regarded as satisfied, with respect to works protected under the Convention and published outside the territory of the state and by an author who is not a national of the state, if from the time of first publication all the copies of the work published with the authority of the author or copyright proprietor carry the symbol ©, accompanied by the name of the copyright proprietor and the year of first publication, placed in a manner and location to give reasonable notice of the claim of copyright. (For discussion of the notice requirements of the U.S. law, see the "Notice, Deposit and Registration" division beginning at ¶ 5000).

The duration of protection is governed by the law of the contracting state, but generally shall not be less than the life of the author and 25 years after his death, or 25 years from the date of first publication. For photographic works, or works of applied art insofar as they are protected as artistic works, the term of protection must not be less than 10 years.

Translations of copyrighted works of authors in signatory countries are accorded special status under both the Berne and Universal Copyright Conventions. Privileges of translation are granted if, seven years after original publication, a work has not been authorized for translation into a language of one of the countries. An attempt to secure permission from the copyright owner to make the translation is a prerequisite. In the event permission is not or cannot be obtained, the translator may obtain a nonexclusive license for translation into the language of the signatory country. Efforts must be made by the country of translation to compensate the author. Special rights are given to translations for those developing countries which have signified their status as such to the United Nations. The period which must elapse between original publication and license for translation is reduced to three years and, in case the translation is to be made in a language not in general use in one or more of the developed countries, one year. These translations may not be exported from the country for which translated.

MEMBERS OF THE UNIVERSAL COPYRIGHT CONVENTION
(Dates of membership to both the UCC and Berne Conventions)

COUNTRY	UNIVERSAL	BERNE	COUNTRY	UNIVERSAL	BERNE
Algeria	8/28/73		Lebanon	10/17/59	9/30/47
Andorra	9/16/55		Liberia	7/27/56	
Argentina	2/13/58	6/10/67	Libyan Arab		
Australia	5/1/69	4/14/28	Jamahiriya	9/28/76	
Austria	7/2/57	10/1/20	Liechtenstein	1/22/59	7/30/31
Bahamas	12/27/76	7/10/73	Luxembourg	10/15/55	6/20/1888
Bangladesh	8/5/75		Madagascar	1/1/66	
Belgium	8/31/60	12/51887	Malawi	10/26/65	
Benin	1/3/61		Mali	3/19/62	
Brazil	1/13/60	2/9/22	Malta	11/19/68	9/21/64
Bulgaria	6/7/75	12/5/21	Mauritania	2/6/73	
Cameroon	5/1/73	9/21/64	Mauritius	3/12/68	
Canada	8/10/62	4/10/28	Mexico	5/12/57	6/11/67
Central African Republic		9/3/77	Monaco	9/16/55	5/30/1889
Chad	11/25/71		Morocco	5/8/72	6/16/17
Chile	9/16/55	6/5/70	Netherlands	6/22/67	11/1/12
Columbia	6/18/76		New Zealand	9/11/64	4/24/28
Congo	5/8/62		Nicaragua	8/16/61	
Costa Rica	9/16/55	6/10/78	Niger	5/2/62	
Cuba	6/18/57		Nigeria	2/14/62	
Cyprus	2/24/64		Norway	1/23/63	4/13/1896
Czechoslovakia	1/6/60	2/22/21	Pakistan	9/16/55	7/5/48
Democratic			Panama	10/17/62	
Kampuchea	9/16/55		Paraguay	3/11/62	
Denmark	2/9/62	7/1/03	Peru	10/16/63	
Ecuador	6/5/57		Philippines	11/19/55	8/1/51
Egypt	6/7/77		Poland	3/9/77	1/28/20
El Salvador	3/29/79		Portugal	12/25/56	3/29/11
Fiji	10/10/70	12/1/71	Romania	1/1/27	
Finland	4/16/63	4/1/28	Senegal	7/9/74	8/25/62
France	1/14/56	12/51887	South Africa	10/3/28	
Gabon	3/26/62		Soviet Union	5/27/73	
German Democratic			Spain	9/16/55	12/5/1887
Republic	10/5/73	12/51887	Sri Lanka	7/20/59	
German Federal			Suriname	2/23/77	
Republic	9/16/55	12/5/1887	Sweden	7/1/61	8/1/04
Ghana	8/22/62		Switzerland	3/30/56	12/5/1887
Greece	8/24/63	11/9/20	Thailand	7/17/31	
Guatemala	10/28/64		Togo	4/30/75	
Haiti	9/16/55		Tunisia	6/19/69	12/5/1887
Holy See	10/5/55	9/12/35	Turkey	1/1/52	
Hungary	1/23/71	2/14/22	United Kingdom	9/27/57	12/5/1887
Iceland	12/18/56	9/7/47	United States		
India	1/21/58	4/1/28	of America	9/16/55	
Ireland	1/20/59	10/5/27	Upper Volta	8/19/63	
Israel	9/16/55	3/24/50	Uruguay	7/10/67	
Italy	1/24/57	12/5/1887	Venezuela	9/30/66	
Ivory Coast	1/1/62		Yugoslavia	5/11/66	6/17/30
Japan	4/28/56	7/15/1899	Zaire	10/8/63	
Kenya	9/7/66		Zambia	6/1/65	
Laos	9/16/55				

SUMMARY

In the past, common law copyright came into effect the moment a song was written, without any necessity for registration or notice in common law form. This is now "The Federal or National System of Protection." It gives the writer protection against the use of his song without his approval. This protection (in the form of the writer affixing the proper notice to his lead sheets and/or cassettes, reel-to-reel copies, etc) lasts for the life of the author plus fifty years (see Chapter 6, The New Copyright Law). Proper notice at this point is simply the symbol ©, year it was written, and writer's name. In published form, the only change in the notice would be of the publisher's name substituted for the writer's, the writer either having contracted his song to a publisher or formed his own company. For example, if he contracted the song to the National League Music Company, the notice would be: © 1988 National League Music Company.

Since the cost is now ten dollars for every song you feel should be copyrighted, it is obvious that a prolific writer can wind up spending quite a lot for copyrights and lead sheets. The new Federal law is really quite adequate in the initial stages of your career. If you have written only a few songs, it can't hurt to use an old idea for proof of ownership of a song. That is, take a lead sheet or a demo tape or cassette of the song, put it in an envelope and mail it to yourself *Registered Mail.* Mark the envelope in a corner with the title or titles of song(s) contained, and when it arrives—DO NOT OPEN IT! Hold onto it for the future should you need to prove date of ownership. Though it is questionable whether this would be considered legal proof of ownership in a court of law, it would at least give the owner proof of possession at the time it was mailed.

There is an organization called The Song Registration Service (SRS) of The National Academy of Songwriters in Hollywood, California that has created a similar "proof of possession" service. For details write to The National Academy of Songwriters, 6381 Hollywood Blvd., Suite 280, Hollywood, California 90028.

Lastly, the new Copyright Law has recognized the fact that many songwriters are finding the ten dollar per song registration far too expensive. They have countered this with a single application form and fee for two or more unpublished compositions containing a single title for the whole collection. If activity on an individual song in the collection warrants it, you can register the song later under its specific title. You can use the same PA form, listing all your titles on the title line.

Performing Rights Societies: When and Why You Need Them

PUBLIC PERFORMANCE ROYALTIES of recorded music are the greatest source of income in the music industry. These performance royalties are based on a percentage scale and are collected by BMI and ASCAP, the two major collection agencies in the United States. Writers in the U.S. must belong to one (and only one), in order to collect royalties for air-play of their songs in the United States. Furthermore, these licensing organizations are set up (either through affiliates or companies with whom they have a licensing agreement) to collect royalties on air-play outside the United States. The United

States Congress came up with its first statute in 1897, but this had little bearing, because copyright owners weren't organized enough to collect royalties from such sources as cabarets and dancehalls for the use of the music.

The following is a short history of the Copyright Act and its bearing on writers and publishers, and how the performing rights societies have been a guiding force since 1914. The United States Copyright Act of 1909 was a reasonably good and fair bill for that era, giving American composers, lyricists and publishers most of the benefits and protection enjoyed by their colleagues in other lands. The Act reflected the pre-World War I technology that affected music performances and delivery of those performances to the public. At that time, there was no radio, television, music systems, cables, satellites, or jukeboxes. The term of copyright protection, built into the 1909 Statute, was significantly shorter than that of most other countries, but there was little argument, because America's creators were so glad to get copyright protection for non-dramatic performance rights and recording rights. In 1909, the U.S. got a law, but it still did not get any royalties. No one respected our performing rights until ASCAP was founded in 1914 by writers and publishers who organized to get the statute enforced.

Actually the law was not widely enforced until January 1917, when the U.S. Supreme Court ruled in ASCAP's favor in a crucial suit brought by one of ASCAP's founding fathers, Victor Herbert, against Chandley's Restaurant in New York. The years passed, the technology changed, and the world of music evolved to the delight of expanding audiences everywhere. The statute remained the same, however.

By the 1920s, some members of Congress recognized that the statute was unrealistic and began to discuss changes to modernize the obviously obsolete legislation. Laws were passed to remedy economic inequities affecting larger groups, but composers and lyricists had to wait at the end of the line. The obsolete law survived unchanged; everyone recognized American music as both a major cultural and economic force, and it was widely admitted that music was probably our first ambassador internationally. Technology changed at an ever-increasing rate, but the level of copyright protection remained frozen in 1909 terms.

Fortunately, the courts first interpreted the old law reasonably and applied it to new uses—particularly to radio and television. Later, beginning in 1968, the trend was reversed when cable television was held exempt. No one could explain why lyricists, composers, and music publishers should fall behind or be treated as second class citizens, but no one could deny those realities either.

In 1955, Congress funded a series of studies by the Copyright Office. It took nine long years for the first copyright modernization bill of this generation to be introduced. Three years later, the House of Representatives passed a bill that wasn't perfect, but which would have done much to remedy some of the major inequities. The Senate never got to vote on this bill, and it died.

The effort to get a fair bill didn't die, however. On February 19, 1976, twenty-one years after the Copyright Office studies were funded by Congress, fifteen years after they were completed and had demonstrated the areas in which new legislation was needed, and twelve years after the first revision bill was introduced, the Senate unanimously passed a bill which became law January 1, 1978.

The 1909 law had broad exclusions that limited copyright protection to public performances for *profit*. The new law has removed the "for profit" limitation and substituted exemptions for specific situations, such as religious services. The 1909 law created one compulsory license that has long oppressed creators—the proviso that arbitrarily set the recording royalty for a record at $ .02 per record. After 67 years without increase, Congress raised that rate to $ .0275. (For rates over the last ten years, see Chapter 5.) Anyone familiar with the great rise in living costs since 1909 will understand why ASCAP and BMI urged a significantly larger increase in this mechanical rate.

That brings us to the present. (For details of the new Copyright Law, see Chapter 6.) To give you an idea of the growth of performing rights societies, ASCAP writer membership has gone from 13,500 in 1970, to 18,000 in 1977, and to 28,000 in 1988. BMI writer membership is up from approximately 10,000 in 1963, to over 32,000 in 1977, and 50,000 in 1988. Publisher membership in both societies has also grown. By 1988, ASCAP had 10,000 and BMI 30,000 publisher members. ASCAP has also more than doubled its collected performance fees by going from $38 million in 1963 to $161 million in 1982, and by 1986 their collection fees totaled over $252 million, more than six times the figures of 1963. BMI also more than doubled its collected performance fees over a seven year period, going from approximately $15 million in 1963 to $34 million in 1970.

Today, performing rights societies collect most of their licensing income from T.V. and radio use of recorded music. A smaller amount is acquired by wired-music sources such as Musak and major concerts. As of January 1, 1978, juke-boxes and cable T.V. also became licensed for use. Areas long closed to publishers and writers are now open.

Since performing rights societies were formed primarily to provide a service that individuals could not perform for themselves, including collecting royalties for writers and publishers as payment for the use of their music, it is quite obvious why an association with one of these societies would be to the advantage of anyone seriously trying to make a go of it as a writer or publisher. It would be genuinely impossible for an individual to negotiate a license as well as monitor her songs' use with every possible user of her copyrighted work in this country, let alone in foreign countries. Still, the association with these societies is voluntary, *not mandatory*, and the time to choose joining one is up to you.

The most appropriate time to join a licensing society is upon, or shortly after, the actual publication of your composition, whether it be as a record release or concert performance. The societies do not accept full membership prior to publication of a writer's first work, as too often dates change or publication never takes effect.

Don't worry about losing any income credits from these first uses. The societies are monitoring compositions in a "catch all" system and are usually making payment on performances established anywhere from nine months to a year prior to their current payment period. For example, if the societies were making payment to a writer at the end of the second quarter of 1988 (see Chapter 5—BMI and ASCAP royalties for how often writers are paid), it would be for the airplay or performances logged from a period usually nine months before (third quarter of 1987).

This doesn't mean, however, that you should wait nine months to register your compositions and yourself as a writer with the society of your choice. The sooner after publication that your representation is in place, the less likely the opportunity for mistakes to arise.

How to Choose a Performing Rights Society

CHOOSING A PERFORMING RIGHTS society is not as difficult as you might think, but first it would help to understand what a performing right is. It is a right granted by the U.S. Copyright Act to creators of musical works to license these works for public performance for profit. This right is one of a number of separate rights the law gives to copyright owners. The main American performing rights associations are ASCAP (American Society of Composers, Authors, and Publishers) and BMI (Broadcast Music Incorporated). Both organizations are non-profit, and neither has any overwhelming advantage over the other. This chapter will define and explain their activities comparatively, and let you decide which is to your advantage. One thing that should be noted is that neither one is a disadvantage to a beginning writer.

Both BMI and ASCAP share their income equally between writers and publishers. BMI is owned by broadcast stations throughout the country and was established in 1940 by these broadcasters. ASCAP is a membership group. (At the end of this chapter are sample copies of society membership applications and agreements.) Both BMI and ASCAP distribute all of the money they collect, other than what is needed for operating expenses. Both societies use complicated, statistical samplings of broadcasts by stations to determine the amount of money to be paid to each publisher and writer.

Network performances are on a complete count basis; local television and all radio broadcasts are sampled and logged for payment by both BMI and ASCAP. Along with the over 8,000 radio stations in the U.S., there are over 850 T.V. stations, 9,600 cable systems, 100,000 jukeboxes, 800 non-commercial radio stations, 2,500 colleges and universities, 700 symphony orchestras, and numerous background music services, along with 35,000 hotels, thousands of nightclubs, bars, skating rinks, circuses, restaurants, and theme parks where music is performed publicly for profit. The over 8,000 local radio stations in the United States are on the air for an average of 18 hours a day (approximately 53,000,000 hours a year). These music users obtain licenses from BMI and ASCAP for the rights to the use of their music for broadcast or performance of any of the music licensed by them. License fees paid to BMI and ASCAP are based on the size of the music user (i.e. a 50,000 watt radio station pays more than a 5,000 watt station). The user's advertising income also has a bearing on the fee paid. These advertising fees are determined by negotiation between the performing rights society and the user.

BMI Radio and TV

Basically, BMI keeps track of its radio performances by daily logs provided by the stations. Since there are so many stations, it is impossible to keep track of everything every one of them plays every day of the year. Instead, a scientifically chosen, representative cross-section of stations is logged each quarter. Stations which are being logged supply BMI with complete information as to all of the music being performed. These lists or logs are put through an elaborate computer system which multiplies each performance listed by a factor which reflects the ratio of the number of stations logged to the number licensed. For example: If BMI licensed 500 stations of a certain kind, and ten of them were logged during a given period, every performance of a song would be multiplied by fifty and the writer and publisher would receive credit for fifty performances every time the work appeared on a log. Television theme and cue music is logged with the aid of cue sheets prepared by the producer, which list all of the music performed on the program. The number of performances of music in motion pictures on TV, syndicated film series, and certain types of other television shows are counted with the aid of cue sheets and more than 110 *T.V. Guides* printed in various parts of the country. In the field of concert music, BMI secures all the programs of symphony orchestratras, recital hall concerts etc., to ascertain actual performances of music by BMI composers.

BMI personnel do not know which stations are being logged in a given month until after the logging period is over. The selection of stations to be logged is made on the basis of a scientifically chosen sample. Communication with stations to be logged is done by an independent accounting firm.

The licensing of music users, both broadcast and general, is the responsibility of a BMI field staff of over 50 representatives working out of 11 regional offices which cover all of the U.S.. The users with whom they deal include radio and television stations, hotels and motels, restaurants, nightclubs, cocktail lounges and taverns, discotheques, ballrooms, skating rinks, background music services, airline inflight music, theme parks, symphony orchestras, concert halls and promoters, sports arenas, trade shows, and traveling attractions like ice shows, circuses, and rodeos. All of the many kinds of attractions of which music forms a commercial feature are dealt with. These music users are mailed the proper license forms for completion and return.

ASCAP Radio and TV

The T.V. networks are large and well-staffed organizations which are accustomed to keeping records of many phases of their business. Local radio stations come in all sizes, including some that are almost "Mom & Pop" operations, in that they employ only five or six people. There is no FCC requirement that stations must keep logs of music use. ASCAP samples local radio by taping. ASCAP has been taping for more than a quarter of a century, first experimentally, and then on a regular basis. Today, the sample includes 60,000 hours of local radio each year, including college stations not affiliated with National Public Radio, plus 30,000 hours of local commercial TV, 1,200 hours of public TV, and 600 hours of national public radio. Every local radio station has an opportunity to be included in the sample each year, and a station that pays $20,000 is taped twice as much as a station that is a $10,000 customer, a $40,000 user four times as much as that, etc. The taping unit for radio stations is six hours; the design of the survey is such that some stations are taped only once or twice a year and others are covered more often. Some of the smaller stations may not be sampled this year, but may be next year. Of course, the taping covers both AM and FM stations.

Every category of radio stations is sampled every year. All of the stations that pay less than $10,000 a year are grouped in various categories to reflect the kind of community the stations are in and class (size of ASCAP fees) in which it fits. The U.S. Census Bureau divides the country into nine Census Regions, geographically, and ASCAP stations are similarly classified in these regions. ASCAP samples all nine regions, and the taping covers different times of the day. The Census Bureau also uses subcategories within the regions to show various types or counties, parishes or boroughs. Then it classifies them as metropolitan or non-metropolitan. Counties within each region are grouped to reflect the type of county they are, and the stations are grouped accordingly. Once all of the ASCAP licensed stations are so grouped, the survey again has to be designed to cover all the groups properly. This is the work of the independent survey experts, who are also responsible for a periodic audit of the mechanics of the survey, recommendations for changes, and the annual selection of stations to be sampled within each category.

To minimize the chances of a selection which would be less than completely objective, the annual choice of stations to be sampled and the number of sampling units or tapes to be assigned is made by computer. The actual rescheduling of the taping is handled by another outside research firm, which sends instructions directly to people all over the country as to which stations to record and when to record. The ASCAP headquarters and staff are not notified in advance as to which stations are to be taped or when, nor are the stations themselves notified. The obvious reason is to avoid any attempt to influence the music programming for the taping period. Secrecy and surprise are essential to drawing a representative sample.

The tapes are then sent to New York, where skilled "music monitors" at ASCAP headquarters identify the works on the tapes along with the type of performance, such as a "feature vocal." Candidates for these jobs have to prove their substantial knowledge of music by listening to tapes that include a variety of musical works. Although some of the tape monitors may be very strong in one type of music, that is not enough. If the candidate for the job has a good familiarity with several kinds of music, he or she may be hired as a trainee. It will be many months before a trainee is actually identifying tunes and music for the survey. Unidentifiable songs are referred to a *solfeggist*, an expert trained in musical dictation, who transcribes the notes heard on the tape and then searches through files alphabetized by musical notes beginning with *"do"* from the standard diatonic scale.

Basically ASCAP keeps track of its performances in network television by having the stations send in logs of programs that specify exactly what music was used either as feature performance, theme, or background. (See "Cable," PG. 30.) On other shows, such as feature films, the networks indicate what the programming was, and ASCAP can identify the music through logs and cue sheets supplied by other sources, such as from the producer of the movie, and music publishers who have received cue sheets from film and TV producers. Similar sheets are also procured from the producers of syndicated shows and other programs.

Public Broadcasting

Public broadcasting is sampled by ASCAP in a manner similar to that procedure used in commercial broadcasting. Fewer hours are sampled because the fees paid by public broadcasting stations (PBS) are much lower than the fees paid by commercial broadcasting.

Local Television

Local TV stations are far less numerous than local radio outlets. ASCAP samples 30,000 hours of local TV each year, using *T.V. Guide*, audio tapes and cue sheets. The music monitors also identify what is on the local TV Tapes. In the thirteen cities where ASCAP has local offices, TV is covered by tapes, cue sheets and *T.V. Guide*. In other communities, the stations are surveyed by data obtained from those stations, cue sheets and also *T.V. Guide*. Since many local stations carry major network programs which have already been surveyed, those programs are eliminated from the local TV sampling.

Wired Music

ASCAP works on a Census Basis (complete count) for the major wired music services such as Seaberg, Megnatronics, and Gusto Music. The census are based on reports submitted by the services. However, the much larger Musak is sampled. Approximately two-thirds of ASCAP's wired music fees are from Musak. In the 1970's, when Musak was a company of lesser magnitude, it too was handled on a census basis.

An example of wired music use would be the playing of background music over speakers in hotels, on airlines (airlines provide copies of program listings from their in-flight magazine), or when you are on hold on a telephone.

Symphony, Concert, Educational Music

Music performed by symphony orchestra licensees, serious promoters, and those holding educational licenses are surveyed by means of the concert programs provided to ASCAP and BMI by the sponsoring organization or promoters. Such performances are included on a complete count basis, just as network television performances.

Hotels, Nightclubs, etc.

The cost of surveying those tens of thousands of nightclubs, taverns, and hotels under license would be prohibitive. After some research, the ASCAP and BMI sampling experts have found that it is fair and workable to use feature performances on radio and TV as proxies.

In order to arrive at license fees for restaurants, clubs, etc., the societies calculate a number of variables for each establishment, such as whether they play live vs. recorded music, their weekly entertainment expenditures for bands or live DJ and rental equipment, room occupancy, and whether dancing is permitted or not.

BMI and ASCAP Royalties

BMI publishes a payment schedule of performing rights royalties. A copy of this schedule is given to individuals when they affiliate with BMI. If BMI should change its payments structure, a revised schedule is sent to all affiliates. Both BMI and ASCAP pay four times a year (quarterly). ASCAP has a choice of payments on the basis of current performances of the writer's works (same for BMI) or the more complex "four funds" system, which is a spreading out of payments over five years, usually preferred by more established writers. The writer has this choice at the time of signing with ASCAP.

BMI and ASCAP have different systems of payment and rate schedules that can often become complicated. It is advisable to write to them or call for more in-depth information. As an example, ASCAP song performance credits are processed through the society's computer system and calculated on the basis of a four-part formula: 1. Station Weight—based on license fees paid to ASCAP;   2. Use Weight—based on the kind of performance (e.g., feature, background, theme, etc.); 3. Feature Multiplier—additional credits for uses in areas not surveyed, such as restaurants; and 4. Strata Multiplier—to bring total radio credits in line with radio share of income from all surveyed media. Keep in mind that these rates will periodically change. For example, the annualized publisher credit value of one credit in 1976 was $ .94, while in 1983 it was $2.056—over a 100% increase in 7 years. The rate can decrease as well. The rate in 1987 was 2.56. Therefore, if a credit was worth $2.00 and your song had earned 2,000 credits, the writer's share would have earned about $4,000. The publisher receives about the same amount.

When calculating the performance credits for network TV, the above radio formula has a "hook-up weight" replacing the station weight in the formula. The hook-up weight reflects the number of network affiliates carrying the program transmitted by the network.

When a song reaches a certain number of performances, bonuses are given by BMI and ASCAP to both writers and publishers.

Cable—ASCAP

Cable television performances must be distinguished between re-transmissions of programs and those originated by cable. For cable re-transmissions, a statutory license fee exists. The Copyright Royalty Tribunal determines how that fee is to be allocated among the various claimants (including non-music as well as music copyright proprietors). Cable originations are not subject to the statutory compulsory license, and it is expected that they will be licensed in a similar manner to the way in which radio and television is now licensed. ASCAP has licensed major cable originations on an experimental basis and eventually expects to license all cable originations.

Cable fees are divided into those amounts received pursuant to statutory licenses, which are distributed based on performances on local television; and those amounts received as a result of negotiations between the parties in interest, which are distributed based on performances originating on cable.

The Society currently has licenses with major cable networks including HBO and CINEMAX; MTV and NICKELODEON; SHOWTIME and THE MOVIE CHANNEL; and THE DISNEY CHANNEL. License fees are distributed based on a census of performances on HBO, while performances on the other cable networks are surveyed on a sample basis.

BMI distributes the money it receives from those cable television services with which it has a license agreement, based upon performances as indicated on cue sheets and program guides supplied to BMI by the cable service. Cable distributions are made semi-annually.

Neither licensing society currently has licensing agreements with all the cable services, as negotiations are ongoing.

Advances

BMI began advancing money to writers practically from the day it opened its doors in 1940. A writer had the right to negotiate for an advance at any time during his tenure with BMI. Advances were usually based on the activity of the writer's catalogue, and could have been anything from a few hundred dollars for signing or having a song recorded to several thousand dollars for having a song in the top ten, or featured performances on network TV for a number of the writer's copyrights. This money was not recoupable by BMI except out of actual money earned and due writers.

ASCAP began its money advance policy to writers in 1966, and its recoupment factor was the same as BMI's. ASCAP and BMI used trade papers and publishers' information in helping them to arrive at an advance that would be in line with the income potential of the writer at the time he requested the advance.

When Buffalo Broadcasting Case (see Chapter 16) raised the prospects of the licensing societies (and, subsequently, writers and publishers) having their gross income reduced by as much as 25% because of potential syndicated TV royalty losses, the societies tightened their belts by eliminating writer advances, except in the most dire of circumstances. In the recent past, these advances have been made to writers who have money due them from previous or current song activity (such as a chart record or song in a TV show), but because of normal logging and accounting periods, they would not see that money for many months.

BMI accepts into membership any writer who has had at least one song commercially published or recorded. The term of a BMI writer's membership is two years with automatic renewal by BMI unless either party gives notice 60 days prior to the termination of the contract.

ASCAP holds the same procedure regarding a writer's membership, although the contract term is shorter. An ASCAP writer may resign at the end of any year of her one year contract by informing ASCAP in writing three months before the end of the year. ASCAP also requires an annual membership fee of $10.00 for writer members and a $50.00 fee for publisher members. BMI has a one-time $25.00 fee for new publishers, with no "one-time" annual fees for writer members.

Foreign Collections

Just as ASCAP and BMI collect royalties for their members on airplay performances in the U.S., similar licensing organizations perform the same service for foreign countries. To collect royalties on an American owned song played abroad, BMI and ASCAP have agreements with affiliates who collect the local royalties for distribution in the U.S. Both societies deal with about thirty licensing organizations worldwide. Since most foreign countries have only one licensing organization, BMI and ASCAP are often represented in an individual country by the same foreign society. BMI charges 3% to its writers and 3% to its publishers for such collection, while ASCAP charges 3.6% on average. (See the end of this chapter for a list of foreign societies.)

If an ASCAP writer co-authors a song with a BMI writer, both societies will collect and pay their own affiliated writer his portion of the income due him.

Publisher Affiliations

Publishers usually have both a BMI and ASCAP company. This is because the publisher is aware of a writer's desire to have a choice of performing rights societies. If a writer belongs to BMI and has a song the publisher wants, the publisher must have or form a BMI company. This is so the writer and publisher can collect royalties due them, since the song involved must be written and published by affiliates of the same performing rights society.

Additional Services

All societies have services to help and encourage the new songwriter, while honoring the established ones. Among them are:

ASCAP—WORKSHOPS

The ASCAP foundation sponsors ongoing series of songwriter workshops in New York, Los Angeles, and Nashville spanning all genres of music. Each workshop meets once a week for two months and features prominent industry guest panelists who field questions and critique participants' material. All ASCAP workshops are free of charge and open to both members and non-members alike. (For more information, contact ASCAP Public Relations in New York.)

GRANTS TO YOUNG COMPOSERS

To encourage composers under 30, the ASCAP foundation annually awards a memorial fund of Jack and Amie Norworth.

SCHOLARSHIPS

ASCAP grants annual scholarships to universities for music students.

ORCHESTRA AWARDS

Annual cash awards are made for adventuresome programming of contemporary music to symphony orchestras administered by the American Symphony Orchestra League.

STANDARD AND POPULAR AWARDS

Awarded to writers whose works have unique prestige value, but for which adequate compensation would not otherwise be received, or whose works are performed substantially in a medium not surveyed by the society.

NEW COMPOSERS COMPETITION

Annual ASCAP foundation grant to composers of new or previously unperformed symphonic works.

BMI—SONGWRITERS SHOWCASE

BMI sponsors the Los Angeles Songwriters Showcase where songwriters have their songs critiqued by publishers, producers, and record executives and receive a variety of services.

AWARDS

BMI Awards To Student Composers Competition is held to encourage and aid young composers of concert music. BMI holds this competition annually and presents cash awards to the winners.

WORKSHOPS

For writers interested in writing for the musical theatre, BMI maintains the BMI-Lehman Engel Musical Theatre Workshop. Workshops are held in New York City and admission to the sessions is determined by audition and the judgment of a board of workshop directors. There is no cost to the writers.

FOREIGN PERFORMING RIGHTS SOCIETIES

Country	Society	Territory
ARGENTINA	S.A.D.A.I.C.—Sociedad Argentina de Autores y Compositores de Musica	Republic of Argentina
AUSTRALIA	A.P.R.A.—Australasian Performing Right Association Limited	Australia, Australian Antarctic Territory, Nauru, New Zealand, Papua New Guinea, Ross Dependency, Western Samoa, the Islands of Ashmore, Cartier, Christmas, Cocos (Keeling), Cook, Fiji, Heard, Macquarie, McDonald, Niue (Savage), Norfolk, Tokelau (Union).
AUSTRIA	A.K.M.—Staatlich Genehmigte Gesellschaft der Autoren, Komponisten und Musikverleger.	Austria
BELGIUM	S.A.B.A.M.—Societe Belge des Auteurs Compositeurs et Editeurs	Belgium, Burundi, Ruanda
BRAZIL	S.I.C.A.M.—Sociedade Independente de Compositores e Autores Musicais	Brazil
BRAZIL	U.B.C.—Uniao Brasileira de Compositores	Brazil
CAMEROUND	S.C.A.D.R.A.—Societe Camerounaise	Through S.A.C.E.M. (see France)
CANADA	P.R.O.C.A.N.—Performing Rights Organization of Canada, Ltd.	Canada
CHILE	D.A.I.C.—Universidad de Chile, Departamento del Derecho de Autor	Chile
COLOMBIA	S.A.Y.C.O.—Sociedad de Autores y Compositores de Columbia	Colombia
CZECHOSLOVAKIA	O.S.A.—Ochranny Svaz Autorsky	Slovak Socialist Republic
DENMARK	K.O.D.A.—Selskabet til Forvaltning af Internationale Komponistrettigheder i Denmark	Denmark, Faroe Islands, Greenland.

FOREIGN PERFORMING RIGHTS SOCIETIES

Country	Society	Territory
EGYPT	S.A.C.E.R.A.U.—Societe des Auteurs, Compositeurs et Editeurs de la Republique Arabe d'Egypte	Through S.A.C.E.M. (see France)
FINLAND	T.E.O.S.T.O.—Saveltajain Tekijanoikeustoimisto	Finland
FRANCE	S.A.C.E.M.—Societe des Auteurs, Compositeurs et Editeurs de Musique	Andorra, Cameroun, Central African Republic, Chad, Congo (Brazzaville), Dahomey, Egypt, French Republic: France, French Austral & Antartic Possessions, French Guyana, French Polynesia, Guadeloupe, Martinique, Mayotte, New Caledonia & dependencies, Reunion, Saint-Pierre & Miquelon, Wallis and Futuna, Gabon, Gambia, Ivory Coast, Lebanon, Luxembourg, Madagascar, Mali, Mauritania, Monaco, Morocco, Niger, Senegal, Togo, Tunisia, Turkey, Upper Volta, Vanuatu (formerly New Hebrides).
FRENCH POLYNESIA	S.P.A.C.E.M.—Societe Polynesienne des Auteurs, Compositeurs et Editeurs de Musique	Through S.A.C.E.M. (see France)
GAMBIA	B.S.D.A.—Bureau Senegalais du Droit d'Auteur	Through S.A.C.E.M. (see France)
GERMANY	G.E.M.A.—Gesellschaft fur Musikalische Auffuhrungs und Mechanische Vervielfaltigungsrechte	German Federal Republic and West Berlin, Iran, Rumania.
GREECE	A.E.P.I.—Societe Anon. Hellenique Pour la Protection de la Propriete Intellectuelle	Greece
HONG KONG	C.A.S.H.—Composers and Authors Society of Hong Kong Ltd.	Through PRS (see England)
HUNGARY	A.R.T.I.S.J.U.S.—Bureau Hongrois Pour La Protection des Droits d'Auteur	Hungary

FOREIGN PERFORMING RIGHTS SOCIETIES

Country	Society	Territory
ICELAND	S.T.E.F.—Samband Tonskalda of Eigenda Flutningsrettar	Iceland
INDIA	I.P.R.S.—The Indian Performing Right Society Ltd.	Through P.R.S. (see England)
ISRAEL	A.C.U.M.—Societe des Auteurs, Compositeurs et Editeurs de Musique en Israel	Israel
ITALY	S.I.A.E.—Societa Italiana degli Autori ed Editori	Italy, Ethiopia, Libya, Republic of San Marino, Somalia, Vatican City.
IVORY COAST	B.U.R.I.D.A.—Bureau Ivoirien du Droit d'Auteur	Through S.A.C.E.M. (See France)
JAPAN	J.A.S.R.A.C.—Japanese Society for Rights of Authors, Composers and Publishers	Japan
MADAGASCAR	F.I.M.M.E.N.A.	Through S.A.C.E.M. (see France)
MEXICO	S.A.C.M.—Sociedad de Autores y Compositores de Musica S de A.	Mexico
MOROCCO	B.M.D.A.—Bureau Marocain du Droit d'Auteur	Through S.A.C.E.M. (see France)
NETHERLANDS	B.U.M.A.—Het Bureau voor Muziek-Auteursrecht	Indonesia: Borneo (Kalimantan), Celebes, Moluccas, Sunda Isles, Irian Barat, Netherlands (Holland), Netherlands Antilles: Aruba, Bonaire, Curaço, Saba, St. Eustatius and St. Martin, Surinam.
NORWAY	T.O.N.O.—Norsky Komponistforenings Internasjonale Musikkbyre	Bear Islands, Hope Island, Jan Mayen Island, Norway, Spitsbergen
PHILIPPINES	F.I.L.S.C.A.P.—Filipino Society of Composers, Authors and Publishers	Philippine Republic
POLAND	Z.A.I.K.S.—Stowarzyszenie Autorow	Poland

FOREIGN PERFORMING RIGHTS SOCIETIES

Country	Society	Territory
PORTUGAL	S.P.A.—Sociedade Portuguesa de Autores	Azores, Madeira, Portugal.
SENEGAL	B.S.D.A.—Bureau Senegalais du Droit d'Auteur	Through S.A.C.E.M. (see France)
SOUTH AFRICA	S.A.M.R.O.—South African Music Rights Organisation Limited	Botswana, Lesotho, Namibia (formerly South West Africa, Republic of South Africa, including Bophuthatswana and Transkei, Swaziland, Zimbabwe (formerly Rhodesia)
SPAIN	S.G.A.E.—Sociedad General de Autores de Espana	Spain
SWEDEN	S.T.I.M.—Svenska Tonsattares Internationella Musikbyra	Sweden
SWITZERLAND	S.U.I.S.A.—Societe Suisse pour les Droits des Auteurs d'Oeuvres Musicales	Switzerland, Liechtenstein
TUNISIA	S.O.D.A.C.T.—Societe des Auteurs et Compositeurs de Tunisie	Through S.A.C.E.M. (see France)
TURKEY	F.I.S.A.N.	Through S.A.C.E.M. (see France)
UNITED KINGDOM & TERRITORIES	P.R.S.—The Performing Right Society	Anguilla, Antigue, Ascension Island, Bahamas, Bangladesh (formerly East Pakistan), Barbados, Barbuda, Belize (formerly British Honduras) Bermuda, British Antarctic Territory, British Virgin Islands, Brunei, Cayman Islands Central & Southern Line Islands, Channel Islands, Cyprus, Dominica, Falkland Islands, Gambia, Ghana, Gibraltar, Grenada, Guyana, Hong Kong India, Ireland (Republic of), Isle of Man, Jamaica, Kenya, Kiribati (formerly Gilbert Islands), Malawi, Malaysia, Malta, Mauritius, Montserrat, Nevis (see St. Kitts—Nevis), Nigeria, Pakistan (formerly West Pakistan) Pitcairn Islands, Redonda,

FOREIGN PERFORMING RIGHTS SOCIETIES

Country	Society	Territory
UNITED KINGDOM & TERRITORIES (Continued)	P.R.S.—The Performing Right Society	Seychelles, Sierra Leone, Singapore, Solomon Islands (formerly British Solomon Islands), South Georgia, South Sandwich Islands, Sri Lanka (formerly Ceylon), St. Christopher (now St. Kitts—Nevis) St. Helena, St. Kitts-Nevis, St. Lucia, St. Vincent, Tanzania, including Tanganyika & Zanzibar, Tobago (see Trinidad & Tobago) Tonga,Trinidad & Tobago, Tristan da Cunha, Turks & Caicos Islands, Tuvalu (formerly Ellice Islands), Uganda, United Kingdom, Zambia
URUGUAY	A.G.A.D.U.—Asociacion General de Autores del Uruguay	Uruguay
U.S.S.R.	V.A.A.P.—The Copyright Agency of the U.S.S.R.	Union of Soviet Socialist Republics
VENEZUELA	S.A.C.V.E.N.—Sociedad de Autores y Compositores de Venezuela	Venezuela
YUGOSLAVIA	S.O.K.O.J.—Savej Organizacija Kompozitora Jugoslavije	Yugoslavia

Clearance Form

Broadcast Music, Inc., 320 West 57th Street, New York, N.Y. 10019
Att. Clearance Department

COMPLETE FORM IN ACCORDANCE WITH INSTRUCTIONS ON THE REVERSE SIDE AND RETURN BOTH COPIES TO BMI. DO NOT USE THIS FORM TO CORRECT OR REVISE INFORMATION ON A PREVIOUSLY CLEARED WORK. SEND DETAILS IN A LETTER.

FOR BMI USE
DO NOT WRITE BELOW

ENTERED VIA SCOPE

DATE: _____

BY: _____

TITLE — ONE WORK PER FORM

Credit Rate	Mulpt Credit	Clear-ance	BMI	Log U.S./Can.

IF BASED ON PUBLIC DOMAIN - GIVE ORIGINAL TITLE, WRITER AND SOURCE

CHECK IF WORK IS FROM:
☐ MOTION PICTURE OR TV FILM
☐ BROADWAY SHOW
☐ OFF-BROADWAY SHOW

GIVE TITLE OF PICTURE, FILM OR SHOW
(SEE REVERSE SIDE)

WRITER(S) NAME(S)			WRITER(S) ADDRESS(ES)	Perf. Rts. Orgn.	Percentage Share	Mode of Pay-ment	WR
LAST	FIRST	MIDDLE					

SOC. SEC. NO.

SOC. SEC. NO.

SOC. SEC. NO.

SOC. SEC. NO.

SOC. SEC. NO.

PUBLISHER(S) NAME(S)

☐ CHECK HERE IF NO RIGHTS GRANTED BY WRITER(S) TO ANY PUBLISHER.
☐ CHECK HERE IF PUBLISHER IS ADMINISTRATOR ONLY. DO NOT CHECK THIS BOX IF PUBLISHER OWNS PART OR ALL OF COPYRIGHT AND/OR PERFORMING RIGHTS.
NAME(S) OF U.S. ORIGINAL PUBLISHER(S):

	Perf. Rts. Orgn.	Percentage Share	Credit		Orig. Pub.	World Rights
			U.S.	Can.		

IF WORK IS OF FOREIGN ORIGIN, COMPLETE BELOW AND ATTACH AN ADDITIONAL COPY OF THIS FORM:
U.S. SUB—PUBLISHER(S): (PLEASE GIVE TERRITORIES)

FULL NAME OF FOREIGN ORIGINAL PUBLISHER:

PLEASE DO NOT SUBMIT NON-MUSICAL WORKS. THEY CANNOT BE CLEARED BY BMI. FOR SPOKEN WORD MATERIAL WITH A MUSICAL BACKGROUND, SEE INSTRUCTIONS ON REVERSE SIDE.

TYPE OR PRINT NAME AND ADDRESS OF SUBMITTING BMI AFFILIATE.

MAIL CONFIRM-ATION TO:

RECORD LABEL & NO. OF 1ST RECORD RELEASE

ARTIST   RELEASE DATE

DATE SUBMITTED TO BMI

AUTHORIZED SIGNATURE

CLEARED IN ACCORDANCE WITH TERMS ON REVERSE SIDE

INSTRUCTIONS

Fill out columns on left side of page and RETURN TO BMI CLEARANCE DEPARTMENT. DO NOT fill in columns in shaded area. (BOTH COPIES OF THIS FORM MUST BE RETURNED TO BMI).

TITLE   Give complete title of work you are submitting for clearance. If also known under another title, please indicate a/k/a (also known as) and give other title. (ONLY ONE WORK PER FORM).

If this work is based on a Public Domain work, GIVE ORIGINAL TITLE, WRITER AND SOURCE. A LEAD SHEET OR RECORDING MUST BE SUBMITTED WITH THIS CLEARANCE FORM IF THIS WORK IS BASED ON A PUBLIC DOMAIN WORK.

If this work was written for a Full Length Feature Motion Picture or a Film made for TV, or a Broadway or Off-Broadway Show, check appropriate box and give complete title of Motion Picture, Film or Show. Enclose program, name of theatre and/or additional details.

PERCENTAGE   **Indicate share of each writer. All writers' shares should total 100%.**
SHARES
Indicate share of each publisher. All publishers' shares should total 100%.

IF NO RIGHTS HAVE BEEN ASSIGNED TO ANY PUBLISHER, CHECK THE BOX PROVIDED. IN SUCH CASE FULL PUBLISHER SHARE WILL BE DIVIDED BETWEEN WRITERS IN SAME PERCENTAGE AS WRITER SHARES.

If part of publisher share has been granted, indicate percentage due to publisher and percentage retained by writer(s).

WRITER(S)   Give complete name and address of each writer. If pseudonym, give complete name of writer under his pseudonym. Last Name first followed by First Name and Middle Name or Initial. Give Social Security No. of each writer.

Give name of PERFORMING RIGHTS ORGANIZATION (Perf. Rts. Orgn.) with which each writer is affiliated.

PUBLISHER(S)   Give complete name of all publishers and co-publishers.

If publisher acquired this work from a publisher outside the United States, give complete name of the original foreign publisher, territories for which sub-publishing rights were acquired and ATTACH AN ADDITIONAL COPY OF THIS FORM.

Give name of PERFORMING RIGHTS ORGANIZATION (Perf. Rts. Orgn.) with which each publisher is affiliated.

SPOKEN   Spoken word material with a musical background will be cleared only if the music is original (not based on
WORD   a Public Domain work) and if a substantial part of the recording contains background music. A recording
MATERIAL   must be submitted with this Clearance Form if this is spoken word material.

RECORD   If this work has been recorded, give the record label and number, artist and date it was or will be released.

DATE   Give the date you are submitting this work to BMI.

SIGNATURE   This form must be signed by an affiliated writer or an authorized representative of the submitting publisher.

IF ALL OF THE ABOVE INSTRUCTIONS ARE NOT FOLLOWED, THIS WORK WILL NOT BE REGISTERED FOR LOGGING PURPOSES AND THE FORM WILL BE RETURNED TO YOU FOR CORRECTION OR COMPLETION.

CLEARANCE TERMS

THE RETURN OF A STAMPED COPY OF THIS FORM INDICATES THAT THE WORK LISTED ON THE REVERSE SIDE HAS BEEN CLEARED.

A writer submitting this form warrants and represents that (s)he is the writer or co-writer of the work to the extent indicated and that (s)he has not acquired his or her interest in such work by virtue of purchase or assignment from the writer or writers thereof.

Please note that in the event that a work cleared is published or recorded with lyrics which we, in our sole judgment, regard as unsuitable for broadcast use or with musical or lyrical material which we, in our sole judgment, regard as an infringement, we reserve the right at any time to exclude this work in its entirety from the provisions of our agreement and to withdraw the clearance.

We bring to your attention that in the event a clearance form submitted does not properly indicate in the space provided therefor that a work is based on public domain source, we reserve the right, if at any time such work is found to have a public domain source, to allocate to such work a percentage of the normal logging credit or, in the case of a work having little or no original material, to give no logging credit to such work.

Michael Tortora

Michael Tortora
Clearance Dept.

CF-2/87

BROADCAST MUSIC, INC.

320 West 57th Street   New York, N.Y. 10019

Date

Dear

The following shall constitute the agreement between us:

1. As used in this agreement:

    (a) The word "period" shall mean the term from   to

, and continuing thereafter for additional terms of two years each unless terminated by either party at the end of said initial term or any additional term, upon notice by registered or certified mail not more than six months or less than sixty (60) days prior to the end of any such term.

    (b) The word "works" shall mean:

        (i) All musical compositions (including the musical segments and individual compositions written for a dramatic or dramatico-musical work) composed by you alone or with one or more collaborators during the period; and

        (ii) All musical compositions (including the musical segments and individual compositions written for a dramatic or dramatico-musical work) composed by you alone or with one or more collaborators prior to the period, except those in which there is an outstanding grant of the right of public performance to a person other than a publisher affiliated with BMI.

2. You agree that:

    (a) Within ten (10) days after the execution of this agreement you will furnish to us two copies of a completed clearance sheet in the form supplied by us with respect to each work heretofore composed by you which has been published in printed copies or recorded commercially or which is being currently performed or which you consider as likely to be performed.

    (b) In each instance that a work for which clearance sheets have not been submitted to us pursuant to sub-paragraph (a) hereof is published in printed copies or recorded commercially or in synchronization with film or tape or is considered by you as likely to be performed, whether such work is composed prior to the execution of this agreement or hereafter during the period, you will promptly furnish to us two copies of a completed clearance sheet in the form supplied by us with respect to each such work.

    (c) If requested by us in writing, you will promptly furnish to us a legible lead sheet or other written or printed copy of a work.

3. The submission of clearance sheets pursuant to paragraph 2 hereof shall constitute a warranty by you that all of the information contained thereon is true and correct and that no performing rights in such work have been granted to or reserved by others except as specifically set forth therein in connection with works heretofore written or co-written by you.

4. Except as otherwise provided herein, you hereby grant to us for the period:

    (a) All the rights that you own or acquire publicly to perform, and to license others to perform, anywhere in the world, any part or all of the works.

    (b) The non-exclusive right to record, and to license others to record, any part or all of any of the works on electrical transcriptions, wire, tape, film or otherwise, but only for the purpose of performing such work publicly by means of radio and television or for archive or audition purposes and not for sale to the public or for synchronization (i) with motion pictures intended primarily for theatrical exhibition or (ii) with programs distributed by means of syndication to broadcasting stations.

    (c) The non-exclusive right to adapt or arrange any part or all of any of the works for performance purposes, and to license others to do so.

5. (a) The rights granted to us by sub-paragraph (a) of paragraph 4 hereof shall not include the right to perform or license the performance of more than one song or aria from a dramatic or dramatico-musical work which is an opera, operetta, or musical show or more than five minutes from a dramatic or dramatico-musical work which is a ballet if such performance is accompanied by the dramatic action, costumes or scenery of that dramatic or dramatico-musical work.

(b) You, together with the publisher and your collaborators, if any, shall have the right jointly, by written notice to us, to exclude from the grant made by sub-paragraph (a) of paragraph 4 hereof performances of works comprising more than thirty minutes of a dramatic or dramatico-musical work, but this right shall not apply to such performances from (i) a score originally written for and performed as part of a theatrical or television film, (ii) a score originally written for and performed as part of a radio or television program, or (iii) the original cast, sound track or similar album of a dramatic or dramatico-musical work.

(c) You retain the right to issue non-exclusive licenses for performances of a work or works (other than to another performing rights licensing organization), provided that within ten (10) days of the issuance of such license we are given written notice of the titles of the works and the nature of the performances so licensed by you.

6. (a) As full consideration for all rights granted to us hereunder and as security therefor, we agree to pay to you, with respect to each of the works in which we obtain and retain performing rights during the period:

(i) For performances of a work on broadcasting stations in the United States, its territories and possessions, amounts calculated pursuant to our then current standard practices upon the basis of the then current performance rates generally paid by us to our affiliated writers for similar performances of similar compositions. The number of performances for which you shall be entitled to payment shall be estimated by us in accordance with our then current system of computing the number of such performances.

It is acknowledged that we license the works of our affiliates for performance by non-broadcasting means, but that unless and until such time as feasible methods can be devised for tabulation of and payment for such performances, payment will be based solely on broadcast performances. In the event that during the period we shall establish a system of separate payment for non-broadcasting performances, we shall pay you upon the basis of the then current performance rates generally paid by us to our other affiliated writers for similar performances of similar compositions.

(ii) In the case of a work composed by you with one or more collaborators, the sum payable to you hereunder shall be a pro rata share, determined on the basis of the number of collaborators, unless you shall have transmitted to us a copy of an agreement between you and your collaborators providing for a different division of payment.

(iii) All monies received by us from any performing rights licensing organization outside of the United States, its territories and possessions, which are designated by such performing rights licensing organization as the author's share of foreign performance royalties earned by your works after the deduction of our then current handling charge applicable to our affiliated writers.

(b) We shall have no obligation to make payment hereunder with respect to (i) any performance of a work which occurs prior to the date on which we have received from you all of the information and material with respect to such work which is referred to in paragraphs 2 and 3 hereof, or (ii) any performance as to which a direct license as described in sub-paragraph (c) of paragraph 5 hereof has been granted by you, your collaborator or publisher.

7. We will furnish statements to you at least twice during each year of the period showing the number of performances as computed pursuant to sub-paragraph (a) (i) of paragraph 6 hereof and at least once during each year of the period showing the monies due pursuant to sub-paragraph (a) (iii) of paragraph 6 hereof. Each statement shall be accompanied by payment to you, subject to all proper deductions for advances; if any, of the sum thereby shown to be due for such performances.

8. (a) Nothing in this agreement requires us to continue to license the works subsequent to the termination of this agreement. In the event that we continue to license any or all of the works, however, we shall continue to make payments to you for so long as you do not make or purport to make directly or indirectly any grant of performing rights in such works to any other licensing organization. The amounts of such payments shall be calculated pursuant to our then current standard practices upon the basis of the then current performance rates generally paid by us to our affiliated writers for similar performances of similar compositions. You agree to notify us by registered or certified mail of any grant or purported grant by you directly or indirectly of performing rights to any other performing rights organization within ten (10) days from the making of such grant or purported grant and if you fail so to inform us thereof and we make payments to you for any period after the making of any such grant or purported grant, you agree to repay to us all amounts so paid by us promptly on demand. In addition, if we inquire of you by registered or certified mail, addressed to your last known address, whether you have made any such grant or purported grant and you fail to confirm to us by registered or certified mail within thirty (30) days of the mailing of such inquiry that you have not made any such grant or purported grant, we may, from and after such date, discontinue making any payments to you.

(b) Our obligation to continue payment to you after the termination of this agreement for performances outside of the United States, its territories and possessions shall be dependent upon our receipt in the United

States of payments designated by foreign performing rights organizations as the author's share of foreign performance royalties earned by your works. Payment of such foreign royalties shall be subject to deduction of our then current handling charge applicable to our affiliated writers.

(c) In the event that we have reason to believe that you will receive or are receiving payment from a performing rights licensing organization other than BMI for or based on United States performances of one or more of your works during a period when such works were licensed by us pursuant to this agreement, we shall have the right to withhold payment for such performances from you until receipt of evidence satisfactory to us of the amount so paid to you by such other organization or that you have not been so paid. In the event that you have been so paid, the monies payable by us to you for such performances during such period shall be reduced by the amount of the payment from such other organization. In the event that you do not supply such evidence within eighteen (18) months from the date of our request therefor, we shall be under no obligation to make any payment to you for performances of such works during such period.

9 In the event that this agreement shall terminate at a time when, after crediting all earnings reflected by statements rendered to you prior to the effective date of such termination, there remains an unearned balance of advances paid to you by us, such termination shall not be effective until the close of the calendar quarterly period during which (a) you shall repay such unearned balance of advances, or (b) you shall notify us by registered or certified mail that you have received a statement rendered by us at our normal accounting time showing that such unearned balance of advances has been fully recouped by us.

10. You warrant and represent that you have the right to enter into this agreement; that you are not bound by any prior commitments which conflict with your commitments hereunder; that each of the works, composed by you alone or with one or more collaborators, is original; and that exercise of the rights granted by you herein will not constitute an infringement of copyright or violation of any other right of, or unfair competition with, any person, firm or corporation. You agree to indemnify and hold harmless us and our licensees from and against any and all loss or damage resulting from any claim of whatever nature arising from or in connection with the exercise of any of the rights granted by you in this agreement. Upon notification to us or any of our licensees of a claim with respect to any of the works, we shall have the right to exclude such work from this agreement and/or to withhold payment of all sums which become due pursuant to this agreement or any modification thereof until receipt of satisfactory written evidence that such claim has been withdrawn, settled or adjudicated.

11. (a) We shall have the right, upon written notice to you, to exclude from this agreement, at any time, any work which in our opinion (i) is similar to a previously existing composition and might constitute a copyright infringement, or (ii) has a title or music or lyric similar to that of a previously existing composition and might lead to a claim of unfair competition, or (iii) is offensive, in bad taste or against public morals, or (iv) is not reasonably suitable for performance.

(b) In the case of works which in our opinion are based on compositions in the public domain, we shall have the right, upon written notice to you, either (i) to exclude any such work from this agreement, or (ii) to classify any such work as entitled to receive only a fraction of the full credit that would otherwise be given for performances thereof.

(c) In the event that any work is excluded from this agreement pursuant to paragraph 10 or subparagraph (a) or (b) of this paragraph 11, all rights in such work shall automatically revert to you ten (10) days after the date of our notice to you of such exclusion. In the event that a work is classified for less than full credit under sub-paragraph (b) (ii) of this paragraph 11, you shall have the right, by giving notice to us, within ten (10) days after the date of our letter advising you of the credit allocated to the work, to terminate our rights therein, and all rights in such work shall thereupon revert to you.

12. In each instance that you write, or are employed or commissioned by a motion picture producer to write, during the period, all or part of the score of a motion picture intended primarily for exhibition in theaters, or by the producer of a musical show or revue for the legitimate stage to write, during the period, all or part of the musical compositions contained therein, we agree to advise the producer of the film that such part of the score as is written by you may be performed as part of the exhibition of said film in theaters in the United States, its territories and possessions, without compensation to us, or to the producer of the musical show or revue that your compositions embodied therein may be performed on the stage with living artists as part of such musical show or revue, without compensation to us. In the event that we notify you that we have established a system for the collection of royalties for performance of the scores of motion picture films in theaters in the United States, its territories and possessions, we shall no longer be obligated to take such action with respect to motion picture scores.

13. You make, constitute and appoint us, or our nominee, your true and lawful attorney, irrevocably during the term hereof, in our name or that of our nominee, or in your name, or otherwise, to do all acts, take all proceedings, execute, acknowledge and deliver any and all instruments, papers, documents, process or pleadings that may be necessary, proper or expedient to restrain infringement of and/or to enforce and protect the rights granted by you hereunder, and to recover damages in respect to or for the infringement or other violation of the said rights, and in our sole judgment to join you and/or others in whose names the copyrights to any of the works may stand; to discontinue, compromise or refer to arbitration, any such actions or proceedings or to make any other disposition of the disputes in relation to the works, provided that any action or proceeding commenced by us pursuant to the provisions of this paragraph shall be at our sole expense and for our sole benefit.

14. You agree that you, your agents, employees or representatives will not, directly or indirectly, solicit or accept payment from writers for composing music for lyrics or writing lyrics to music or for reviewing, publishing, promoting, recording or rendering other services connected with the exploitation of any composition, or permit use of your name or your affiliation with us in connection with any of the foregoing. In the event of a violation of any of the provisions of this paragraph 14, we shall have the right, in our sole discretion, by giving you at least thirty (30) days' notice by registered or certified mail, to terminate this agreement. In the event of such termination no payments shall be due to you pursuant to paragraph 8 hereof.

15. No monies due or to become due to you shall be assignable, whether by way of assignment, sale or power granted to an attorney-in-fact, without our prior written consent. If any assignment of such monies is made by you without such prior written consent, no rights of any kind against us will be acquired by the assignee, purchaser or attorney-in-fact.

16. In the event that during the period (a) mail addressed to you at the last address furnished by you pursuant to paragraph 19 hereof shall be returned by the post office, or (b) monies shall not have been earned by you pursuant to paragraph 6 hereof for a period of two consecutive years or more, or (c) you shall die, BMI shall have the right to terminate this agreement on at least thirty (30) days' notice by registered or certified mail addressed to the last address furnished by you pursuant to paragraph 19 hereof and, in the case of your death, to the representative of your estate, if known to BMI. In the event of such termination no payments shall be due you pursuant to paragraph 8 hereof.

17. You acknowledge that the rights obtained by you pursuant to this agreement constitute rights to payment of money and that during the period we shall hold absolute title to the performing rights granted to us hereunder. In the event that during the period you shall file a petition in bankruptcy, such a petition shall be filed against you, you shall make an assignment for the benefit of creditors, you shall consent to the appointment of a receiver or trustee for all or part of your property, or you shall institute or shall have instituted against you any other insolvency proceeding under the United States bankruptcy laws or any other applicable law, we shall retain title to the performing rights in all works for which clearance sheets shall have theretofore been submitted to us and shall subrogate your trustee in bankruptcy or receiver and any subsequent purchasers from them to your right to payment of money for said works in accordance with the terms and conditions of this agreement.

18. Any controversy or claim arising out of, or relating to, this agreement or the breach thereof, shall be settled by arbitration in the City of New York, in accordance with the Rules of the American Arbitration Association, and judgment upon the award of the arbitrator may be entered in any Court having jurisdiction thereof. Such award shall include the fixing of the expenses of the arbitration, including reasonable attorney's fees, which shall be borne by the unsuccessful party.

19. You agree to notify our Department of Performing Rights Administration promptly in writing of any change in your address. Any notice sent to you pursuant to the terms of this agreement shall be valid if addressed to you at the last address so furnished by you.

20. This agreement cannot be changed orally and shall be governed and construed pursuant to the laws of the State of New York.

21. In the event that any part or parts of this agreement are found to be void by a court of competent jurisdiction, the remaining part or parts shall nevertheless be binding with the same force and effect as if the void part or parts were deleted from this agreement.

Very truly yours,

BROADCAST MUSIC. INC.

ACCEPTED AND AGREED TO:

By ....

Assistant Vice President

....

1986-1995

No.

Rec'd

Agreement Between

AND

American Society
OF
Composers, Authors & Publishers
1 LINCOLN PLAZA
NEW YORK, N. Y. 10023

Dated:

AGREEMENT made between the Undersigned (for brevity called *"Owner"*) and the AMERICAN SOCIETY OF COMPOSERS, AUTHORS AND PUBLISHERS (for brevity called *"Society"*), in consideration of the premises and of the mutual covenants hereinafter contained, as follows:

1. The *Owner* grants to the *Society* for the term hereof, the right to license non-dramatic public performances (as hereinafter defined), of each musical work:

Of which the *Owner* is a copyright proprietor; or

Which the *Owner*, alone, or jointly, or in collaboration with others, wrote, composed, published, acquired or owned; or

In which the *Owner* now has any right, title, interest or control whatsoever, in whole or in part; or

Which hereafter, during the term hereof, may be written, composed, acquired, owned, published or copyrighted by the *Owner*, alone, jointly or in collaboration with others; or

In which the *Owner* may hereafter, during the term hereof, have any right, title, interest or control, whatsoever, in whole or in part.

The right to license the public performance of every such musical work shall be deemed granted to the *Society* by this instrument for the term hereof, immediately upon the work being written, composed, acquired, owned, published or copyrighted.

The rights hereby granted shall include:

(a) All the rights and remedies for enforcing the copyright or copyrights of such musical works, whether such copyrights are in the name of the *Owner* and/or others, as well as the right to sue under such copyrights in the name of the *Society* and/or in the name of the *Owner* and/or others, to the end that the *Society* may effectively protect and be assured of all the rights hereby granted.

(b) The non-exclusive right of public performance of the separate numbers, songs, fragments or arrangements, melodies or selections forming part or parts of musical plays and dramatico-musical compositions, the *Owner* reserving and excepting from this grant the right of performance of musical plays and dramatico-musical compositions in their entirety, or any part of such plays or dramatico-musical compositions on the legitimate stage.

(c) The non-exclusive right of public performance by means of radio broadcasting, telephony, "wired wireless," all forms of synchronism with motion pictures, and/or any method of transmitting sound other than television broadcasting.

(d) The non-exclusive right of public performance by television broadcasting; provided, however, that:

(i) This grant does not extend to or include the right to license the public performance by television broadcasting or otherwise of any rendition or performance of (a) any opera, operetta, musical comedy, play or like production, as such, in whole or in part, or (b) any composition from any opera, operetta, musical comedy, play or like production (whether or not such opera, operetta, musical comedy, play or like production was presented on the stage or in motion picture form) in a manner which recreates the performance of such composition with substantially such distinctive scenery or costume as was used in the presentation of such opera, operetta, musical comedy, play or like production (whether or not such opera, operetta, musical comedy, play or like production was presented on the stage or in motion picture form): provided, however, that the rights hereby granted shall be deemed to include a grant of the right to license non-dramatic performances of compositions by television broadcasting of a motion picture containing such composition if the rights in such motion picture other than those granted hereby have been obtained from the parties in interest.

(ii) Nothing herein contained shall be deemed to grant the right to license the public performance by television broadcasting of dramatic performances. Any performance of a separate musical composition which is not a dramatic performance, as defined herein, shall be deemed to be a non-dramatic performance. For the purposes of this agreement, a dramatic performance shall mean a performance of a musical composition on a television program in which there is a definite plot depicted by action and where the performance of the musical composition is woven into and carries forward the plot and its accompanying action. The use of dialogue to establish a mere program format or the use of any non-dramatic device merely to introduce a performance of a composition shall not be deemed to make such performance dramatic.

(iii) The definition of the terms "dramatic" and "non-dramatic" performances contained herein are purely for the purposes of this agreement and for the term thereof and shall not be binding upon or prejudicial to any position taken by either of us subsequent to the term hereof or for any purpose other than this agreement.

(e) The *Owner* may at any time and from time to time, in good faith, restrict the radio or television broadcasting of compositions from musical comedies, operas, operettas and motion pictures, or any other composition being excessively broadcast, only for the purpose of preventing harmful effect upon such musical comedies, operas, operettas, motion pictures or compositions, in respect of other interests under the copyrights thereof; provided, however, that the right to grant limited licenses will be given, upon application, as to restricted compositions, if and when the *Owner* is unable to show reasonable hazards to his or its major interests likely to result from such radio or television broadcasting; and provided further that such right to restrict any such composition shall not be exercised for the purpose of permitting the fixing or regulating of fees for the recording or transcribing of such composition, and provided further that in no case shall any charges, "free plugs", or other consideration be required in respect of any permission granted to perform a restricted composition; and provided further that in no event shall any composition, after the initial radio or television broadcast thereof, be restricted for the purpose of confining further radio or television broadcasts thereof to a particular artist, station, network or program. The *Owner* may also at any time and from time to time, in good faith, restrict the radio or television broadcasting of any composition, as to which any suit has been brought or threatened on a claim that such composition infringes a composition not contained in the repertory of *Society* or on a claim by a non-member of *Society* that *Society* does not have the right to license the public performance of such composition by radio or television broadcasting.

2. The term of this agreement shall be for a period commencing on the date hereof and expiring on the 31st day of December, 1995.

3. The *Society* agrees, during the term hereof, in good faith to use its best endeavors to promote and carry out the objects for which it was organized, and to hold and apply all royalties, profits, benefits and advantages arising from the exploitation of the rights assigned to it by its several members, including the *Owner*, to the uses and purposes as provided in its Articles of Association (which are hereby incorporated by reference), as now in force or as hereafter amended.

4. The *Owner* hereby irrevocably, during the term hereof, authorizes, empowers and vests in the *Society* the right to enforce and protect such rights of public performance under any and all copyrights, whether standing in the name of the *Owner* and/or others, in any and all works copyrighted by the *Owner*, and/or by others; to prevent the infringement thereof, to litigate, collect and receipt for damages arising from infringement, and in its sole judgment to join the *Owner* and/or others in whose names the copyright may stand, as parties plaintiff or defendants in suits or proceedings; to bring suit in the name of the *Owner* and/or in the name of the *Society*, or others in whose name the copyright may stand, or otherwise, and to release, compromise, or refer to arbitration any actions, in the same manner and to the same extent and to all intents and purposes as the *Owner* might or could do, had this instrument not been made.

5. The *Owner* hereby makes, constitutes and appoints the *Society*, or its successor, the *Owner's* true and lawful attorney, irrevocably during the term hereof, and in the name of the *Society* or its successor, or in the name of the *Owner*, or otherwise, to do all acts, take all proceedings, execute, acknowledge and deliver any and all instruments, papers, documents, process and pleadings that may be necessary, proper or expedient to restrain infringements and recover damages in respect to or for the infringement or other violation of the rights of public performance in such works, and to discontinue, compromise or refer to arbitration any such proceedings or actions, or to make any other disposition of the differences in relation to the premises.

6. The *Owner* agrees from time to time, to execute, acknowledge and deliver to the *Society*, such assurances, powers of attorney or other authorizations or instruments as the *Society* may deem necessary or expedient to enable it to exercise, enjoy and enforce, in its own name or otherwise, all rights and remedies aforesaid.

7. It is mutually agreed that during the term hereof the Board of Directors of the *Society* shall be composed of an equal number of writers and publishers respectively, and that the royalties distributed by the Board of Directors shall be divided into two (2) equal sums, and one (1) each of such sums credited respectively to and for division amongst (a) the writer members, and (b) the publisher members, in accordance with the system of distribution and classification as determined by the Classification Committee of each group, in accordance with the Articles of Association as they may be amended from time to time, except that the classification of the *Owner* within his class may be changed.

8. The *Owner* agrees that his classification in the *Society* as determined from time to time by the Classification Committee of his group and/or The Board of Directors of the *Society*, in case of appeal by him, shall be final, conclusive and binding upon him.

The *Society* shall have the right to transfer the right of review of any classification from the Board of Directors to any other agency or instrumentality that in its discretion and good judgment it deems best adapted to assuring to the *Society's* membership a just, fair, equitable and accurate classification.

The *Society* shall have the right to adopt from time to time such systems, means, methods and formulae for the establishment of a member's status in respect of classification as will assure a fair, just and equitable distribution of royalties among the membership.

9. **"Public Performance" Defined.** The term *"public performance"* shall be construed to mean vocal, instrumental and/or mechanical renditions and representations in any manner or by any method whatsoever, including transmissions by radio and television broadcasting stations, transmission by telephony and/or "wired wireless"; and/or reproductions of performances and renditions by means of devices for reproducing sound recorded in synchronism or timed relation with the taking of motion pictures.

10. **"Musical Works" Defined.** The phrase *"musical works"* shall be construed to mean musical compositions and dramatico-musical compositions, the words and music thereof, and the respective arrangements thereof, and the selections therefrom.

11. The powers, rights, authorities and privileges by this instrument vested in the *Society*, are deemed to include the World, provided, however, that such grant of rights for foreign countries shall be subject to any agreements now in effect, a list of which are noted on the reverse side hereof.

12. The grant made herein by the owner is modified by and subject to the provisions of (a) the Amended Final Judgment (Civil Action No. 13-95) dated March 14, 1950 in U. S. A. v. ASCAP as further amended by Order dated January 7, 1960, (b) the Final Judgment (Civil Action No. 42-245) in U. S. A. v. ASCAP, dated March 14, 1950, and (c) the provisions of the Articles of Association and resolutions of the Board of Directors adopted pursuant to such judgments and order.

SIGNED, SEALED AND DELIVERED, on this......................day of..., 19........

Owner { ....
        ....

AMERICAN SOCIETY OF COMPOSERS,
AUTHORS AND PUBLISHERS,

Society {

By ....
                    President

FOREIGN AGREEMENTS AT THIS DATE IN EFFECT

(See paragraph 11 of the within agreement)

COUNTRY	WITH (Name of Firm)	EXPIRES	REMARKS

TITLE: (DURATION IN MINUTES)

LIST PRODUCTION/FILM TITLE IF ANY

| COMPOSER (AFFILIATION) | AUTHOR (AFFILIATION) |

CHECK   ORIGINAL COPYRIGHT

ONE   ARR. OF PUBLIC DOMAIN WORK   ARR: (AFFILIATION)

COPYRIGHT OWNER   PUBLISHER (AFFILIATION)

MEMBER CONTROLLING PERFORMING RIGHTS IN THE U.S.A.

PERCENTAGE OF PUB. FEES CLAIMED: (IF ON ASSIGNMENT. PROVIDE COPY INDICATING EFFECTIVE DATE)   DATE OF COPYRIGHT

COPYRIGHT ENTRY NUMBER

DO NOT WRITE IN THIS SPACE

ENTER REMARKS AND SUB-PUBLISHING AGREEMENTS ON REVERSE.

BMI
WRITER APPLICATION

APPLICATION WILL NOT BE ACCEPTED UNLESS ALL QUESTIONS ARE FULLY ANSWERED AND SIGNED IN INK

PLEASE
PRINT

Mr.
1. FULL <u>LEGAL</u> NAME: Ms. _____
Miss   (First Name)   (Middle Name)   (Last Name)
Mrs.

2. ☐ HOME ADDRESS:
_____
(Street)   (City)   (State)   (Zip Code)   (Phone Number)

3. ☐ BUSINESS ADDRESS: (If same as above, write "same")
_____
(Street)   (City)   (State)   (Zip Code)   (Phone Number)

(Check one address to which all mail is to be sent)

4. DATE OF BIRTH: _____ CITIZENSHIP: _____
(Month)   (Day)   (Year)   (Country)

5. LIST ALL PEN NAMES WHICH YOU HAVE USED OR WILL USE AS A WRITER:
_____
_____

6. Are you now or have you ever been a writer-member or writer-affiliate of BMI, ASCAP, SESAC, or of any foreign performing rights licensing organization? If so, state name of organization and the period during which you were a member or affiliate:
_____

7. Is your spouse, parent, brother, sister, child or any other relative a writer-member or writer-affiliate of any organization specified in Question 6? If so, give name, relationship to you and organization:
_____

8. **COMPLETE THE ENCLOSED CLEARANCE FORM** listing one composition written by you, either alone or in collaboration with others, which is commercially recorded or being performed or likely to be performed and return it to BMI with the application. A supply of clearance forms for reporting other songs will be sent to you when the processing of your application has been fully completed.

I warrant and represent that all of the information furnished on this application is true. I acknowledge that any contract consummated between me and BMI will be entered into in reliance upon the representations contained in this application, and that the contract will be subject to cancellation if any question herein contained is not answered fully or accurately.

Date: _____

SOCIAL SECURITY NUMBER: _____
(If no Social Security Number is listed, application WILL NOT BE ACCEPTED.
Foreign nationals should request Form 1001 from BMI for completion.)

SIGNATURE: _____
(Full Legal Name)
(If applicant is under 18 years of age, the parent or legal guardian must sign below:

Guardian Signature: _____

BMI	BMI	BMI
Writer Administration	Writer Administration	Writer Administration
320 West 57th Street	10 Music Square East	8730 Sunset Blvd., 3rd Floor West
New York, NY 10019	Nashville, TN 37203	Los Angeles, CA 90069
212-586-2000	615-259-3625	213-659-9109

PLEASE RETURN COMPLETED APPLICATION AND CLEARANCE FORM TO THE BMI OFFICE FROM WHICH IT WAS RECEIVED.

FOR INTERNAL BMI USE ONLY

CODE NO.:

D. OF C.:

PERIOD:

ENTERED VIA SCOPE

BY: _____

VERIFIED: _____

JINGLES	1
TV	2
THEATRE	3
SERIOUS	4
JAZZ	5

2-87

APPLICATION FOR WRITER-MEMBERSHIP
IN THE

AMERICAN SOCIETY of COMPOSERS, AUTHORS and PUBLISHERS
One Lincoln Plaza, New York, N.Y. 10023

	FULL □	STANDARD □	AUTHOR
I hereby apply for membership as a	ASSOCIATE □	POPULAR PRODUCTION □	COMPOSER

in the American Society of Composers, Authors and Publishers. If elected, I agree to be bound by the Society's Articles of Association, now in effect and as they may be amended, and I agree to execute agreements in such form and for such periods as the Board of Directo shall have approved or shall hereafter approve for all members.

The following information is submitted in support of this application:

1. Full Name: Mr.   Miss
   Mrs. Ms. _____
   _____(First Name)_____ _____(Middle Name or Initial)_____ _____(Last Name)_____

2. Pseudonyms, if any (no more than four)

   _____

3. Home Address:

   □ _____
   _____(Street)_____ _____(City)_____ _____(State)_____ _____(Zip Code)_____ _____(Area Code & Te

   Business Address (if same as above, write "same"):

   □ _____
   _____(Street)_____ _____(City)_____ _____(State)_____ _____(Zip Code)_____ _____(Area Code & Te

   Please check to which address your mail is to be sent.

4. Date of Birth: _____

   Place of Birth: _____

5. Citizen of: _____

6. Social Security #: _____

7. I am □, or have been □, a writer or publisher member or affiliate of ASCAP, BMI or SESAC, or of a foreign performing rights licens organization (Check one of applicable)

   If you have checked one of the boxes above, please state the name of the organization with which you were affiliated, relationship, and period of your affiliation, and attach a copy of your release if applicable: _____

   If publisher member or affiliate, please list firm name_____

8. I have □, do not have □, a relative (including brother, sister, husband, wife, child or any other relation) who is affiliated with an organizat referred to in item 7.   (Check the applicable box)

   If you answered affirmatively, please give the name of any such person, relationship to you and organization with which affiliated: _____
   _____

9. I have □, have not □, paid a record company or publishing company to have the works which form the basis for my membership publis or recorded. (Check the applicable box).

   If you have answered yes to the above, please indicate which works were included and to whom payment was made:

   _____
   _____

10. The musical works of which I am composer or author are listed on the opposite page. I represent that there are no existing assignment licenses, direct or indirect of non-dramatic performing rights in or to any of the works so listed, except with publishers of such works. If th are assignments or licenses other than with publishers, I have attached true copies. I have read the Society's Articles of Association make this applicaton with full knowledge of their contents.

   I warrant and represent that all of the information furnished in this application is true. I acknowledge that any contract betwe ASCAP and me will be entered into in reliance upon the representations contained in this application, and that the contract will subject to cancellation if the information contained in this application is not complete and accurate.

Signature_____ Date_____

WRITER'S LIST OF WORKS

W

List of Domestic Copyrighted Musical Compositons Owned by the Applicant

TITLE	YEAR OF COPYRIGHT	COMPOSER	AUTHOR	PUBLISHER

The New Copyright Law

THE LONG AWAITED new copyright law took effect on January 1, 1978. One of the long sought after features of this new law was the extended protection of the copyright period over the old law.

Songs copyrighted before January 1, 1978 will retain the first term of 28 years of protection and a renewal term of forty-seven years, totaling seventy-five years. Songs copyrighted after the new law date will have the copyright protection for the life of the writer plus fifty years.

This "life-plus-50" period applies to songs that have more than one writer, as well those that have a single writer, the only difference being that the term "life" is meant to be the life of the last surviving writing partner. An example would be if two writers composed a song in 1980 and one writer died in 1985, the other in 1995. The song would be protected until 2045, which is 50 years after the death of the last surviving member of that writing team.

With this new law, the United States is beginning to catch up to other countries in copyright protection. Most countries covered by the agreements like the Berne Convention have had a "life-plus-50" year policy as a minimum term for many years. The new copyright law replaces the antiquated fifty-six (twenty-eight plus twenty-eight renewal) term. Songs renewed in 1977 or before did not have to be renewed again and automatically got the longer forty-seven renewal term.

Songs created for hire (such as television or film music and commercials) after January 1, 1978 are protected for seventy-five years from publication, or 100 years from creation, whichever term expires first. The new law extends copyrights to the end of the year in which they would terminate. In other words, a song that would normally lose copyright protection on May 6, 2020 would now change to December 31, 2020.

Under the old law, songs not published or copyrighted were protected under "common law" copyright. The new law practically does away with common law by stating that songs created, but not copyrighted or published, before January 1, 1978 will be protected by the new federal law for the life plus fifty years period.

Songs already in their renewal term at the same time the law was signed (Oct 19, 1977), automatically and immediately had their renewal terms extended for an additional nineteen years, for a total period of seventy-five (twenty-eight plus twenty-eight renewal plus nineteen years extension). The new law drops the renewal clause for all songs copyrighted after the law took effect. In place of it, the new law generally permits the author to terminate the transfer of his copyright after 35 years by serving notice to the person or organization to whom he transferred those rights. For songs existing prior to January 1, 1978 which a songwriter has assigned the *renewal term* (second 28 years) of copyright to a publisher, the new law provides (with specific notice) that the writer can reacquire part of the renewal rights back (specifically, 19 years of the 47 years renewal total). This gives the writer a position of renegotiation for those 19 years with the publisher.

Recognizing the fact that a major portion of writers' income is derived from airplay (known as "performances"), Congress expanded the copyright owners' public performance right with respect to copyrighted music by defining the terms "perform" and "perform publicly" to a greater degree than those terms had previously been interpreted by the courts. In addition, they eliminated the limitation that an infringing public performance must be for profit.

Prior to the new copyright law, users of music could often argue that their use of music was not directly profiting them. One example might be a store owner in a mall playing music over a speaker that is being heard by people either in or near the store, or music played in a restaurant. Since the old law did not specifically define "for profit," the courts often had to reevaluate that limitation to consider what was and was not a copyright infringement under the 1909 law.

Several cases were brought before the Supreme Court right in the middle of World War I involving the unlicensed performance of copyrighted music. Fortunately, these cases ended with the court rejecting the claim of hotel and restaurant owners that since they were not charging admission to hear music at their establishments, they had not infringed. The veiled attempt to mislead the court was not overlooked, as the judgment made it clear that the music was being provided for the purpose of profit and was part of a total price for which the public paid through higher prices of food.

These judgments opened the door for successful copyright infringement cases against users of music in such diversified atmospheres and businesses as nightclubs, racetracks, roller-skating rinks, and theatres, as well as in increasing numbers of restaurants and hotels. Still, there remained the difficult task of dealing with the many nonprofit organizations who were often well-financed and therefore able to pay appropriate royalties.

The new law, while eliminating the "for profit" limitation, created a list of exempt performances. Thus a great number of users fell under the new law's doctrine stating that any public performance of copyrighted music, except for those that have been specifically exempt by statute or license, constitutes an infringement of the owner's rights. Since public performance in some cases can be construed as "partial" public performances, places such as private clubs are considered partially public and are therefore governed by the copyright law. The new law further clarifies that performances at schools, camps, etc., are subject to the copyright law.

Although the 1909 law regarding the term "public performance" was not specifically defined (not a great deal was defined under that law), the courts resolved that for copyright purposes, musical performances, even in private clubs, could be considered "public performances." This became all the more apparent when one considers that the only reasons a club might be considered private is because it is catering to a special segment of the population or because of state liquor laws. An even greater degree of protection came into being with the new law, however, when a definition in the statute made it clear that a performance is considered to be public for purposes of the copyright law if the performance occurs "at a place opened to the public," or at any place where a substantial number of people outside a normal circle of a family and its social acquaintances are gathered."

The new law helps cover musical performances at many places which were not covered in the old copyright law. The new law states: "To perform a work means to recite, read, play, dance or act it either directly or by means of any device or process." Therefore, the public performance of copyrighted music by almost any means is subject to the new law. It is interesting to note that when the copyright law of 1909 went into effect, there were no TV's, jukeboxes, or even commercial radio. Therefore, protective provisions in the law for the unforeseen marvels of the future were not even considered.

How, then, were so many infringements and potential infringements dealt with? As stated above, judicious interpretation of the then current laws, along with varying degrees of common sense on the part of the court, helped greatly. Copyright infringement suits were often successfully prosecuted on the basis of unlicensed musical performances, regardless of the technological medium with which they reached the public.

In one case, however, it was not the ambiguity of the old law that hurt copyright owners, but a specific exemption in it. In 1909, the only <u>mechanical</u> devices capable of playing even a crude kind of music were penny arcade machines. Copyright owners of the time were so pleased to have some form of protection that one can only speculate as to why they made little effort to eliminate a provision in the law that gave an exemption for the playing of music by means of "coin-operated machines." Years later, along came the jukebox, and with it a potentially lucrative area of income for writers and publishers, except for one thing: The coin-operated machine provision in the law gave it an exemption, and it became quite a controversial one.

Although the exemption was a limited one (it was only applicable if the jukebox was wired for use without a coin or was in a place where admission was charged), it became a rallying cry for those lobbying for new copyright laws. When the new law did take effect in 1978, the so-called jukebox exemption was eliminated and replaced by a compulsory license and fee.

The jukebox operator is now required to obtain a license from the copyright office or licensing societies. He pays a yearly blanket fee of $50 to the societies based on the number of jukeboxes he owns (see Chapter 4). This royalty is only for the music used. No performance royalty is due the owners of the recordings (record companies, producers, etc.) whatsoever. The only current exemptions relating to jukeboxes are, if: 1. A list of the music is not affixed to the jukebox or posted where the list can be readily examined by the public; 2. The patrons are not permitted to make the choices as to the music to be played; 3. A direct or indirect admission charge is made; 4. The jukebox is not activated by the insertion of coins or other monetary units.

The new law also allows the creator copyright registration for unpublished lyrics. The old law stated that lyrics, without music, could not be registered. Also, the Notice of Use used when a song is first recorded is no longer required. Instead, the person wishing to distribute any records of the first recording of that song must, within 30 days after the pressing of the records, serve notice to the copyright holder of his intention to release the record to the public. This notification is done by the record company either in the form of a letter requesting the copyright holder (often a publisher) to send a mechanical license, or by sending their own mechanical license form to the copyright holder. Releasing a record without notification to the copyright holder or without negotiating and signing an appropriate mechanical license can be considered an infringement of the copyright owner's rights.

COPYRIGHT INFRINGEMENT

A copyright infringer is subject to a civil action in Federal Court for an injunction, and libel for the copyright owner's actual damages, the infringer's profits or statutory damages, plus court cost and attorney's fees. In copyright infringement cases involving the performance of music, the copyright owner will usually obtain a judgement for statutory damages, rather than actual damages or profits. Ordinarily, statutory damages will not be less than $250 or more than $10,000 for each copyrighted song performed publicly without a license.

The new copyright law doubled the maximum statutory damages from the $5,000 limit of the old law. Damages for copyright infringement are not measured by the usual small amount which the infringer might have paid under a performing rights license. It is important to note that a copyright infringement suit is not a suit for breach of a license agreement which the copyright infringer refused to accept when it was offered. If the license fees were the only gauge of damages for copyright infringement, there would be practically no financial incentive for any music user to obtain a license, since it would not cost any more to infringe than to have a license. In addition to civil liabilities for copyright infringement, the copyright law also includes the following criminal sanctions: "Any person who infringes a copyright willfully and for purposes of commercial advantage or private financial gain shall be fined not more than $10,000 or imprisoned for not more than one year or both."

Another major feature of the new law is the changes in the Mechanical Royalties for Phonograph Records. The new law gives an increase for the statutory Compulsory License regarding sound recordings.

The mechanical royalty rate was raised from an interim rate of .0275¢ in 1978 to .04¢ in July of 1981. By January of 1983, it was .0425¢ and moved up to .045¢ on July 1, 1984. Then on January 10, 1986, it was raised to .05¢ or .95 of a cent per minute of playing time. Therefore, to garner a higher royalty rate than the .05¢ rate, a song would have to be at least six minutes long.

In March of 1987, after almost five months of negotiations, the National Music Publisher's Association (NMPA), the Songwriters Guild of America (SGA), and the Recording Industry Association (RIAA) hammered out a new and historic statutory mechanical royalty rate structure that, for the first time, was tied to the consumer price index. The trade organizations petitioned the copyright royalty tribunal to adopt the proposal for adjustments to the rate over a ten-year period. In June of 1987, the system was approved by the tribunal for adjustment of the rate every two years effective November, 1987. Regardless of any changes in the consumer price index, the rate cannot decline below .05¢ per song or exceed the previous rate by more than 25% for any two-year span.

The new statuatory mechanical rate is .0525¢ or .01¢ per minute of playing time or fraction thereof, whichever amount is greater. The new rate is applicable to all phono records made and distributed on or after January 1, 1988, regardless of the date upon which the license was issued or phono record was released.

CABLE AND THE ROYALTY TRIBUNAL

When the copyright law states that a royalty must be paid, it means that there is a chain of payments to the copyright owner. The chart on the next page will show how payment is made for the major domestic and foreign sources of income to the writer and publisher under the old and new Copyright Law.

As you can see, some new areas of income have opened up to the publisher and writer, namely the jukebox, cable TV, educational institutions and public broadcasting industries. All were previously exempt from having to make any kind of royalty payments on the music they used.

Cable TV systems are expected to negotiate with the licensing societies for payment (see Chapter 4). The tribunal will review secondary transmission cable television rate formulas every five years, or more often if changes in the nation's economy require it, or if FCC regulations change.

Although Public Broadcasting Stations (PBS) do not have to pay the same rates as the commercial broadcasters (NBC, ABC, CBS), rates have been formulated between music licensees and the PBS. PBS is non-commercial TV, generally educational. Payments are made directly to music owners or licensees.

The Royalty Tribunal's function is to periodically review and revise, if necessary, the rates in compulsory licensing of cable TV programming, Public Broadcasting, and jukeboxes. The tribunal consists of five members chosen by the President of the U.S. for a seven year term. The Tribunal's obligation is to maintain a fair balance between the creators and the users of music.

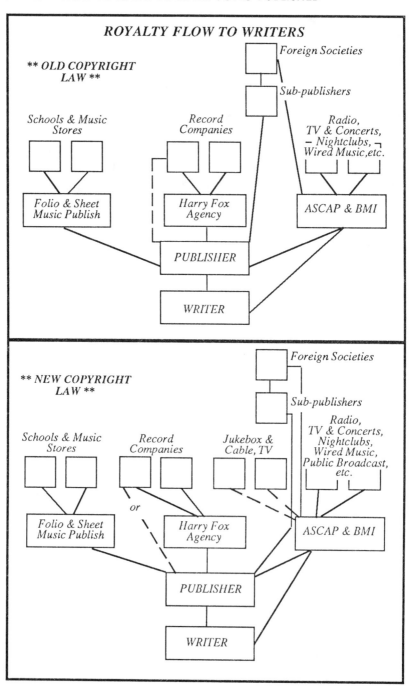

How To Present Your Song

THE PRESENTATION OF A SONG to publishers is one of the least understood areas of the music business, especially with the beginning writer. There are various ways to present your song to publishers.

One way is by live performance. Live performance is where the writer is a member of a group or is a single vocalist with an opportunity to showcase his songs at a night club, disco or similar showplace. This is the most unusual and least likely prospect, because of all the contacts and planning that go into arranging such a showcase. The average individual doesn't have these contacts and would most likely need proper management to acquire them.

The basic way to present your song is on a demonstration tape, called a "demo" in the industry. Almost all publishers today will review only a demo, whereas in the past publishers would accept lead sheets and listen to songs played live on a piano as demonstrations of the song. This was especially true in the 1950s before recording techniques made demos a suitable alternative to lead sheets. Many publishers have professional managers who do not even read sheet music, so hearing a demonstration tape is the only way they can review the song.

Most writers do a demo at home by playing a guitar or piano and singing along on a home tape machine. However, the better demo you make, the better are your chances of having a *good* song picked up by a publisher. A bad song can be enhanced just so much by a good demo, but a good song will shine through and have a greater chance for acceptability on a good demo. Demos can be categorized into two groups—home demos and studio demos. It should be noted that a publisher usually prefers a demo done in the studio, although with today's high-tech electronic music equipment, a well-prepared and produced home demo can be of sufficient quality to properly represent your song.

The following is basic knowledge you should have regarding your home demos. The advantages and disadvantages should be noted, so you may choose what best suits your situation. First, it is obviously less expensive to record on your home tape set up. The disadvantages are lack of sound quality and possible lack of professional performance if you are not really a good musician, singer, or both. One advantage of a recording studio is that they may be able to help you find qualified musicians and singers to do your demos. They also often have bulletin boards in the lobbies with musician and singer referrals. With this in mind, a very important consideration is your belief in your own ability and how seriously you intend to approach a writing career.

If you were a carpenter, you would have to buy certain tools in order to do your job. The same is true for making a demo. It must be a *quality* demo. Since the cost of using a recording studio can become prohibitive, you will have to invest in *quality* equipment for your home studio.

The thing that sets this era apart from the past (for songwriters) is the development of the cassette recorder/mixer. Instead of big, bulky 4-tracks, you can now use cassette 4-track machines the size of a small briefcase. (MIDI setups will be discussed later.) If you have decided that home demos are the way for you to go, the choices are varied. There are units that are 4-track cassette recorders and mixing boards which allow you to record two tracks at one time, overdub on the other two tracks, punch in and out, and ping-pong. Many also have "B" noise reduction and a pitch control. Some include Dolby "C" noise reduction, which ignores low frequencies and helps eliminate tape hiss in the mid- and high-frequencies, plus 6 source mixing, 4 independent tape outputs, and stereo effect return.

More sophisticated machines have DBS noise reductions, standard cassette 1 $^7/_8$ ips tape speed, variable pitch and zero return, allowing the user to set replay guidelines so the unit will rewind when the tape reaches a preset point such as the end of a chorus or song. This feature, combined with the foot switch operated punch-in, makes it easy to make repeated passes over a verse or chorus until you get it right. There are also 6-track mini studios which have added features such as effect send, and allow for an external signal processing unit (reverb, echo, EQ, etc.) to be added. There are many additional choices with even greater features. You should consider choosing the machine that is right for your budget and musical needs. Some of the writers with whom I work have recommended Tascam, Fostex and Teac's lines of product, many of which fit the specifications noted above. If you were looking to put together a good quality, relatively inexpensive setup for demos on an even higher level than the cassette recorder/mixer level, the following would get you on your way:

1. You still need a cassette recorder/mixer, price $350-$450.
2. MIDI keyboard synthesizer with 128 sounds, price $650-$800.
3. Electronic MIDI drum machine, price $350-$400.
4. MIDI sequencer, price $250-$500.

The above is a MIDI setup and, as you can see, can be put together for about $1,600. MIDI is an acronym for <u>musical instrument digital interface</u> and was developed in the early 80s. It was intended to allow a synthesizer, electronic instruments and computers to digitally communicate information to other instruments so a musician could play either or both instruments from the original keyboard. On the next page you'll find a basic MIDI setup with options like an echo unit.

Remember, a good demo, even a home demo, has one objective: It must show the song off to its best advantage so that the publisher can hear your song's possibilities for artists he is "casting"(considering which artist or group a song may fit). This does not mean that the more instrumentation and harmonies you put down on tape, the better your chances. It often has the reverse effect by distracting many publishers from the song itself.

The instrumentation used should be totally dependent on the type of song you've written. For example, if you've written a song that you believe would be good for Aretha Franklin, you would not use a

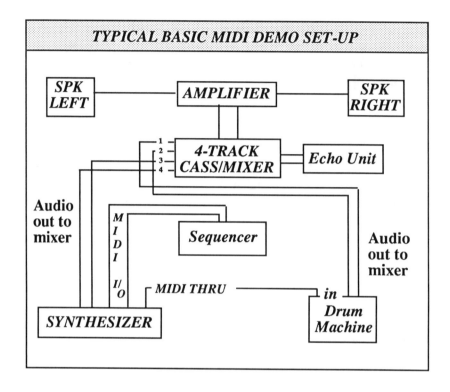

"fuzz tone" guitar sound or a rock drummer to make your demo. The same applies if you had a song for a group like Bon Jovi—you wouldn't use lush background strings or female background vocals. Often a sparse demo is more effective than a full production if that is what your song requires.

In making your demos, several basic rules apply: First, always make your lyrics as vocally clear as possible, and make sure your melody and lyric are out in front of the instrumental track so they can be clearly heard and understood. After all, you're showcasing your song, not your arranging, playing, or singing talents. Instrumentation is strictly to enhance a song in the demo phase of its presentation.

At the beginning, your contact with most publishers will be by mail, so your presentation is not only the presentation of your song, but your introduction to him. Remember, he may be getting hundreds of tapes every few weeks from people all over the country trying to do the same thing. This is not to discourage you, but you should know that your competition is enormous in quantity. What you must believe is that hard work, perseverance, and quality will see its just reward.

Once you feel really confident in the song itself, you're ready to consider how it should be demoed and for whom it might be appropriate. If you don't read or write music, get some opinions from any musicians you might know regarding the kind of instrumentation that might work with the song, and combine it with your own ideas. You may try two or three different instrumentations before you settle on what sounds best. For example, drums, bass, piano, rhythm guitar is one possibility, or drums, steel guitar, fiddle and bass, etc.—in short, whatever sounds best for the song. The same applies to vocal arrangements (yes, vocals, both lead and background, have to be worked out ahead of time, although there's always a degree of spontaneous change during the recording). The decision whether to use three male background singers or two female, one male; one female soul singer with two high-voiced females; or two male soul singers; these are just some of the limitless possibilities for the imagination when making a demo. Also, if you're not the only singer available, think in terms of the type of lead vocalist you'd like for your song. For example, if you have a great song for Whitney Houston, don't have one of your male friends who sounds like Bruce Springsteen sing the demo. If you can't find someone who sounds a little like Whitney Houston, use a female singer so the publisher can at least relate to the possibilities of a female singing the song. This is your decision, so before you begin to get into any kind of demo, put the song down on tape with just a guitar or keyboard and your vocal. Listen to it alone and with others. People always hear their songs differently when someone else is also listening, as opposed to when they listen alone. What sounded great alone may sound wrong, incomplete, weak, or even embarrassing when played for others.

Other aspects of the writer-publisher relationship will be covered in subsequent chapters, but competition is mentioned here because presentation of your song has to be as professionally done as possible in terms of common sense and business sense. This doesn't necessarily mean the $500 demo, but it does require the following:

1. A good cassette tape of your song.
2. Lyric and/or lead sheets (see the examples that follow).
3. A cover letter of introduction (more on this later).
4. A stamped, self-addressed return envelope for your tape, lead sheet, and hopefully, a comment letter from the publishers.

If you don't read and write sheet music accurately, then you should have someone do it for you. Professionals can be found in the phone book under "Music Arrangers" or "Music Copyists." A lead sheet will usually cost $10.00 to $30.00 a copy, depending on the length of the song. The best way to have someone transfer your song to a lead sheet is by giving that person a tape of the song. If possible, provide a lyric sheet for the copyist, and try to have her play the completed lead sheet for you before final payment. Lead sheets aren't entirely necessary when sending tapes to a publisher, as long as you've included a lyric sheet. But if you intend to copyright the song, it is an alternative to sending tape copies (see Chapter 3). Also, if a publisher is interested in the song, he may request a lead sheet. And always have your name, address, and phone number somewhere on the lead sheet (possibly under your copyright notice).

To get back to the home demo operation, a few basic hints are in order. Where you record your demo is important. Try to record in a room with no phone, or take it off the hook. A room without a carpet is best for acoustics; the more things there are in a room, the more sound is soaked up. A room without windows, such as a basement or loft, is best for keeping unwanted outside noise from leaking into your recording. You should also lock the door or leave a note on it to keep unwitting visitors out of your recording session.

Use a stopwatch to keep track of the length of your songs. What often starts out as a three minute song when you write it, could become a seven minute song after you arrange it, add an instrumental introduction and/or instrumental break, or even slow down the original tempo. A safe time for a Top 40, pop R&B, pop country, A/C song is 3-5 minutes.

If you do have a basement, loft, garage, or any relatively soundproofed room, your musicians are the next consideration. Many young writers have groups that they play with, but that doesn't mean you need to use every member. All of the instruments may not fit your song. If you are not part of a group, decide what instruments you'd like to use and consider the following: 1) Put up notices on local bulletin boards at stores, schools, and parks etc., and 2) check with local music schools or music teachers (if local schools do not have a music department to draw from). If you can pay musicians, all the better, and it may help you to get musicians faster. You should audition any musician with whom you're not familiar. Even if he knows his instrument well, he may not play your type of music (again, the case of the rock drummer for an Aretha Franklin type song).

On the next two pages, you'll see examples of how a lyric sheet and a lead sheet should look.

I USED TO SAY "I LOVE YOU"

Words & Music By Jay Warner

Whenever moonlight and music got into this heart of mine,
I'd tell the girl I was holding, the words she was looking to find.
The words had less and less meaning, each time I said them in vain.
And then you walked on, into my life, and the words found
  meaning again.

I used to say "I love you," when I didn't know what else to say.
I used to say "I love you," but I found out there's a better way.
I used to say "I love you," it was easier than being me.
Now I don't say I love, love, love,
  but lovin' you is all I see.

I know you've been through the same thing, and don't want it
  to happen to you.
A guy who easily says "I love you," can easily leave you too.
But you and me we've had some time in each others arms and eyes.
We never once had to say the words, but I know that we
  both realize.

(CHORUS)
We used to say "I love you," when we didn't know what else to say.
We used to say "I love you," but we found out there's a better way.
We used to say "I love you," to others when it wasn't real,
Now we don't say I love, love, love, but love is what we really feel.

Copyright © 1975 HANDSHAKE MUSIC

(Sample format for a lyric sheet)

Copyright © 1975 HANDSHAKE MUSIC

When using home equipment as well as studio equipment, the more musicians and singers you use, the more important and critical the mix becomes. This relates to certain kinds of music, but more specifically, to rock material. The home demo will sound better if you think in terms of making everything blend. This is especially true of a live mix, rather than a studio mix where the sounds you take onto the tape are mixed (sorted out) later (assuming you are not using contemporary sequencing equipment such as the MIDI setup).

Have your musicians run the song down *without a vocal* and listen to it as if it came from the radio. Would the lead guitar be that much louder than the others in a record? Are those drum riffs really necessary to help the song? *Simplicity often helps a song more than overcrowding.* Is that synthesizer tone a proper working sound against the other instruments for the song? Is the keyboardist playing choppy "Stevie Wonder type" riffs when he should be playing more sustained chords? Is the bass obscuring, or obscured by, other instruments? You will run into all of these situations, and many more, on your own, and they can make the difference between a good or bad home demo. If you have home equipment with a separate mixer, it is a little easier, but you still have to record your musicians with a proper level to allow for good mixing later. A keyboard that is too soft will have to be boosted in the mix to the point where a lot of hiss will occur. A guitar that is too loud will distort and have to be lowered in the mix to the point where its original effect will be lost.

If you are using one mike to your tape recorder, position it with your musicians in a semi-circle around the mike. Do a test run to hear how the balance sounds. Move the microphone closer or further away, depending on what instruments you want to bring into position sound-wise on the tape. When doing vocals, get a comfortable position at the mike, either sitting or standing; try not to move around too much while singing or the sound level of your voice will rise and fall accordingly on the tape. Don't emphasize words containing the letter "P" because they will "pop" on the tape. Sing words like "impossible" and "please" softly on the "p." Always face the microphone, and do not use a hand-held mike—put it on a mike stand, and don't touch it during recording. Unlike artists you see in performances, recording requires no outside noises, and holding a mike creates crackling sounds from the move-ment of the cable to such interference as the tapping of a ring on your finger.

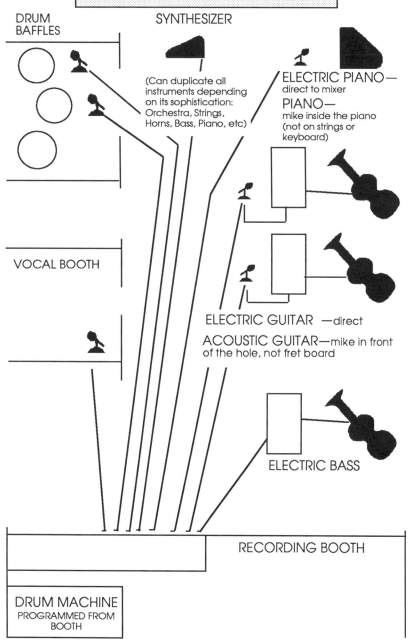

MIKING OF INSTRUMENTS IN THE STUDIO
& ADDITIONAL ELECTRONIC EQUIPMENT

DRUM BAFFLES

SYNTHESIZER

(Can duplicate all instruments depending on its sophistication: Orchestra, Strings, Horns, Bass, Piano, etc)

ELECTRIC PIANO— direct to mixer

PIANO— mike inside the piano (not on strings or keyboard)

VOCAL BOOTH

ELECTRIC GUITAR —direct

ACOUSTIC GUITAR—mike in front of the hole, not fret board

ELECTRIC BASS

RECORDING BOOTH

DRUM MACHINE PROGRAMMED FROM BOOTH

Recording in the Studio

If you are considering recording in a studio, you should have a basic knowledge of studio costs. Smaller studios (usually those with 8 and 16 track equipment) will charge approximately $40.00 to $75.00 an hour, plus tape costs and tax. This includes a professional engineer's services. A well-rehearsed song demo (with your own band) should take about two to three hours in the studio.

If your vocals are going to be put on tape separately from the band (which is the most professional way to do it), rehearse your band instrumentally. This way they'll get used to hearing the song without vocals for your demo session. As mentioned before, studios usually have a list of singers and musicians who do regular demo work for anywhere from $15.00 to $25.00 an hour, or $25.00 per song. They are generally quite capable, as they do this type of work on a regular basis. All recordings are done on 8- or 16-track two inch tape, transferred to 2-track stereo quarter inch tape, and then transferred to cassettes. Tapes will cost about $3–$5 per song. Union scale for musicians and singers on demos is less than for masters, and while below scale pay to union members is technically not allowed, the practice is common. Many writers use non-union musicians and pay them about $25.00 per song, regardless of how many hours it takes to record the song. A recording session bill may vary depending on:

1. Use of trained musicians who can read charts or lead sheets vs. inexperienced musicians who may be unfamiliar with recording practices.
2. Vocalist capabilities.
3. Your ability to mix and get your desired sound in a reasonable period of time.

An example of a recording bill could be as follows:

1 Song—16 tracks

Studio Time:	2 hr. per song	@ $75/hr	=	$150.00
Mixing Time:	1 hr.	@ $75/hr	=	$75.00
Musicians:	4 musicians & 1 vocalist	@ $25/ea	=	$125.00
Tape Costs:				$100.00
Tax:				$17.00
			TOTAL	$467.00

When choosing a studio for demos, keep several things in mind: Convenience in terms of how close the studio is to your home should not be a primary concern. Ask people you know who may have used a studio if they can suggest one or two. Check the phone book and call several studios to get rate differences. Ask for their rate schedule including per hour costs for day and night. The rates usually vary depending on how many tracks this would include. Get tape costs. When you get a couple of comparison ideas and decide which studios you want to take a chance on, make an appointment to see them. This may seem like a waste of time for just a demo, especially since you don't have a lot of knowledge of what to look for in a good studio, but that is not the concern. If the studio is a good value compared to the others you have checked out, you can start building a relationship with the manager and engineer right at this first meeting. They are always looking for new business. If you show enough concern for your recordings to check out their studio before you record, they will believe that you could become a regular customer and give you all the more attention. They could be very important to you if you intend to continue recording demos. You will establish a relationship that could be the difference between an average demo and a really good one. Since you have shown enough interest, the manager and engineer may give you tips and ideas on how to make your recording better, which in turn will bring you back to their studio. This could help you write better songs, since these people are hearing all kinds of material regularly, and their opinions and suggestions are closer to professional than most people can get. The studio may also have suggestions about publishers with whom they deal who could be beneficial to you.

When you show an inclination to return, you may be able to work out a rate or deal even below their regular rate. At the time you examine the studio, check on the availability of house musicians and singers (if you're not using your own band) and the costs.

A working relationship with an engineer will help you relate to him what you want done, and will help him show you the abilities and limitations of the equipment. It is not essential to become an engineer yourself. However, the more you understand about things like mikes, inputs, sound levels, compressors, monitors, earphones, tape speed, editing, "punching out" or "punching in," etc., the better equipped you'll be to work closely with an engineer and get the sound you're trying to achieve.

Sending Your Songs To A Publisher

When sending your song, be sure to be selective with a publisher; if you've written thirty songs, you can't send him all thirty, or even ten. Read the trade papers—*Billboard* and *Cash Box* (addresses for subscriptions are at the end of this chapter). The trades feature Top 100 Charts, which will give you an idea of which artists are currently doing well and actively recording. You can use this information to get an idea which of your songs would be good for the artists who record outside songs. (See Chapter 10 for the use of the trades.)

Never send more than three or four songs to a publisher, for he will rarely play more than three or four songs at one time for producers and artists. Let him focus his concentration on a couple of your songs, rather than a whole collection. The ideal situation is to send one or two of your *best* songs. If they have quality or show a degree of writing talent, even if they are not considered "hit songs," a good publisher will usually respond by asking to hear more. Leave space of about four seconds between your songs, if possible, to allow the publisher to go on to the beginning of a new song easily. Otherwise, some publisher will "fast-forward" the tape too far into the next song and listen to the song from that point, which is obviously to the writer's disadvantage.

Your cover letter is an important part of your presentation because it introduces the *person* sending the song, whereas the tape and lyrics sheets are introducing only the song. The letter should not be too long (no more than a page), and should contain the following information in the following order:

1. Introduce yourself.
2. Describe what you have sent.
3. Describe your music background, if any.
4. Name or describe the artist you feel best suits the song.
5. Make it clear that if there is no interest in your song, the material can be returned in the enclosed stamped, self-addressed envelope.
6. Mention that any comments would be appreciated.

This form is only necessary when approaching a publisher for the first time. Subsequent contacts with that publisher eliminates the need for 1 and 3.

Following is one of many possible approaches for a first letter to a publisher:

LETTER #1

Dear Mr./Ms._____

Enclosed please find a tape and lyric sheet for two songs that I have recently written. I am a graduate of the Julliard School of Music and have played with several groups here in Brooklyn. Of the over twenty songs in my catalogue, there are several that I believe have strong hit potential.

The first song, entitled "Who Do You Think You Are?" would be great for a male top 40 group like Bo Donaldson and the Heywoods. The second song is entitled "Southern Nights" and has a pop-country feel, possibly for Glen Campbell.

Also enclosed is a stamped, self-addressed envelope that you may use to return this material to me should the material not meet your current requirements. I would be most grateful if you would include any comments regarding my songs or general comments that would help me create exactly what you are looking for.

Very truly yours,

The following is a possible second letter.

LETTER #2

Dear Mr./Ms. _____
    Thank you, Mr./Ms. _____, for your kind attention in taking the time to review the material I recently sent to you. Enclosed are two new songs that may be of interest.
    The first is entitled _____ , and I think it would be great for a female Top 40 pop artist like Cyndi Lauper or Madonna. The second is a rock & roll song entitled _____, possibly for Starship.
    Thank you again, Mr./Ms. _____, and please let me know your thoughts on this new material at your earliest convenience.

Very truly yours,

    All of the information covered in this chapter is essential to presenting your song to a publisher. Set a pattern for yourself from the stage of how, where, when, and with whom to record your songs, to the letter you send accompanying your tape. All of these things are time-consuming, exciting, frustrating, costly, or even inconvenient, and are only the first steps in dealing with a publisher, but they can be the most important. So, handle them according to how committed you are to having your hit song published.

Billboard

New York
1515 Broadway
New York, N.Y. 10036
212-764-7300

Nashville
14 Music Circle E.
Nashville, Tenn. 37203
615-748-8100

London
71 Beak Street
W1R 3LF
01-439-9411

Los Angeles
9107 Wilshire Blvd.
Beverly Hills, CA 90210
213-273-7040

Tokyo
19-16 Jingumae 6-Chome
Shibuya-ku, Tokyo 150
03-498-4641

Cash Box

New York
330 W. 58th Street (Suite 5D)
New York, NY 10019
212-586-2640

Hollywood
6363 Sunset Blvd. (Suite 930)
Hollywood, CA 90028
213-464-8241

Nashville
21 Music Circle East,
Nashville TN 37203
615-244-2898

Japan
3rd Floor of Chuo-Tatemono Bldg.
2-chome, 11-1, Shinbashi, Minato-ku
Tokyo, Japan 105
504-1651

United Kingdom
Flat 3, 51 Cleveland Street
London W1P 5PQ
01-631-1626

R&B Report
6430 Sunset Blvd Suite 1201
Los Angeles, CA 90028
213-461-4773

How To Pick A Publishing Company

IN ORDER TO KNOW what to look for in a publisher, you should have a degree of experience with different publishers. This means a basic relationship with several publishers to understand the way they work. You can have a knowledge of what makes a good publisher (which is provided herein), but after that, first-hand experience is the best teacher. To start with, a good publisher is often one who was at one time, and may still be, a writer himself. This lets you know that he is likely to understand many of the problems a writer faces. A cardinal rule to remember is that the relationship you are attempting to build with a publishing company is not dependent on the company, but on the individuals with whom you deal. If your publisher leaves the company after you've built your relationship with him, you're often starting from scratch again. Therefore, try to get to know more than one key person in the company. The music industry has very mobile employees, and although the publishing area is relatively stable compared to most areas of the music industry, you will still see quite a number of people moving from company to company. This change can be to your advantage if you have placed a few songs with a publisher and feel he has done a good job prior to his leaving. When he goes to a new company, you will already have the contact there. You can keep track of this movement by watching the trades in sections referred to as "Exec-utive Turntable" *(Billboard)* or "Executives on the Move" *(Cash Box)*.

Assuming you're starting from scratch, your main concerns in picking a publisher are as follows: The size of the company catalogue. If it is huge—thirty to forty thousand songs—you may not get the kind of personal attention you feel your songs merit, even if the company is interested in acquiring songs from you. This is because large companies may not have enough professional managers to handle all the songs in their catalogue (even though many songs may be very old, dated, and left unpromoted).

Obviously each company has marketing considerations that may supercede promotion of your song (for example, if the company has a past active catalogue that has proven sales ability, such as a collection of songs by *Lennon & McCartney* or *The Beach Boys).* These kinds of catalogues are continually promoted because there is always the possibility that an old hit with a fresh arrangement and production will become a new hit.

A staff writer-artist or writer-producer is considered a major priority with a publishing company. They're a priority because a publisher usually has a financial investment in these multi-talented writers by virtue of signing them to staff writing contracts, and because as writer/artist or writer/producer, they will be an outlet for a good percentage of their own songs. The writer/artist will more than likely record a good percentage of his songs, and the writer/producer will more than likely produce records on other artists with some of her songs. This puts pressure on a publisher to get cover records (among other areas of exposure we will cover later) to show the writer that he is generating income from more sources than just his own recordings.

From the above, you can see why a new writer with interest from a company in one or two songs would still not be considered a priority. This is not to say that all large publishing companies are a bad direction for the new writer. However, a lot does depend on the relationship you build with the person who picks up your songs and the person who will be running with your songs (often not the same person in larger companies). On the other hand, large companies often have easier access to producers, managers, etc., simply because of their well-established names. Initially, their enthusiasm is your only guide to how much exposure they will try to give your songs. There are many good, active publishing companies, but their effectiveness with your songs depends on your relationship with the people and their enthusiasm for the songs.

To find out approximately how many songs a publisher has, contact the societies BMI and ASCAP and ask for information regarding the specific publisher. Remember, all publishing companies have at least one BMI or ASCAP affiliate for their writers' convenience, so by calling just one, you may not get a true evaluation. A publisher may have 3,000 songs in their ASCAP company and 25,000 in their BMI company. (Of course, you can also ask the publisher about the size of his catalogue.)

Another area to look into is how many writers the company has on staff or in co-publishing deals. This is of primary concern in order to get an idea of the size of the company, but should not affect your overall considerations regarding dealing with that company. What might be of more concern is the type of writers the company has.

Many people don't realize that a lot of publishers, though maintaining that they look for and have all types of music, are strong in only one or two categories. For example, if a company's catalogue and writers are heavily loaded with R & B material and very little country or Top 40, then you as a Top 40 or country writer may not get proper exploitation of your song. Another example is if you're a country writer and the publisher you're considering doesn't have a Nashville office or affiliate company in the proximity (such as Memphis or Muscle Shoals). That publisher may not have the necessary contacts and push to consistently have your songs heard there. Unlike New York and Los Angeles, where almost all kinds of contemporary music are recorded (pop, Top 40, jazz, R & B, country), Nashville is very heavily into country. Therefore, it is advisable for a publisher dedicated to country music to have an affiliate in or to be based in the Nashville area. More and more, Nashville, Muscle Shoals, and Memphis are locations where producers are recording pop and R & B songs with their artists. Many of these songs are being produced to crossover from the straight country market to the pop Top 100 charts. Unless your songs are considered pure country, a Nashville office should not be a primary concern.

When dealing with small publishing companies, your main concern should be their effectiveness in exploiting copyrights. Being small can mean that they are just getting started, have limited contacts, or that they depend on an income from a single writer (who could be owner or part owner of the firm). On the other hand, the small company could be successful and quality-oriented rather than quantity-conscious. In this case, their catalog could be strong, but relatively small. Check to see if they have an in-house or affiliated record production division. If so, they are also a potential outlet for the songs they acquire and possibly the songs you write. Try to find out if the acts they produce are self-contained (that is, singer/songwriters who write for themselves) or are acts needing outside songs.

How do you find out? Usually the same way you learn about a big company. Talk with the representatives of the company. Find out what others in the industry think of the *person* you spoke with and the *company*. You should find out about both because you'll often hear good things about one and bad things about the other.

Investigate any leads the publisher may have given you. Follow the trade papers (*Billboard* and *Cash Box*) to see which publisher names appear next to a writer's song. The last is not all inclusive, because many times a publishing company name can and is inadvertently omitted from the label copy. But if it is there, then you know that the publisher is getting activity.

Some publisher may cite names of writers to impress you with their associations, where the associations no longer exist. Writers come and go from publishers like baseball players change teams. When their contracts are up, they move to what will seem to be and may be, greener pastures. This is often based on the success or exposure they have received with the publisher they are leaving; therefore, it is not a negative note when you find out that a publisher *used* to have a well-known writer. Give the publisher credit for recognizing talent earlier than others! This may be the very publisher who could build your career in the same manner, and everyone has to start somewhere.

You should have more than one objective when looking for a publisher. The first, of course, is to find a publisher who likes your songs. Another key objective should be to let your songs open the door for you, so that regardless of the activity the song gets, it has impressed the publisher enough for him to consider giving you a writing assignment.

One of the signs of a good publisher is his ability to spot good creative talent, and if you feel a good vibe from your meeting, a suggestion as to a writing assignment could stimulate the conversation beyond the one-song-do-or-die situation. No publisher can get a record on every song he likes, but if he likes what you are doing, you could get a response something to the effect of: "I like what you are doing. There is a major pop/country female artist looking for a great ballad with a poetic lyric. I need songs within three weeks. Would you like to take a shot at it?" You now have inside information, a project, and a potential relationship with a publisher.

When you notice plaques, sheet music, or gold records on a publisher's walls, take note of the kind of songs these hits are. Are they the kind of songs you're writing? Does the publisher have a music room, or at least a piano or guitar in his office? If he does, he is more likely to work with writers and help them, or at least provide a place for a writer to work out ideas on the premises. Be observant, and everything you notice about the publisher and his office will make your decision-making process easier, and will help you to determine if he is the publisher for you. Of course, when talking about the publisher for you, it's in terms of signing with a publisher exclusively. Until you reach the point in your writing career where you are in demand, every reputable publisher is necessary. It doesn't hurt, however, to make mental notes as to which publisher you would prefer to sign with, when and if the opportunity arises.

The most difficult thing to ascertain about a publisher is his track record, because he's usually the only one from whom you can obtain information about individuals and specific hits in which he has been involved. So many people are usually involved in the making of a hit that it's often hard to find out how the song really got recorded. In my own experience, I received a song from my boss entitled "Who Do You Think You Are." He had received the song from one of our company executives who had heard it in England and acquired it for our catalogue. I sent the song to the producer of the *Heywoods* on ABC Records. He, in turn, played it for the group, and they made it into a top ten record—with the help of the producer, arranger, engineers, musicians, promotion people, disc jockeys, etc. Get the idea?

To further complicate the situation, the group who doesn't know, and usually doesn't care, how the producer gets the song can easily misinterpret the origin of the song. A recording artist has access to songs from many sources, and often several people, rather than one, may be responsible for that hit. In my case, either one of the executives who gave me the song could be credited. Also, since the song was already out in England, someone from the group could have heard it. In other cases, if a song is on an album, the act might have heard it that way, or in some instances, directly from the writer. Roberta Flack was traveling on a plane when she heard Lori Lieberman's Capitol recording "Killing Me Softly" on the in-flight head phones. She thought it would be such a tremendous song for her that she recorded it. The rest is history.

Along with these possibilities, artists are constantly deluged with songs from their producers, studio musicians, managers, arrangers, publicity people, relatives, friends, record company executives, and A & R people. It seems hopeless, doesn't it? Fortunately, the real secret of an active publisher's track record as far as you're concerned is not based solely on whether or not he really placed that top five smash. What you really should find out is how well he services the people who make the records. Being a good, active publisher is like being a good baseball player. The ballplayer's job is to get a hit with a man on base. If you got the hit and the man on base is thrown out at home, it is not your fault. You did your job to advance him. The same applies to a good publisher. His job (among others discussed in Chapter 9) is to place songs with producers, artists, and record companies, etc. If he does this effectively, then he is someone you will want to run your songs. It is not his fault if the producer's production isn't great, or the artist is lacking, or the record promotion is weak, etc. You have to understand that a publisher expects certain things regarding his day-to-day dealing with music people, and only a small percentage of the songs he plays for people ever get recorded—let alone released and chart bound. (A graph in Chapter 9 shows the ratio of songs received vs. recorded.) The main idea is that a good publisher gets out and sees people who may be recording. He should constantly be on top of who's coming up for a recording session, and send out songs appropriate for those acts.

The next area to consider about a publishing company is the opportunity for you to write in other areas. When you're at a point of writing proficiency where you are capable of writing beyond the so-called "hit song" category, then you will want a publisher who is diversified as well. This is not to say that because you feel you can write a commercial jingle, a theme for a movie, or specific music for TV shows, that you are actually capable of it. Most writers who are attempting to write in the contemporary area will usually get an opportunity along the way to write a "spec"or speculations commercial or some incidental music for a pilot film from a publisher or person who was attracted to that writer by his ability in contemporary songwriting. These "spec sessions" are what we call "paying dues," and they are necessary training and proving grounds for writers who want to get into these diversified writing fields.

It usually takes many years to get one or two chances at this kind of writing, and it is not the same as approaching a publisher with a song for a possible hit. Many people are capable of writing contemporary songs, but few without the training necessary ever make it in the more exacting area required for commercials, TV, and film music. If you are associated with a publishing company with outlets for these areas, it is obviously more beneficial to your writing career.

What you must develop are writing or composing capabilities suited to these directions, and make the publisher aware of your capability and desire to write for a TV show. Saying it is one thing. Proving it is another. Rarely will a publisher think of you for a music scoring project in a film or TV show by hearing a song you write. It is important you distinguish between the two as almost separate writing careers. Rarely, too, have traditional TV or film composers ever been able to write a hit song.

Finally, there is the question of advances when dealing with a publishing company on a song-by-song basis. There are several things to consider. First, if this is the first or second song that you are contracting with the particular publishing company and you have no previous track record, an advance is unlikely and should not be anticipated. Of course, it won't hurt you to ask for one. A publisher will have a number of expenses regarding your song, even without an advance. All of this is still based on speculation. At this point, it is only the publisher's belief in the song that is your opportunity. Until the song has justified itself with some activity, you are in no position to deal. The publisher will be spending money to make lead sheets, demo the song, copyright the song (assuming none of these have been done), as well as phone calls and mailing costs over a period of time.

To counter this situation, you can request that your contract incorporate a clause requiring the publisher to advance you a certain amount of money upon their placing this song for a first recording. If you have a track record of sorts, such as a few songs on different albums, a single release that shows some life, or writing associations with known professionals, then your opportunities for an advance are better. This advance can be anywhere from $100 to $1,000 per song, depending on the song's capabilities. It would be questionable whether to base a deal on the haggled amount of an advance, because you can easily lose sight of the main reason for dealing with any publisher—DO THEY RUN SONGS WELL? WILL THEY EXPOSE YOU AND YOUR SONG TO THE PUBLIC? If they are going to do this sincerely, then that should be enough for you at this stage of your career.

How A Publishing Company Works

THE BASIC FOUNDATION OF ANY company is its catalogue of published songs and its currently available writers (if any). To operate a publishing company, funding is necessary for the following items:

1. Catalogue acquisitions
2. Writer royalty advances
3. Cost of demonstration tapes (demo's)
4. Copyright costs
5. Lead sheet costs
6. Advertising and promotion of new songs & records
7. Recording studio costs (some publishers have their own 8- or 16-track facilities)
8. Equipment costs (recorders & speakers, etc.)
9. Usual office expense (telephone, stationery, phones, recording tape, taxes, rent, office supplies, electricity, etc.)
10. Legal fees

11. Trade publications and research materials
12. Computer equipment for administration and accounting
13. Staff salaries

As you can see, owning and operating a publishing company can be an expensive proposition requiring a significant investment. A publishing company with a medium-size catalogue (2,000 tunes) and four or five executives and employees could run up a $300,000 budget per year, and that is based on a minimum number of acquisitions beyond the existing catalogue.

Buying certain established catalogues has several advantages for a publishing company with available capital. First, it is a short cut to a bottom line of income from the copyrights obtained. Second, it gives added stability (or in the case of a new company, initial industry respect) as a viable publishing company because the company now controls copyrights of some proven value. This is obviously based on the fact that the catalogue bought has some proven income value and audience acceptability. Third, it gives a new operation immediate access to advances and deals from such sources as individual foreign markets for sub-publishing deals or an overall deal with one licensee for the whole world outside of the publisher's territory. It also enables the publisher to gain advance money from print publishing licenses, as well as licensing income from TV and film uses, for established past catalog. Finally, a publishing company that is connected with either a record label, film production company, commercial jingle house, or other musical user, has a built-in use for a percentage of its catalogue. It can earn back the purchase price in a much shorter period of time— which means earlier and bigger profits.

With this in mind, you may wonder why a person with a good catalogue would want to sell it. In the first place, smaller individually owned catalogues often become available when the owner dies and the relatives sell it for quick cash (especially if they have no inclination to become active in the music industry). Partnerships break up and a percentage of the company becomes available. Fear of decrease in the catalogue value may prompt a sale. The inability or lack of desire on the part of an owner to promote his catalogue may also lead to the sale decision. Sometimes the simplest rule of business will prevail: The company has no intention of selling, but is made an offer by an acquisition-minded company that is too good to refuse.

Major publishing companies differ from independent companies in many ways and philosophies. Major publishing companies obviously have large staffs and more copyrights, but they also have more categories of music that must be attended to. For example, an independent company may specialize in R & B, rock and roll, and pop because of the expertise of its small staff of key people, but a major company may also have standards, country, jazz, etc. This means that they will have more people who only work on the standard catalog, while others promote the jazz, and so on. Also, some majors will have one or more people working solely with film or TV companies for use of their compositions.

There will usually be four key categories of people working in any size publishing company: The director or head, the professional manager, the administrator, and the bookkeeper. Of course, in large companies or majors, there are entire departments that cover these categories, rather than one or two individuals.

The head of a publishing company (often President or Vice-President by title) is responsible for overseeing the company regarding profit and loss, initiating and finalizing negotiations for writers (although in large companies, this task might fall to a vice president of the professional staff) and catalogue acquisitions, the maintenance of relationships with foreign sub-publishers and the general decision-making regarding the review of contracts with current sub-publishers (in large companies, this might be the function of the business affairs department, usually another name for a collection of lawyers), and picking up new sub-publishers. Especially in small companies, the head of the company will also negotiate synchronization and performance licenses with film and TV companies who are desirous of using his songs. Additionally, he will negotiate print licenses for sheet music and folio use of his songs, as well as licensing deals with advertising agencies for the use of his copyrights in commercials. In large companies, these duties are usually handled by the business affairs people and/ or the administrative staff.

If a publisher's song comes out and seems to have hit potential, the publisher may authorize the buying of space for advertising in the trades. He also authorizes the news releases for trade paper articles. These releases will include information about new writer signings, catalogue acquisitions, or any new promotional items of information that he wishes the industry to be aware of. If there is a record label affiliate, the publisher acts as liaison between projects on the label requiring songs and the publishing company as a possible supplier of those songs. If there is a film company associated with the publisher, the same liaison situation applies regarding the finding of appropriate material for film soundtracks or theme and background music for TV shows. Although again, in large companies these are duties that are likely to be delegated to a subordinate or professional staff member.

The professional manager or professional staff is the backbone of an active publishing company. If you have such a person, or persons, coupled with an energetic head of operations, then you have a great "one-two punch." In smaller companies, the head of operations often takes on the responsibilities of professional manager. A professional manager is the person who, for the most part, deals directly with the writers, from the inception of a writer's idea to the finished version. He initiates the direction that a demo will take, and is usually responsible for the actual production of the demo, including hiring the musicians and scheduling the studio. He makes the contacts with producers, artists, A & R people, managers; in short, anyone connected with the responsibility of recording a song. He previews the material that has the most hit potential from his catalogue for particular artists, and is responsible for having it placed or playing it for them. He also previews all new material that comes in from unsolicited sources, such as new writers not associated with the company. Since his day-to-day activities are most important to the writer, it is the professional manager who the writer should attempt to build a relationship with.

As mentioned above, the publisher has many responsibilities relating to the exposure of his catalogue. Part of the reason for this is that there are many areas of exposure to pursue, and a full service publishing company will pursue them all. On the next page is a chart outlining these areas of pursuit and the general order in which they flow.

As the chart illustrates, there are four initial categories for the exposure of songs: Recording artists, film companies, TV companies, and commercials. Getting to the artists, however, can encompass as many as six categories of industryites, such as attorneys, managers, record producers, A & R executives at record companies, studio engineers, and the artists themselves. This does not include the occasional non-industry friend, relative, etc., who a publisher may use as a conduit to an artist.

CHART OF EXPOSURE OUTLETS FOR A SONG

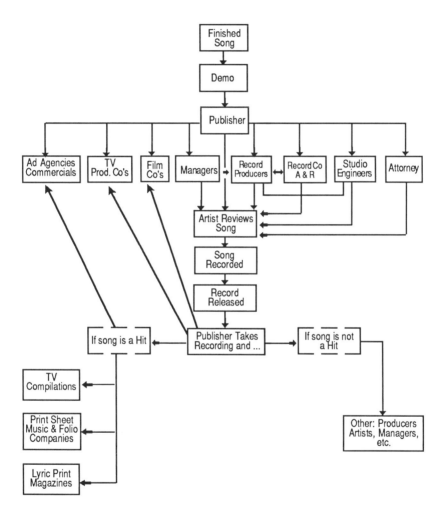

Once an artist has received a song she wants to record, records it, and it is released, the publisher is again faced with the task of continuing the exposure of the song. When it is released, the publisher then may approach film and TV companies to use the song in a strategy of "cross-pollination." That is, the song could be put in the film to promote the record while the record is promoting the film.

If the recording begins to show signs of success, a publisher will attempt to have sheet music printed. I say "attempt" because certain types of songs do not lend themselves to the printing of sheet music. Also, print publishers are usually reluctant to rush R & B songs into print unless they are top 20 hits or are crossing over to pop, since the R & B enthusiast has traditionally not been a heavy buyer of sheet music.

When a song is a hit, the publisher can then pursue TV advertised compilation recordings and advertising commercials for his song, as well as lyric print magazines that only print hits. If the song is not a hit, the publisher will more than likely theorize that the song is still great, but the record or promotional support wasn't, and start pursuing new artists to record the song as if it had never been out! Keep in mind that few people know of a record's previous existence if it was a failure, and therefore, it is as if the song is getting an opportunity to be recorded for the first time.

It is essential for a professional manager to be organized in several categories. First are his contact lists: All of his associates or people with whom he may one day deal, including producers, managers, record executives, artists, publicists, engineers, promotion people, studio managers, musicians, writers, advertising agencies, disk-jockies, A & R staffers, performing rights societies, and TV producers, as well as other domestic publishers.

Second, his catalogue must be organized for quick and easy accessibility to particular songs, including where and how he files his demos, lead sheets, cover versions of songs, sheet music, and tape copies of new material by writers.

The third category to be organized is his daily casting, which includes people who are currently looking for material, the direction to take musically, and the type of artist, etc.

The professional manager would then draw his ideas for songs from his *master catalogue list,* usually printed with the writer's name at the top of the page and all of his songs the publisher controls underneath. He writes his suggestions in a larger casting book under the title of the artist and/or producer's name. From this list, he draws the most likely titles for the artist and enters those titles in a book that might be called "Daily Casting Log." This book contains space for each casting completed, and often has three or four castings per page, arranged according to the date they were completed and sent out. The casting space would contain the producer, the artist, whether delivered in person or by mail, the date, and a list of the tunes. (More details on this in Chapter 11.)

This system necessitates still another book to transfer all the "Daily Casting Log" information into a "Producers Book." That way, the publisher can refer to his producers book (with a page for each producer) to see over a period of time what songs went to a specific producer, when they went, and for which artist (since most producers have produced more than one act over a period of time). A space would be provided for the producer's reaction to the tune next to the title.

Of course not all professional managers are this organized. Some may have no system at all and either cast from ideas off the top of their head (not a bad idea if they are successful and really know their catalog) or push the same favorite songs. Since you may wind up with one of these people being responsible for your songs, it is wise to inquire as to the professional manager's system. I have found that the more organized and thorough a person is, the more persistent he is likely to be, and that is the kind of individual you want running your songs.

To summarize, a professional manager will have three general categories to organize with sub-categories:

1. Contacts
2. Catalogue
3. Castings
   a. Master Catalogue List
   b. Casting Book
   c. Daily Casting Log
   d. Producers Book

While following the daily routine of phone calls to producers, A & R people, managers, etc., doing casting and letters to accompany tapes to be sent to producers, reading the trades for information on new artists and producers, the publisher must also keep in contact with his writers. One way is to keep them aware of activity on their catalogue—

when this is feasible time-wise. It motivates the writer to continue to write. Often, a publisher will call one of his writers just to inform him that he just found out a certain artist is looking for songs and ask if the writer has anything new that might fit the artist, or if the writer has any suggestions of songs already in the catalogue.

A publisher may also develop associations with Broadway or off-Broadway show producers. The soundtracks for shows are very lucrative. Many publishers do everything they can to represent the songs from shows in hopes that the show may be a winner, which would give the soundtrack a great market value. Adding to this incentive for the publisher is the fact that over the years, various songs from Broadway shows have been hit singles on the national charts ("Memory" from CATS). And, several cast albums have done well, even though the show was not a great success. Music from films such as BEVERLY HILLS COP and LA BAMBA has proven the value of publisher involvement in contemporary films, as these among others have produced big selling hit songs.

The publisher is also involved in the promotion of product to the market. When a song is finally recorded and out as a single or an album, a publisher may sometimes hire independent promotion people to work the record in conjunction with the record company's own in-house promotion staff. Some publishers prefer not to hire promoters and will instead give a perc to a record company's promotion individuals so that they will make an even greater effort in promoting the publisher's song. The same people may try to have a song that the publisher controls receive more airplay in the hopes that the song will be pulled from the album and made into a single. This kind of strategy also applies to a publisher who has a song recorded on the "B" side of the release. If the "A" side is not doing well, the publisher may ask his promotion people to promote the "B" side in the hopes of having the "dying single" flipped (although this is a less common practice today than it was in the past). Further areas of the professional manager's daily involvement may include association with advertising agencies for the use of material from the catalogue for commercials, as well as TV producers for the use of material and/or writers regarding upcoming TV projects and soundtracks for films.

As you can see, a good hustling publisher has a number of ways to gain enormously from his catalogue. A more recent, but highly profitable income source is the TV marketing package. These packages have been around since the early 70s, but few publishers were getting quantative use out of them until the "publisher-approach system."

To understand this system requires a short explanation of TV marketing. A TV marketing package is a one, two, or three record compilation of one or more recording artists' more popular songs (for example, *The Four Seasons*) advertised on TV and sold either through the mail or in stores. The usual procedure is for a marketing company to put its concept together regarding which songs to use, approach the record company that owns the masters, and lease them. Then they would approach the publishers to request a mechanical rate for each published song used in the package. Some packages contain 20-30 songs, which could mean as many as 20-30 publishers to contact.

The "publisher-approach" system is initiated by a publisher going through his catalogue and creating a package from tunes he controls. After conceptualizing the album, he would approach the record labels and marketing company separately with a fully conceptualized package. A publisher can save months of work for everyone while improving his own company's income from the package, since he has the songs and recognizes the income potential.

Since the marketing companies put packages together on the basis of hit products, they often have to deal with an excessive number of publishers. If a publisher puts a package together based on established copyrights in his catalogue, the marketing companies are dealing with only one publisher—therefore a very simple process. (See TV Marketing Diagram on the next page.)

A related area of income for publishers is record clubs, which sell their product through subscriptions in magazine advertisements. A publisher's main contact with these clubs is for rates negotiation . The rates are negotiated rather than statutory because premium records are sold at such reduced prices to the public that manufacturers claim they can't maintain costs and still pay full writer/publisher royalties. You'll see more on this in the contracts review section.

Although not under the control of the publisher, but still a source of income, is the printed music market—the printing of sheet music and songbooks of a publisher's best copyrights. Publishers do not have their own printing division, since it is a very costly operation to run. A publisher will have a print licensing deal with a major print publisher such as Hal Leonard Publishing Corp. or Warner Bros. Music, etc. The print music business has changed dramatically, from

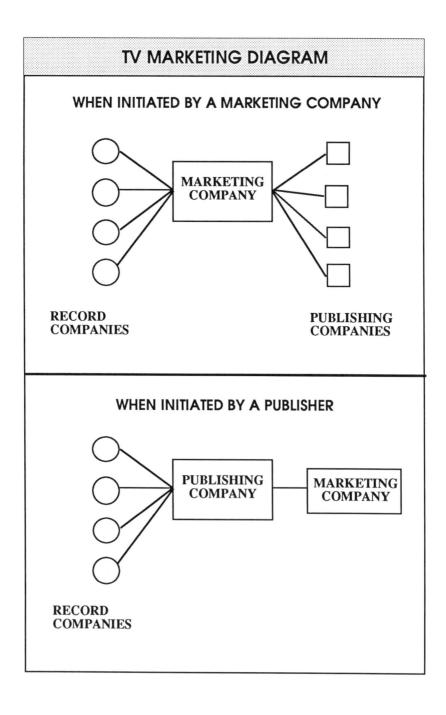

sheet music sales on newsstands to mass merchandising of sheet music and books on radio and TV. Just like the TV package concept of recordings, the possibilities for packages is endless.

To give you an idea of the scope of printed music, the entire recording industry estimated $4 billion in retail sales in 1984. Of that, $266 million was in the area of printed music. Today's print area includes sheet music, songbooks of past and present hits or matching record albums, editions for concert, stage, or marching bands, instrumental books, choral arrangements, and guitar books. Sheet music is usually printed when a song hits the singles charts, but it's not uncommon for an active publishing/print house to get the ball rolling on the basis of favorable reviews in the trades, or when a major artist is coming out with a new album.

A good sale of a songbook is 5,000 to 50,000 copies, and with the increasing number of musicians and singing groups trying to make a living in the music industry, songbook and sheet music sales can't help but increase. The sheet music sales on a Top 5 record are governed by the melody of the song. A non-melodic hit may sell only 5,000–10,000 copies, whereas a melodic song can reach 100,000 or more. Schools have opened up a large market, especially when you consider that there are almost 30,000 school bands in the country. Publishers who stay on top of their catalogues' activity find that the print area broadens the exposure of their songs, as well as bringing in additional income.

From the cost breakdown side of things, the in-store price of sheet music is $2.95 per song. The store paid about $1.78 to acquire the sheet music from the print publisher, who paid the publisher $ .50–$ .60 each in song royalties. The publisher pays the writer $ .08–$ .10 (depending on the publisher's contracts with the writer).

One problem a publisher faces is that competition has become very keen from writers and recording artists. The writer/artist who records her own songs has forced publishers to take new measures in dealing in today's market. In the period of the late 1950s, publishers used to control what was recorded because they were the only regular suppliers of songs. With the advent of the writer/artist and independent writer/producer, many publishers were bypassed in the contemporary market—especially those who decided not to change with the times and sat back relying on royalties from their past catalogue.

Today, an aggressive publisher will not only attempt to sign writer/artists and writer/producers, but he often gets his company into the record production end as well. Wes Farrell was an early example of this kind of publisher. Starting as a writer himself, he saw a trend coming and began producing artists such as the *Partridge Family*, *The Brooklyn Bridge*, and Paul Anka, among others, using songs from his publishing company's catalogue.

Another of the successful independents was the Entertainment Company, headed by publisher Charles Koppelman (now the president of the SBK Entertainment World, the company that acquired the former CBS Records publishing catalogue). Having an extensive catalogue, they have used their songs in their own productions of Barbra Streisand, Glen Campbell, and Dolly Parton, among others.

Good publishing requires promotion, and today that can mean everything from finding writer/artists and getting them record deals to buying trade space and hiring promotion people to work your records.

The third person essential to a publishing company is the administrator. Administration is a very exacting and time consuming job. The more capable the administrator, the smoother the entire publishing operation runs. The responsibilities of the administrator center around the paperwork that is so essential to a well-run organization. These basic functions include copyrighting new songs, administering and organizing all songwriter and individual song contracts, and acting as a direct liaison to the sub-publishers for new material to be sent abroad. BMI and ASCAP must be dealt with regarding new and past catalogue items. The administrator must handle licensing agreements for TV packages, premium and record club releases, and correct label copy for new single and album releases. The administrator issues mechanical licenses to record labels for songs that have been recorded and are being released in the United States. Their responsibilities include the issuing and coordinating of film and TV licenses for the company's copyrights. Although the executive of small- or medium-sized independent companies may negotiate the licenses, paperwork and follow-up are usually in the administrator's hands.

The administrator also keeps records of network TV usage of published songs that are from her catalogue. In general, she must supervise all paperwork, from the filing of Form PA's to generally advising the staff on copyright law regarding contracts, compulsory licenses, copyright terms and renewals (again, as it pertains to large major companies, the business affairs department handles some of these functions). The administrator is also responsible for having lead sheets made, and researching through the Library of Congress to handle copyright ownership disputes. When her company contemplates the purchase of an already established catalogue, the research necessary can be staggering. Sometimes hundreds of hours are required just to read the various contracts to verify who owns what percentage, who has sub-publishing options, and which songs are sub-published from other countries for the U.S. Advances due writers, status of recoupment, and probability of recoupment must all be evaluated. All of these things must be broken down into their simplest, categorized form and made available to the publishing company executives, who require a summary to determine the value of a catalogue, and that is predicated on who owns what songs for how long and what kind of contracts and advances are made against those copyrights.

The last category of personnel in the publishing company is the bookkeeper (or bookkeeping department) who are responsible for all payments, from salaries of the staff to royalties paid to writers and co-publishers. Publishing companies normally pay royalties twice a year, usually within sixty to ninety days after June 30th and December 31st. All monies accrued during those six month periods are credited to the various publishing companies and writers affiliated with the publisher, and before the payments are made, all contractually agreed upon deductions (such as administration fees, advances, demo costs, etc.) are made. Bookkeepers work closely with the administrative staff in regard to percentages and deductions relating to the individual songs, since the individual contracts can vary as to what percentages of ownership each party is entitled to and what deductions their contract calls for.

How To Make Publishing Contacts

THERE ARE MUSIC PUBLISHERS in every state in the country, but the ones with whom you want to deal are, for the most part, located in only three places—New York, Los Angeles, and Nashville. That is because these are the main music centers of the U.S., and publishers in these places are at least close to the music scene. Proximity to the music capitals is no guarantee of publisher effectiveness, but a good active publisher would probably not be in Podunck, Iowa.

The publishers you do find in other cities are, for the most part, not really active publishers at all, but people who for one reason or another formed their own publishing company (Chapter 12 shows how to form your own publishing company). A percentage of the publishers in New York, Los Angeles, and Nashville are also not really publishing in the active sense, but are songwriters or writer/artists who formed companies to control their own copyrights or because they couldn't interest an active publisher in their work. That leaves a very small percentage of *real* publishers.

How do you find them? The best way to start is to be based in one of those three music capitals, which may not be practical, assuming you don't already live there and can't get there often. There are a number of ways to get lists of publishers. Some lists will be small and others will contain hundreds of names. *Billboard Magazine* publishes a "Buyers Guide" which includes almost every name of every company in the industry, but it will take you quite a bit of time sorting out the ones that are the real active publishers. One logical tip is that in all three cities, the record companies, publishers, studios, etc., are located in close proximity to each other. So if you see a company listed on Broadway in New York, or on Sunset Blvd. in Hollywood (or more properly, Los Angeles), they are probably active publishers. If a publisher's address is listed as a P.O. Box number, then they probably are not. One reason is that most of the songwriters/publishers almost always work out of their house and wouldn't have an office in the business area. Lists may also show legal or accounting firms as addresses reoccurring for many publishers, which indicates that these individuals are being managed or represented through their attorney or accountant. If you are planning a trip to New York, Los Angeles, or Nashville, consult the key areas of recording companies and publishers shown on the maps at the end of this chapter. This will enable you to make appointments in advance (with both publishers and A & R people), while knowing the proximity of one company to others. Knowing where you're going can mean the difference between two appointments and five appointments per day.

You can also obtain New York, Los Angeles, and Nashville telephone directories to help you zero in on some companies. Local recording studios may also be of assistance, as well as local disc jockies, but these methods are not the most recommended.

One of the best way to become familiar with the major players is to subscribe to the trades. The trades print weekly the top songs in the country in all areas (Top 40, R & B, and Country), as well as the names of the songwriter of the recording, the producer, and the publisher. You still have to learn which artists usually don't write their own songs or you'll wind up contacting publishing companies that don't actively run songs. For example, if John Smith has a song on the charts written by John Smith and published by John Smith Publishing Co., it is not to your advantage to send anything there, since it is probably his own publishing company. On the other hand, if you see a song on the charts by Barbara Mandrell, written by Joe Boyland, and the publisher is National League Music, then at least on this occasion the artist took an outside song. To help you get a jump on getting your songs to receptive artists, the following is a list of some current artists in all types of music who record outside songs. While you are making publisher contacts, it helps to have some artist or artists in mind for your song. If your song is strong and your song-to-artist matchup is valid, it might make the difference between a publisher being interested or not interested in your material, especially if he is looking for material for a particular artist now.

1. Whitney Houston
2. George Strait
3. James Ingram
4. Jets
5. Linda Ronstadt
6. Cher
7. Al Jarreau
8. Ricky Skaggs
9. Johnny Mathis
10. Smokey Robinson
11. Crystal Gayle
12. Gladys Knight & Pips
13. Madonna
14. Waylon Jennings
15. Olivia Newton-John
16. Starship
17. Kenny Rogers
18. Ann Murray
19. Eddie Money
20. Glen Campbell
21. Barbra Streisand
22. Jeffrey Osborne
23. Barbara Mandrell
24. Frankie Valli
25. Laura Branigan
26. Donna Fargo
27. Art Garfunkel
28. Rod Stewart
29. Tanya Tucker
30. Aretha Franklin
31. Tammy Wynette
32. Conway Twitty
33. Dionne Warwick
34. The Judds
35. T.G. Shepard
36. The Pointer Sisters
37. Steve Waroner
38. Emmy Lou Harris
39. Diana Ross
40. Ronnie Milsap
41. Natalie Cole
42. Stephanie Mills
43. Reba MacEntire
44. Phyllis Hyman
45. Michael Jackson
46. Lee Greenwood
47. Patti LaBelle

The trades also have regular articles on publishing companies and their activities, including articles on publishing personnel being hired. In *Billboard* the column is called "Executive Turntable," in *Cash Box* it is "Executives on the Move," and the *R & B Report* has a very descriptive "who's where" section. Reading this information regularly will give you names of publishers and professional managers whom you can try to contact.

The following is a list of columns, charts, and general information of interest from the two major music trade papers, *Cash Box* and *Billboard*:

CASH BOX

Cash Box Top 100 Singles Chart—Records based on airplay and sales that are the nation's top 100 singles of the week. Lists artist, label, producer, and songwriter.

New Faces To Watch—Write-ups on artists who just hit the charts.

Executives On The Move—Column with pictures of record people taking on new positions that week.

East Coast/Points West—Happenings in recording and performing on both coasts.

Album Releases—Information describing the "pick hits" of the week, along with "records to watch for" which arc considered possibilities.

Single Releases—Same as album releases, except they list the writers, publishers, licensing societies, and producers.

Country Albums—The Top 50.

Country Singles—The Top 100.

Country Singles and Album Reviews—Albums list producers; singles list writer, publisher, licensing societies, and producer.

Indie Feature Picks—Country Single and LP releases worth noting on independent labels.

Country Roundup—Activities of country artists that week.

Black Album Charts—Top 75.

Black Singles Charts—Top 100.

Black Contemporary—Information on R & B artists' activities and new recordings.

Top Albums—200 Top albums of the week with artist and label.

International Section—Information on record and publishing activities and artist performances overseas, along with the United Kingdom's top ten singles and LPs (Melody Maker Magazine) and top ten singles and LPs of a different country each week.

Jazz—Column on jazz artists and LPs in the Top 40.

Dance—Top 75 12" dance singles and featured releases of the week.

Music Videos—Top 40 chart of music videos based on TV rotation at various stations and networks.

BILLBOARD

Executive Turntable—Same as *Cash Box's* "Executives On The Move."

Commentary—Very informative column—each week a topic of interest to the music industry is presented by industryites. The subjects vary from publisher and writer concerns over source licensing, to the archaic New York cabaret laws that permit only three musicians to perform in an unlicensed establishment.

Hot Country LP's—The Top 75.

Hot Country Singles—The Top 100, including producer, songwriter, publisher, licensing society, and print music company.

Hot Adult Contemporary—Top 40 singles of the week.

Black—Column on activities by black artists.

Top Black Singles—Top 100 R & B Records, with writer and publisher names of songs.

Top Black Albums—The Top 100.

Audio Track—Columns concerning which artists and producers are currently recording and where.

Hot Dance Charts—The Top 50 dance singles. Actually two charts–one based on club play, and the other on 12" single sales.

Jazz Blue Notes—A column on jazz artists' activities in two charts; the Top 15 jazz LP's and the Top 25 contemporary jazz LP's.

MTV Music Videos Chart

New Companies—A column listing new companies opening offices that week. Most are small organizations in local areas (not L.A., N.Y., or Nashville). They range from record labels to management and booking agencies. Sometimes a good starting point for you if one of these companies is in your local area. Can give you a little insight into actual music business functions.

Top Album Picks—Lists artist, label, and producer with some of the albums' suggested best cuts.

Top Singles Picks—Lists songs, artist, producer, publisher, writer, and label of this week's best new releases.

Top LP's—Top 200 albums of the week.

Hot 100—Top 100 singles of the week; lists producers, labels, writers, publishers, and sheet music companies.

Inside Track—Column on week's activities and rumors of possible future industry activities.

Hits Of The World—Top Singles and LP charts for the UK, Canada, and alternating weekly, such countries as Italy, West Germany, Australia, Netherlands, Japan, and France (usually prints 6 of 8 countries each week).

International—Interesting group of articles on activities in foreign countries, often relating to publisher and songwriter rights, new laws, and protections of copyrighted works in those countries.

The best way, of course, to make publishing contacts is through introductions. Most publishers will attempt to pick up individual songs from writers, and they stress that they prefer receiving songs from unknowns through referrals and introductions. There can be other contacts you or your family or friends may have to someone in the music business who knows a publisher. Although it is often a very indirect route, it can be an enormous time-saver and contact-maker in the long run. Even a causally associated reference to a publisher usually carries more weight than an unsolicited tape. For example, your mother, whose sister in Los Angeles is the neighbor of a marketing director to a record company, knows a publisher. Your tape and introduction letter may change hands many times, but it is still coming through an introduction of sorts.

Another form of introduction (but not necessarily a first choice) is through a music business attorney—not a criminal attorney or corporate attorney, but a *specialist* in the music business field. This breed of attorney is found almost exclusively in the key music cities. Finding an attorney who will make introductions for an unknown writer can be as difficult as finding a good publisher. An attorney cannot earn much from introductions, so they must believe that your success is imminent or they will not earn much from future business with you. Some attorneys will represent new songwriters (especially if they have artist capabilities and good quality presentations) because the attorney knows he will make a fee for any contract work that occurs from a successful introduction.

Be aware that attorneys do not usually perform work for no charge, so question a music attorney up front as to business procedures. That is to say, if they like your materials (these not-so-expert music experts are going to judge your material), would they make appropriate introductions for you? Are they charging you for a meeting or to talk to you on the phone? Or will they help you with the understanding that should you hook up with someone who can help you, they will charge you a certain fee for the paperwork they negotiate on your behalf?

Some attorneys charge an hourly rate, others just one flat fee for the contract they review and negotiate. Keep in mind that most single song publishing contracts from publishers may not necessarily require an attorney's negotiation. In many cases, an attorney can review it and make some recommendations to you of compromises that might be in order. (Chapter 13 dissects a standard single song agreement to help you.) Depending on what you already know about such agreements, you may decide you do not need their input at all.

Publishers do not mind making appropriate changes, and reputable publishers will usually recommend that you review the contracts with someone more familiar with them than yourself. Remember, you are negotiating for one song, and some attorneys (and writers) may nit-pick a contract to death. If your attorney is being paid by the hour, and it seems to be taking an inordinate amount of time to finalize a two-page agreement (most single song contracts are only two pages long), then maybe the next time you should work out a flat fee deal. Nit-picking is not only costly in legal fees, but it can hurt your relationship with a publisher as well. The real value of the attorney here is that he is considered a relatively respected source for introductions to publishers.

A very good source of introductions, and sometimes even direct contact, to publishers is the Los Angeles Songwriters Showcase. Meetings are held once a week, and you do not even have to perform your song. Cassettes are played for producers and publishers who attend the meeting looking for new and exciting material. Of course this is another case of having to be there in person, but it is something you could plan as part of a future trip. The Los Angeles Songwriters Showcase is sponsored by BMI. (Contact BMI or the Los Angeles Songwriters Showcase for specifics. See Appendices.) The directors of the Songwriters Showcase are Len Chandler and John Braheny. Attending the Los Angeles Songwriters Showcase can also create an invaluable opportunity to meet other writers for collaborating.

This leads to another way to make publisher contacts. Aside from all of the benefits resulting from shared experiences in writer collaborations and the opportunities collaborations afford you for honest and conscientious evaluation, a writing partner may have a contact you don't!

There are many songwriter associations throughout the United States that may be of help with recommendations. The National Academy of Songwriters (NAS mentioned in Chapter 3) can also be of help. The NAS, as well as the LASS, put out newsletters with information that both writers and publishers read. Recording studios (even local ones) may be helpful with contacts when you are planning on doing studio demos (this would certainly be an added incentive to use their studio).

A long shot, but nevertheless another way of making contacts, is entering and winning a song festival. Writers often come to the attention of publishers and other music business individuals by placing a song high in a song competition. On many occasions a winning song will be recorded as part of the prize. Even without winning, being a finalist can make for the opportunity to meet industry pros.

Another way of contacting publishers is through BMI and ASCAP. If you contact someone in these licensing organizations who works with writers, she may be able to recommend specific publishers who are looking for new material and with whom an affiliation might be worthwhile. BMI also has a musical theater workshop, and both ASCAP and BMI have workshops for pop music in N.Y. and L.A. (see Chapter 5).

If you do live in or near any of the "music capitals," the same sources can be used, but you obviously have the added advantage of possibly being able to meet with some of the people whom you wish to contact. Very honestly, it's not the easiest thing in the world to get in to see a publisher when you consider all the other people who are also trying. He will usually see some people whom he considers a priority, or at least more worthwhile than most of the multitude. Making yourself a priority with him starts from the minute you call for an appointment. It is a combination of what you say and how you say it.

First, you *must* know the name of the person you're calling. If you ask for the professional manager or the person who handles new writers on publishing, you will not get past the receptionist! If you don't know the name and can't get it from previously mentioned sources, then call the company and ask the name of the individual, THEN HANG UP. You can then call back later and ask directly for him. Next you will probably get his secretary. This is where tact and references come in. If he doesn't know you, tell his secretary that you are a songwriter and "would like Mr. Warner to hear your material." She will probably instruct you to drop off the material or mail it in. Don't be discouraged or argue, because this is what most writers have to do. Some publishers will require you to call in several weeks, others will call you if they like what they hear. Still others may request that you don't call at all and they will respond by letter or by returning your tape in a few weeks or months.

If you are fortunate enough to have a track record in any area of the business, or if someone will recommend you, take a different approach. Call the publisher and the conversation with the secretary should go something like this:

"Hello, is Mr. Warner in, this is Tony Hart." (It's psychologically important to say your name right after you say the name of the publisher. This gives an air of respectability to you and makes the secretary assume you know the publisher. She may even connect you directly.) The secretary will usually ask, "What is this in reference to?" You say, "Mr. Johnson from BMI suggested I call him. I have some original material he thought Mr. Warner should hear." This sentence immediately sets up credibility because you have a reference and you are *not* saying you're a songwriter. Saying that you are a songwriter does not impress a publisher, because many people claim they write, but few write professionally. In saying, "I have some original material," you're phrasing it as if you could be the writer or representative of the writer, which carries more weight. In saying, "he thought Mr. Warner should hear it," you are not only giving a reference, but a recommendation.

If you have a track record, they key phrase lies in regard to who you've worked with by saying, for example, "I have some original material and I've written with [   ]" or "I've worked with [   ] and had songs recorded by [   ]." By saying this before the secretary can interrupt, you give her some information that she'll pass on to her boss. *Don't ever give false references or track record* because it's a small music business and it could backfire on you. However, there's nothing wrong or unjustified about relating your accomplishments, no matter how small, to a publisher. He just might pick up the phone and make an appointment to hear your songs. If you don't get an appointment, at least he might remember your name when your tape reaches his desk. It's always nice to be able to have a person meet with you and hear your songs, as it helps to build a rapport with the publisher. This happens infrequently until a publisher has first heard and liked one of your songs.

Recording studios in the music capitals can be of more help than those in small towns or other cities because they often produce demo records for publishing companies. Getting to know someone at a recording studio could give you a good reference. Often, a phone call to a studio will put you in contact with someone who will refer you to someone else, and all without ever meeting them or playing anything for them. The songs must have professional potential for you to get somewhere, but to start opening doors, it only takes perseverance.

NEW YORK

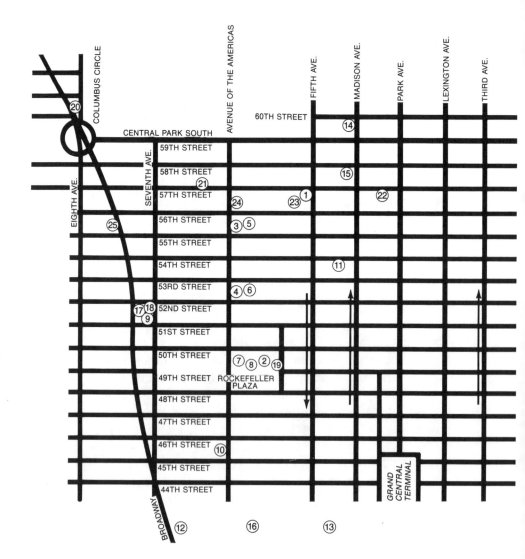

NEW YORK MAP KEY

1. Arista
   6 West 57th Street

2. Atlantic
   75 Rockefeller Plaza

3. Capitol
   1370 Avenue of the Americas

4. Columbia
   51 West 52nd Street

5. EMI/Manhattan
   1370 Avenue of the Americas

6. Epic
   51 West 52nd Street

7. Elektra
   75 Rockefeller Plaza

8. Geffen
   75 Rockefeller Plaza

9. Polygram/Mercury
   810 7th Avenue

10. RCA
    1133 Avenue of the Americas

11. Warner Brothers
    3 East 54th Street

12. Profile
    740 Broadway

13. Island
    14 East 4th Street

14. Chrysalis
    645 Madison Avenue

15. A & M
    595 Madison Avenue

16. Virgin
    30 West 23rd Street

17. SBK Ent. World
    810 7th Avenue

18. Chappell/Intersong
    810 7th Avenue

19. Warner Brothers
    75 Rockefeller Plaza

20. Famous & Ensign
    1 Gulf and Western Plaza

21. Jobette and Stone Diamond
    157 West 57th Street

22. Trio Music
    117 East 57th Street

23. Arista Music
    6 West 57th Street

24. Screen Gems
    1370 Avenue of the Americas

25. MCA
    1755 Broadway

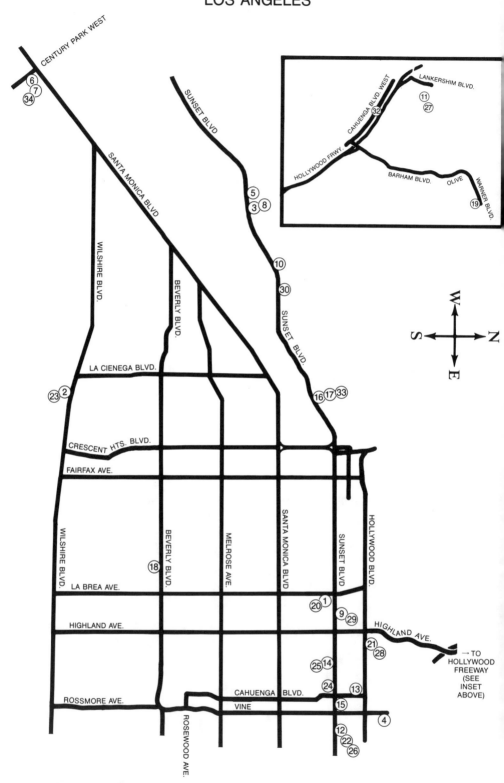

LOS ANGELES

LOS ANGELES MAP KEY

Record Companies		Publishers

1. A & M
1416 North LaBrea (A)

2. Arista
8370 Wilshire Blvd. (B)

3. Atlantic
9229 Sunset Boulevard

4. Capitol
1750 North Vine Street

5. Chrysalis
9255 Sunset Boulevard

6. Columbia
1801 Century Park West (C)

7. Epic
1801 Century Park West

8. Elektra
9229 Sunset Boulevard

9. EMI/Manhattan
6920 Sunset Boulevard

10. Geffen
9126 Sunset Boulevard

11. MCA
70 Universal City Plaza
Universal City (D)

12. Motown (E)
6255 Sunset Boulevard

13. Solar
1635 N. Cahuenga Blvd.

14. Island
6525 Sunset Boulevard (F)
2nd floor

15. RCA
6363 Sunset Boulevard

16. Mercury
8335 Sunset Boulevard

17. Polydor
8335 Sunset Blvd. (G)

18. QWest
7250 Beverly Boulevard,
Suite 207

19. Warner Brothers
3300 Warner Boulevard,
Burbank (H)

20. Almo-Irving
1416 North laBrea (A)

21. Bug
6777 Hollywood Blvd.

22. Chappell
6255 Sunset Blvd

23. Careers Music
8370 Wilshire Blvd. (B)

24. Famous Music
6430 Sunset Boulevard

25. Island music
6525 Sunset Blvd. (F)

26. Jobete Music
6255 Sunset Blvd. (E)

27. MCA Music
70 Universal City Plaza
Universal City (D)

28. Peer International
6777 Hollywood Blvd.

29. Screen Gems/EMI
6920 Sunset Boulevard

30. Warner Bros. Mus.
9000 Sunset Blvd. (H)

31. Columbia Music (C)
1801 Century Park West

32. Private I Mus.
3575 Cahuenga Blvd. W.

33. Polygram Mus.
8335 Sunset Blvd. (G)

34. SBK
1801 Century Park West

NOTE:

The letters (A-H) indicated in parentheses with some of the record companies and publishers indicate an affiliation between the companies. For example, (A) is found next to A & M (record company) and Almo-Irving (publisher), indicating that they are affiliated companies. Likewise, (B) Arista Records is affiliated with Careers Music, (C) Columbia Records is affiliated with Columbia Music, etc.

NASHVILLE

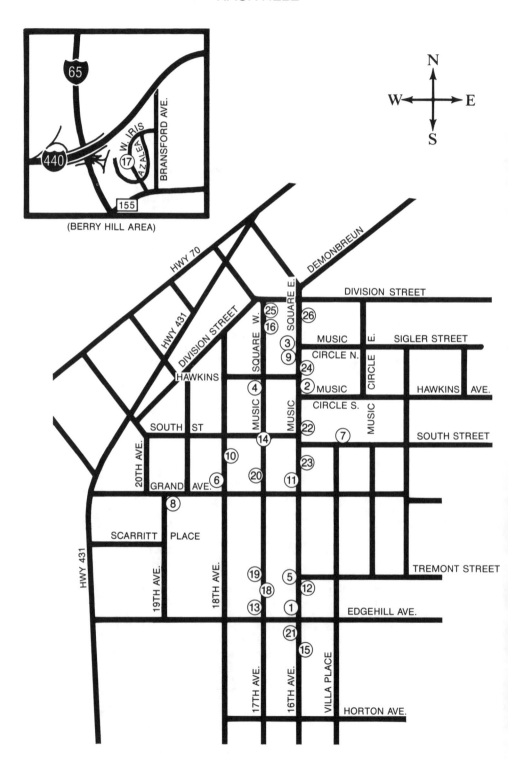

(BERRY HILL AREA)

NASHVILLE MAP KEY

Record Companies	Publishers	Performing Rights Societies
1. Capitol/EMI America 1111 16th Ave. S	8. Almo-Irving 1904 Adelicia	25. ASCAP 2 Music Square W.
2. CBS/Epic 34 Music Square E	9. MTM 21 Music Square E	26. BMI 101 Music Square E.
3. MTM 21 Music Square E	10. Merit 815 18th Avenue S	
4. RCA 30 Music Square W	11. DeJamus 63 Music Square E	
5. Evergreen 1021 16th Avenue S	12. SBK 1015 16th Avenue S	
6. Polygram 901 18th Avenue S.	13. Famous 1233 17th Avenue S	
7. MCA Records 1614 South Street	14. Warner/Chappell 44 Music Square W	
	15. Screen Gems 1207 16th Avenue S	
	16. Tree 8 Music Square W	
	17. Boyland Music 602 W. Iris	
	18. MCA Music 1114 17th Avenue S	
	19. Jobete Music 1109 17th Avenue S	
	20. Acuff Rose/ Opryland Music 66 Music Square W	
	21. Picalic 1204 16th Avenue S	
	22. Rick Hall 47 Music Square E	
	23. Welk Music 54 Music Square E	
	24. Writers Group 23 Music Square E.	

How To Run Your Own Songs

RUNNING YOUR OWN SONGS is done with two goals in mind: One, as a writer, you're running songs to publishers; and two, as a writer/publisher, you're running songs to producers, A & R people, managers, and artists. The difference is what your contacts, financial capabilities, time schedule, track record, and songs are like. Obviously, if you're like the majority of writers, either getting started or having written a short time, your contacts are probably limited to publishers. If you handle these dealings wisely, your contacts and reputability will increase. Of course, things happen much faster if your songs are really good. In any case, here are some tips for running your own song.

Organize your contacts

Every writer has his own system for contact lists, but the following, based on my experience, works well. A phone book itself is not enough. You need a card file system arranged alphabetically, but with cross-references. The following is an explanation of an index chart:

RECORD COs	Alphabetical
PUBLISHERS	Alphabetical
WRITERS	Alphabetical
PRODUCERS	Alphabetical
ADVERTISING AGENCIES	Alphabetical
MANAGERS	Alphabetical
MUSICIANS	Alphabetical
ARRANGERS	Alphabetical
RECORDING STUDIOS	Alphabetical
LAWYERS	Alphabetical
TRADES	Alphabetical
SINGERS	Alphabetical
PROMOTION & PUBLICITY	Alphabetical
BOOKING AGENTS	By city, alphabetically
RADIO STATIONS	By city, alphabetically

Therefore, if I wanted to put Barry Manilow in my book, I would insert a card for him under M in the *Producer* section, under M in the *Singer* section, and under M in the *Writer* section, since Barry does all three. I also carry a much smaller simplified phone book as part of my appointment book.

Organize your files at home and at appointments

Being organized is definitely an asset in terms of dealing with publishers. You should have a desk drawer or file that will hold file folders of letter or legal size. Each folder should be for one song and should contain copies of your lyrics, lead sheets, and copyright forms regarding that song. If you are making a cassette of the song, a copy of the cassette should also go into the file. The song title should be on top of the file with a number so that as you write, each new song would receive the next consecutive number. You then prepare a master list of your song titles that might look something like this:

Song Number	Title	Date Written	Written With	Date Copyrighted
21	Daydreaming	9-26-87		10-16-87
22	Tomorrow	11-21-87		12-21-87
23	My Baby	11-21-87	Fred Sands	12-21-87
24	Katherine	11-30-87		12-21-87

Next, take the original tape copies of your songs and put several of your master copies on one cassette. Label the box with the titles and corresponding code numbers, and you'll have a safety copy from which to make duplicates. *Never take your original out of the house*, except to copy it, and *never leave it with anyone*. Set up a shelf or space where you can file tapes of your songs and put the code number on the binding of the box so they can be located quickly. Keep a separate file folder for copies of all letters you send out to publishers; use another folder for the replies. The procedure should be to send a letter, a tape copy, and a lyric or leadsheet with a stamped, self-addressed envelope. To keep track of songs you play for publishers or send to them, get a simple standard steno book, mark its cover as "Volume One," and date it. As you send out songs, each page will look something like this:

<u>To Producer</u>   <u>For Artist</u>

Clive Davis   Patrice Rushen
                               "Somewhere" (S) 9-6-88

_____

Michael Masser   Whitney Houston
                               "Take Me Down"
                               "I Just Wanna Love You"
                                    (S) 9-8-88

_____

Peter Asher   Linda Ronstadt
                               "Lady of the Night"
                               "Star Crossed"
                                    (B) 9-9-88

By doing this, you can see at a glance how long a publisher or producer has had your tape, and when it might be appropriate to contact them for a follow-up. A reasonable time period is 1-2 weeks. If you wait any longer than that, the tapes seem to get lost. Less than that and it's probable your contact has not even had a chance to listen, if they have received it at all. (Alas, the postal service is not moved to greater efforts by our impatience.) By the way, the "B" in the circle simply means "Brought personally to someone's attention." The "s" means "sent."

Also note that there are never more than three songs sent to any one contact at a time, and usually only two. There is a psychological reason for this: Each song becomes a basis for comparison, even subconsciously. Therefore, someone looking for a hit and hearing one song on a tape that interests him will rarely find more than that one song on that particular tape by reason of comparison. Therefore, give yourself two shots, maybe three, but don't expect them all to be considered equally strong.

As you keep this log for awhile, the system will become automatic. It will also become more involved, because you will be dealing with more publishers and more of your songs. Where you were once showing five songs to eight contacts, you now may have forty songs and twenty contacts. After awhile, you'll whittle down the number of listeners to the ones you feel you can send songs to and receive replies from on a fairly regular basis. However, if you're sending songs that don't *have* it, even the most receptive listener will quit replying. When you begin seeing publishers and producers, etc., and sending songs on a regular basis, you may find a further song file breakdown is necessary. To do this, go through your steno book and enter each publisher's or producer's name at the top of a separate page in a loose-leaf binder with alphabetical indexes. This way, you transfer all of your mailing and appointment information to an alphabetical listing by publisher or producer. It would look something like this:

CONTACT: _Steve Bedell_

TITLE	ARTIST SUBMITTED FOR	DATE SENT
This Is Our Night	Footloose	1-8-86
Tragedy		
Valentine	Footloose	1-29-86
Don't Waste The Night		
Someone For Me	Footloose	2-22-86
Hold On		
Who's It Gonna Be		
Tell Me What I'm Gonna Do		
Bad Boy		
Game of Love	Bev. Hills Cop II	3-4-86
That's The Way I Want It		
Eye to Eye		
Time Talks	Summer School	3-4-86
Who Do You Love		
Midnight Squeeze		
Built For Speed	Bev. Hills Cop	3-11
Time Talks		
Safari	Summer School	3-11
Hard On Addiction		
Say You Do		
Private Domain		

With this system, you avoid the embarrassment of sending the same song to a publisher twice, especially if he didn't like it. You also learn which of your material he might like, so you can either write something else like it, or you may already have something similar for him.

It is also a way to gauge if an artist is likely to be looking for songs for a new LP without any factual information, by keeping track of when they last released the LP. For example, if you make a note that Dolly Parton's last LP was released approximately in May of 1991 (because you sent songs for her in March of 1991), she will probably be considering songs again between January and July of 1992. (Most established artists cut an LP once every 12-18 months, with an average of 1-3 months of production and at least a month to prepare the LP for release. Her May 1991 LP might have taken three months to record and release, so January through March 1991 would have been the best time for submission of material.)

The ideal time to submit songs is a month or two before the artist begins recording and right when they're cutting the record, before they've finalized the songs. Too early, and some songs may be forgotten, even if they are liked. Too late, and—well it's too late! The best way to keep track is by watching the trades and keeping a list of specific artists for whom you feel you have material, or by the factual information you acquire about certain artists when you send material to a publisher for that artist and make a note in your contact file.

This type of record keeping gives you a further insight, over a period of time, about which publishers you find yourself sending the most material to, and who is considering what. It also makes following up on any interested publisher much easier on you because you will have a visual record before you. Over six months' time you may have sent one particular publisher eleven songs in five packages. By referring to your publisher's corresponding page, you can see if there are any notations indicating interest which may require follow-up at this time. For example, a publisher may have liked your song, but did not have an artist for it at that time.

A final point to remember is that all of us, whether seasoned professionals or budding beginners, become emotionally attached to the product we are trying to "sell." By keeping accurate visual records, you will be able to objectively review your progress instead of forging ahead up a blind alley.

Research the person with whom you're dealing

This can be an added help for your meetings with publishers. It always makes for quicker and more natural relationships when you know something about the publisher before you meet him, such as where he is from, where he worked before his current position, if he was previously in another area of the business, such as producing, managing, or writing with some chart success (it happens often).

Upon meeting a publisher for the first time, if often breaks the ice and impresses the individual if you have knowledge of him. It also makes him assume you've been around awhile, even if you haven't. If you know he worked for Capitol Records three years ago, then you might comment "Didn't you work at Capitol a few years ago?" He'll say "yes" and probably start talking about it. Finding out this type of information is not always easy, but as you meet more and more people, they will tell you about other people in the industry. If you collect records, you'll often find a name on the record (whether it be writer, arranger, producer, etc.) who is also now a publisher. You can learn a lot about the publishing company from records, both 45's and albums. Read the liner notes on the albums you buy, and make notes on songs associated with the publishers you are dealing with or want to deal with and what songs they've had hits with. It may be valuable as an ice-breaker and make the publisher more receptive to you and your songs. Even if you do not collect records, you can learn this information by visiting local record stores or reading the trade papers.

Handling yourself in a meeting

Personality and your presentation are the keys to a good meeting. Even if the publisher doesn't like those particular songs, your attitude and professional manner will set you apart from the everyday individual he would consider a waste of time. If he respects you, he may think you could have a song he can use in the future.

When in a meeting, don't try to over-explain your songs. The song itself is the final decision-maker, but you can mention an artist or two whom you might have in mind for it. If it's not a studio demo, let the publisher know it, not by apologizing, but by telling him that you did it at home and tried to gear it for a certain direction.

If you have three or four songs you want the publisher to hear, try to make sure they are on one tape with corresponding lyrics or lead sheets. The ideal form of presentation for multiple songs is to have a cassette of each song. Go to a meeting with six or seven songs, each on a different cassette. Then, in your meeting, play it by ear. Always start with *one of your best* songs. It is your introduction to the publisher, and even if he doesn't hear it as a hit, he will hopefully begin to respect your writing ability. The second song should be your *best* song. If he doesn't like it, pick one more good song from your remaining four or five and see what he says. If after three songs he doesn't like any, don't push him to hear more. If he likes you, you will get an opportunity to play more of your songs. If he doesn't, it wouldn't matter how many songs you played that day. If he does like the second or third song, play one more from your remaining pile. If he likes the way you write, he will ask you to play more songs for him. If you are playing a tape, you lose some of the maneuvering ability after the second song, but you can put five or six songs on the tape and suggest he skip #3 or #4 to go to a song you think he'll like better.

Be sure to leave 4-5 seconds of space between songs. Most publishers have an auto-locating device on their cassette machines that will stop at the beginning of the next song only if there is a space between songs. You don't want the listener starting a song 8 bars in, since they may not have time or patience to look for the beginning.

Make sure your tape copy is just that—a *copy*. Leave your original tape at home. You may have to leave this tape with him. See that you use a virgin tape. Don't overtly contradict his opinion of your song. You may not agree, but it won't help your relationship to have him feel that you're insulted by his opinions. Many publishers won't give you an opinion at all, so anything the publisher says could be of value for your future writing. After a second or third song is turned down, ask him if there is a specific type of material he is looking for. Many publishers will say "Just a hit," but if he does say something like "We're looking more for an uptempo Madonna type of song," you just might have one song remaining in your case or at home. It gives you an opportunity for one more shot at that meeting, but don't waste it with a song you don't really believe that strongly in. If he's turning down your songs without explanation and you feel he is *not* trying to rush you out the door, ask him how he feels you can improve your writing. He might just give you some tips. If it seems like he is rushing you out, asking that question wouldn't get you a helpful answer anyway.

A secretary can often make the difference between you seeing or not seeing her boss, so it requires a good deal of tact, diplomacy, and friendliness on your part.

Conscientious secretaries are often rushed, either by their duties or their bosses, but many secretaries will be patient with you if you make them feel like they are a great help to you. Personality can go a long way toward making the contacts you seek. If you sense a secretary is not rushing you, ask them about their boss: "What kinds of writers have they signed in the last year or so?" "Is the company most successful in placing R & B or country?" Intelligent questions will be beneficial to your future association. It is better to act like a prospective client than a novice writer. Many secretaries will actually encourage their boss towards one writer over another based upon how they are treated.

Should the "vibe" in that all-important meeting be good, and the listener indicates interest in a song, it could be timely to inquire if it would be possible to write with one of their writers or someone they would recommend. The value of such a collaboration is often greater than the acceptance of the song that interested them in the first place. A writer collaboration with a writer recommended by a publisher can be a great door-opener because it gives you continued access to the publisher and, through the collaboration, other potential contacts.

Since the collaborator will almost assuredly be more experienced than you, the benefits are enormous. If the publisher does not have someone they can put you with, or seems reluctant to do so but likes a song of yours, make him aware of your desire to collaborate in the future, and perhaps he will consider a recommendation at a later date.

How To Publish Your Own Songs

IN GENERAL, there are three types of people who start their own publishing companies. The first is the established songwriter whose contract with an established publisher may be running out or who has just reached a degree of success where he can renegotiate his contract with his publisher. In doing this, the writer makes a deal with the existing publisher to *co-publish* his future songs. Most successful writers who are involved in having their own publishing company either have administration deals with another publisher (see Chapter 14), or have co-publishing deals with a publisher, thereby splitting the copyright ownership of their existing catalogue. Some writers own and operate 100% of their publishing company, but that involves a lot of demo costs, promotion, filing, and accounting costs (depending on the writer's activity and catalogue).

The second group of people who start their own publishing companies are the artist/writers. They have little or no time to devote to publishing their own songs, but are often in a position to own some or all of their publishing. In most cases, they will co-publish with a reliable publisher who will administer and exploit their catalogues for them. Some artist/writers even hire a professional individual to run a publishing company for them.

The third group consists of the new or yet-to-be-established writer or writer/artist. He often forms a publishing company because of what he feels may be a lack of interest in his work by other publishers.

BMI and ASCAP encourage the formation of new publishing companies. They both state that anyone can become a publishing member by proving he is actively involved in the music publishing business. This means having a least one piece of music used or commercially published and/or recorded, distributed, and promoted. ASCAP charges a $50.00 fee for publisher membership, and BMI charges a $25.00 fee. There is no license requirement to become a music publisher in the United States. The following is a list of functions that the new writer/publisher can handle himself:

1. **Filing for Publisher Membership.** Contact your preference of either BMI or ASCAP, and request publisher application forms. Choose a name for your company and check with ASCAP and BMI to make sure the name you've chosen isn't already in use. (You may also have to comply with local, county, or state business requirements, but those are beyond the scope of this book—seek legal advice.) After receiving, completing, and returning your application, your chosen affiliate will send you a publisher agreement, which is the legal form that registers your publishing company and the songs in your catalogue. BMI will hold your cleared publishing name for 90 days, ASCAP for 60 days, and if you call or write for extension, ASCAP will hold it another 30 days. The "name hold" will be dropped if you do not join a society within that period.

2. **Necessary operational forms:**
   A. *From BMI or ASCAP*, you'll need to obtain their index cards for filing individual songs, writers' membership forms, and writer clearance forms (*for yourself or other writers' songs you may sign to your company*).
   B. *From the Library of Congress:*
   Form PAU or PA for "Registration for a Claim to Copyright" in either unpublished (PAU) or published (PA) form.
   C. *General forms* such as single song agreements for the acquisition of other writers' songs for your publishing company, and mechanical license forms which give record companies the right to reproduce and distribute your music on records while paying you royalties.

3. **Organizing files on songs, tapes, lead sheets, and copyrights:**
The filing system explained in Chapter 11 is just as workable for
you as a publisher, the exception being that you need a file for
all publisher affiliation papers, and a cost and income file.

4. **Making demos of your songs** was explained in Chapter 7.

Controlling your own copyrights is to your benefit if your
catalogue is a money-making operation, and even then you're often
better benefitted by a full-time professional administration and placement organization.

Having your own publishing company affords you no greater
protection for your songs than not having one. You still must have
Federal copyright protection and you must follow the same songwriter
procedures for copyrighting your company's songs. Having your own
publishing company is of no great value to you if the majority of your
contacts are other publishers. If you have no track record as a writer and
few contacts as a publisher, you may have to give up the publishing
share to an artist or publisher who is interested anyway. This not only
requires an assignment of copyright as well as a songwriting contract,
but is a waste of time and money on your part. Expense-wise, many of
the costs for a writer and writer/publisher will be the same, such as
demos, copyrighting costs, mailing, lead sheets, copying, phone bills,
etc. One cost that is not the same is the publisher membership fee to
either BMI or ASCAP.

Having your own publishing company also requires a talent
beyond writing. That is the ability and objectivity to pick which songs
would best suit and have the most hit potential for the artist or producer
you're contacting. Even with a fair number of contacts, bad casting has
hurt more than one writer/publisher in getting his songs recorded.

Running Your Own Songs

Established publishers perform a service very few writers can
perform on their own—that is the contact and playing of songs to artists,
producers, and managers. If you can perform this service for yourself,
you can bypass the immediate necessity for a publisher (at least until
such time as the paperwork and administration duties drive you crazy).

Many of the areas previously discussed, such as reading the
"trades," getting introductions, going to recording studios, and meeting

people at record companies are all essential for developing relationships with artists and producers. These people aren't in the phone book or readily accessible to the general public. Established publishing companies often have people with what they call "good ears" just for this purpose, which is a delicate and critical area of the business requiring tact in dealing with people, as well as the ability to hear what would be a good song for the artist.

What happens on average to 200 songs sent out by a publisher?

Person receiving songs	# of songs	Held	Recorded	Made Albums	Made Single
A & R	(30)	3	1	0-1	
Producer	(120)	8	4	1-3	
Manager	(20)	3	1	0-1	1
Artist	(20)	3	1	1-2	
Record Exec.	(10)	1	1	0-1	
TOTALS		18	8-9	2-8	1

The above chart gives you an idea of the frustrations writer and publisher alike face in getting activity. Explore the chart breakdown based on 200 songs sent out. A good publisher will try to deal with the producers and artists more than the other categories, since they usually have the last word in what is recorded. Managers and A&R people still have to convince their artists and producers. Record executives, who do get involved in song decision-making, are obviously harder to reach than producers. A wise publisher having an association with a key record executive, will only send that executive one or two of the best things he has for a specific act, thus limiting the quantity. Although, if a president of a record firm likes your song, the chances are better that it will be recorded. Overall, however, songs sent to record executives are at best a small percentage of the actual number of songs sent out by an active publisher.

While contacting producers, managers, A & R people, and artists, the following form can be used to get the necessary information from these people regarding the artist or artists for whom they may need material.

Producer_____ Phone#_____

PRODUCER'S QUESTIONNAIRE

1. WHO'S COMING UP FOR RECORDING:

Artist	Label	Single	Album
1._____	_____	_____	_____
2._____	_____	_____	_____
3._____	_____	_____	_____

2. WHAT DIRECTION:

1. Pop R&B	Disco	Funk R&B	Top 40	MOR	Rock	Country Crossover	Country	Other
2. Pop R&B	Disco	Funk R&B	Top 40	MOR	Rock	Country Crossover	Country	Other
3. Pop R&B	Disco	Funk R&B	Top 40	MOR	Rock	Country Crossover	Country	Other
4. Pop R&B	Disco	Funk R&B	Top 40	MOR	Rock	Country Crossover	Country	Other

3. FEEL & TEMPO

1. Uptempo	Medium	Ballad	Rhythm Ballad	Doesn't Matter
2. Uptempo	Medium	Ballad	Rhythm Ballad	Doesn't Matter
3. Uptempo	Medium	Ballad	Rhythm Ballad	Doesn't Matter
4. Uptempo	Medium	Ballad	Rhythm Ballad	Doesn't Matter

4. PRIORITY:

#1 _____   #2 _____   #3 _____   #4 _____

5. HOW MUCH TIME:

#1 _____   #2 _____   #3 _____   #4 _____

6. ADDITIONAL NOTES ON DIRECTION, EXAMPLES ("BON JOVI" TYPE), & MY SUGGESTIONS

#1. _____

#2. _____

#3. _____

#4. _____

7. PUT WRITERS ON ASSIGNMENT   No☐   Yes☐

8. WHAT WRITERS_____

9. SEND MATERIAL TO: (If address not already on file) _____

_____

_____

The following questions are questions to ask that contact on the phone. Since a phone conversation doesn't usually afford you the luxury of filling out a whole form such as this (especially with a busy producer), use the following shortcuts. Write the contact's name and phone number before the call at the top.

QUESTIONS

1. *Who's coming up for recording?* This is the obvious first question after a few social amenities. Next—*Are you doing a few sides or a whole album?* (Check the category he replies to.)
2. *What is the direction he wants to take the artist in musically?* (Circle the category he states).
3. *Is there a particular feel he wants, such as uptempo or ballads?* (Circle again).
4. *Which artist* (if there is more than one discussed) *is the priority?* (meaning who is he recording first). (Check the number corresponding to the artist he mentions from Question #1).
5. *How much time do I* (the publisher) *have for each project?* (artist #1, 3 weeks to send songs; artist #2, 6 weeks, etc.).
6. From # 6 down, make notes *after* you conclude the telephone conversation regarding your own song suggestions while the conversation is still fresh in your mind. Also, make note of whether you should have any of your writers write something specifically for the project, which writer to ask, and where to send the material if the contact has requested it to be sent to a specific place. Sometimes a contact will have a summer house, or he is recording in a studio for several weeks in another city and requests songs be sent to him there. With a sheet like this, dated and numbered, you can go back several months later to check on a past casting project and follow-up for future projects.

Print works

When your new publishing company does get off the ground with one or more songs recorded and released, and a song reaches a level of acceptance where it is profitable to consider having sheet music produced, a print deal with a major music print publishing house is essential. Since you are the publisher, the time for this is your decision, but you would have to find a print company that is in agreement with you. Usually a song that hits the Top 100 charts will make some extra money if sheet music is printed. The higher the song rises on the charts, and the more records it sells, the more likely that the percentage of sheet music income will be greater. Although most new publishers do not print their own sheet music, here is a cost factor to give you an idea of how you could do it if you so desired. First, a professional musical arrangement of the song must be made (usually for vocal/piano with guitar chords) which will cost $75 to $125. Then the finished arrangement goes to a musical "engraver," now a computerized process, which costs about $25 per page, with three or four pages for each song. Print costs run about $500 for 5000 copies of a single color, 4 page song. Total costs will run about $675 to $725 for 5000 copies, but will decrease with additional copies since the plate costs, etc., are only one-time charges. This is only for producing the sheet music, and doesn't include any cover art for the song sheet. Without a distributor to put the sheets in stores for sale, there is no real purpose in printing them. Also, since today's market requires a hit record, you normally couldn't sell sheet music on a new song until the public, disc jockeys, record distributors, and stores become familiar with your title via its record activity.

Collections on mechanicals

This simply means royalty collections from record companies for records sold containing versions of your song. As you can imagine, that can be quite a full-time job in itself, and therefore a company called the Harry Fox Agency acts as a representative for many publishers in collecting royalties for each publisher from the record companies. They pay the publisher both his publisher's share and the writer's share of the songs listed owned by that publisher. It is the publisher's responsibility to pay his writers their share. The Harry Fox Agency works on a fee basis, and generally 4.5% is deducted before they forward the royalties to the publishers. At the time an artist has recorded a song you publish, the record company will contact you for a mechanical license. This is simply a form which refers to the compulsory licensing provisions of the copyright law and states the agreed-upon royalty. (The current rate, called the "Statuatory Rate", is 5 $1/4$¢ per song for each record sold.) This includes the writer and publisher shares which are split equally. If you are the sole writer of the A and B side of a single, the total of 10 $1/2$¢ per record would be yours.

Where collections on mechanicals becomes time consuming (and, of course, less profitable) is when you have co-written a song. More than money is involved in these instances. As an example, if you co-write a song, unless you have an agreement with your co-writer to either publish her share or co-publish and administer her share, then she is entitled to do whatever she wishes with it, including giving the administration rights on her share to another publishing company. Therefore, on one side of a record you would receive .0131¢ as co-writer and .0131¢ as co-publisher, and your writing partner is given the same, minus any administration fees she is paying to a third party administrator.

Every move in publishing requires paperwork, from registering copyrights and filing forms with the licensing societies to signing co-writers' songs to your company. Companies that have smaller catalogs or companies with large administrative departments sometimes elect to collect mechanical royalties directly from the labels. The advantage is that they can get paid sooner (usually by at least three months) and do not have to pay the Harry Fox fee of 4.5%.

A new writer/publisher closely tracking the activity of songs will almost always know when a record will be released and can choose to license it himself. Don't assume the record company will immediately send you a license or a license request. You often have to request a license from them.

Ideally, you should have your own form to send to the record company, because the mechanical license terminology of a record company's license can be very pro-record company. It is often a case of not what is *in* the license, but what is *not* in it that can hurt you. For example, you should request that no more than 50% "reserves" be withheld from royalties during any one payment quarter. Reserves are the money the record company holds back from royalties in case the distributor returns a record because he couldn't sell it. Also, you should request that all reserves be liquidated within 18 months. The record companies usually want 2 to 2 1/2 years to liquidate, but they certainly should know what they have sold in a year and a half.

Contrary to public opinion, mechanical licenses can and should be negotiated with record companies. If you have a song being released on record, it might be worth contacting a reputable publishing company to have them administer the rights. The 15% fee most publishers charge for this service is worth every penny when you realize all of the pitfalls confronting you in mechanical licenses alone.

Unlike attorneys who get a fee for negotiating contracts, publishers only earn their percentage if you make money. They are not on an hourly retainer, so the better deal they cut for you, the more money their 15% is worth. For example, you may have the only song on an LP being released, whereas the other seven songs are by the writer/artist who has what is called a *"controlled composition clause"* (see Chapter 17) in his recording agreement. This clause forces him (quite unfairly) to deliver his finished LP at three quarters of the statutory rate. Therefore he has to grant the record company the authority to grant him less than $ .0525 per song (8 songs x $. 0525 per cut equals $ .42 per LP at statutory), which would come out to $ .039375 per cut and 31 $1/2$¢ an album. He will also be pressured by his record company agreement to use his best efforts to get the owner of the eighth song to grant the label a reduced rate.

A knowledgeable and aggressive publisher administering your song will obviously fight to retain full statutory for you, and more than likely will succeed, because he will have greater clout with the label than a new writer. Don't forget, the more a publisher can earn for you, the more their 15% is worth to them.

The statutory rate is the top royalty payable under current copyright law to a publisher per song. Aside from controlled composition clauses, there are other times when record companies will try to get a "rate" that is lower than the statutory rate per copy. (For example, when two or more of the publisher's songs are used in TV Marketing Packages.) The decision regarding this is strictly up to the publisher, but the consequences of his decision can, on occasion, affect the use of his song on record. If a publisher decides not to grant a reduced rate, and the record company has more songs recorded for their album than they need, they might drop the publisher's songs from the album in favor of another song with *equal* potential, but with a lower rate. This doesn't happen very often, as most record producers don't over-cut for their albums, and even if they do, they're not inclined to agree with the record company to drop a really good recording because the record company can't get the rate it wants. With TV packages, a marketing company may be more inclined not to use a song unless they get a reduced rate. Publishers will often give a rate if the marketing company agrees to what is called a "Favored Nation Clause." That is a clause whereby the songs in that particular album collection are all being acquired for the same reduced rate (usually anywhere from 50 to 75% of the current statutory rate).

One last thing to remember about mechanical licenses is that the granting of a rate to one record company for one recorded version of your song in no way changes the standard rate on other recorded versions, either before or after you grant a rate. The rate will only be in effect for the version for which you granted the rate.

Foreign Publishing

When you have a record out, there is always the possibility of it being released in a foreign country or covered by a foreign artist in her country. This occurrence would then require the establishment of a "subpublisher" (a company in a foreign country who represents your songs and collects the income on those songs for you). Obviously, arranging to have a subpublisher in each country would be a difficult task at best, so most small publishers have an arrangement with an international publisher like Warner Chappell, Screen Gems EMI, etc., to represent their song throughout most of the world.

Don't, however, overlook the active independent publisher if your research tells you they have territory-by-territory deals, since they may provide you with a network of hand-picked companies in each territory. The majors may have more than one weak affiliate among their worldwide offices, and that weak affiliate could be in the very country in which your record is released.

A subpublishing deal is also a great door opener to an active company, and the only way to justify an administration deal (see Chapter 14) when your lack of track record would normally preclude such an association with a publisher.

Each foreign publisher has a percentage payment system. Some vary quite a bit from the norm of a 50/50 split. Some deals range to 25% for the subpublisher and 75% for the original publisher's share.

If you suddenly find you have one or more recordings "happening" overseas, note that once a year at the end of January most of the active music publishers around the world meet to do business in Cannes, France at a convention called MIDEM. The expense is often prohibitive (usually $4,000-$6,000) for a writer, but should you find yourself in Europe at that time of year, MIDEM is something to behold. Over a 5 day period, the Palais de Festival comes alive with thousands of record company and music publishing people rushing here and there to do deals. This is often where the American publishers who represent you come to meet the subpublishers who will be representing their catalogue, territory by territory, for the next few years.

SUMMARY

Many new writers believe that since the efforts of a writer placing a song with the publisher are identical to a publisher placing a song with an artist, producer, or record company executive, there is really no reason why they should give up 50% of the income possible from their song. In some cases, the writer would be correct in his thinking if he had the contacts that a full-time and active publisher has. However, since new writers don't, the need for a good publisher is obvious.

If you want to move into other areas of the industry, then by all means it is quite possible and has been done by many successful people who started as writers. But by being your own publisher, much of your time will be spent in administration, bookkeeping, and promoting, as well as many other areas that will take time from what you originally wanted to do—*write.*

Publishing Contracts

PUBLISHING CONTRACTS have been known to confuse and scare writers more than any other form of agreement. There is usually very little justification for this, since any reputable publisher must follow certain guidelines that managers, record companies, and producers don't have to adhere to. An example of this is that a manager can, if he so chooses, give a client a contract with a grossly inflated percentage for himself. If his client is foolish enough to agree to it, then it is usually legal, though exorbitant. A publisher, on the other hand, is governed by the copyright law and a standard for the industry. He is forced to retain a maximum 50% split of almost all income with the writers. This is only one instance whereby all publishers have pretty much the same language in their contracts.

The reason most writers have become so guarded when reviewing a songwriter's contract is that most individual publishing contracts are signed by new and upcoming writers who for the most part are signing one or two songs to a publisher for little or no advance. On that basis, a writer usually can't afford an attorney or doesn't want to go through the trouble to retain one. So he reads the contract himself (often his first) and is shaken by what, in reality, are generally standard form paragraphs regarding the rights and royalties. (This is not to say that, like any business, there aren't people who represent themselves to be publishers, but by the nature of their business practices, are really *song sharks*. For example, anyone who charges a writer a fee for publishing or exploiting her song is a song shark; no reputable publisher would do so. Most song sharks prefer not to have a signed agreement as a legal document. This is contrary to their thinking and can inhibit their activities.)

For this reason, a basic publishing contract is presented herein, with a brief layperson's description of the various paragraphs. It contains the basic clauses you'll find in most contracts. Remember, some contracts will have more and some less, so this is only meant to give you a better working knowledge of a publisher's rights as well as your own. Keep in mind, most publishing companies have taken a clear-cut position regarding ownership percentages on songs by new writers. Jobete Music, for example, requires 100% of publisher's share for their company to pick up a song. Some, like Screen Gems–EMI and Warner Bros. Music, give writer advances if the song merits it. Most publishers that give advances pay in the area of $200 to $500 a song. Some publishers will not give reversion clauses, usually because of advances. As a writer, your main concern regarding a contract should be the reputability and effectiveness of the publisher, the length of contract, the advance (if any), and the royalty schedule. This is not to say that all clauses or contracts are equal in their rights to writers and publishers, but it often comes down to the fact that the more impressive your track record or the more in demand your writing services are, the more open a publisher will be to negotiate certain clauses in a single song agreement.

The following contract areas defined are:

- Publisher (ASCAP or BMI)
- Legal full name and pseudonym
- Song title and sale section
- Advance
- Sheet music copies income
- Songbook, folio percentage income
- Foreign royalties income
- Free goods
- Mechanicals, synchronization rights, and other percentages of income
- Performing society royalties
- Writer
- Writer's respective share
- Terms of control
- Royalty statements
- Suit regarding infringements.

> **Ed. Note:** The contract quotations are shown in bold print; the explanation is separated by a line and is in lighter print.

(Basic Publishing Contract)

(A) AGREEMENT entered into this _____ day of _____
(B) 19_____, by and between _____hereinafter
(C) designated as the Publishers, and _____
author(s) and/or composer(s) hereinafter jointly designated as
the Writer.

(A) Make sure the date of the contract is the date you *sign* and not the date it is drawn, which can sometimes be the difference of a month or two. Most publishers will not begin working on a song until contracts are in force. You would not be giving the publisher or yourself a fair chance for an appraisal of the publisher's song-placing abilities if the full one-year period (assuming it's a one-year deal) is not utilized in full.

(B) The publishing company name. If you're signing different songs with different publishers, and are not yet affiliated with BMI or ASCAP, make certain that all songs go into a company that affiliates with the same licensee. As previously mentioned, all active publishers have at least one BMI and one ASCAP licensed company. If you were to become a member of BMI, and the publisher has your songs placed in his ASCAP company, your royalties could be delayed due to confusion.

(C) Your full legal name and/or pseudonym.

WITNESSETH:
The Writer hereby sells, assigns, transfers and delivers to the Publisher, its successors and assigns, the original musical composition written and composed by _____
(D) _____ (hereinafter referred to as the "Composition"), at present entitled (E) _____,
which title may be changed by the Publisher, including the title, words and music thereof, and all rights therein, and all (F) copyrights and the rights to secure copyrights and any extensions and renewals of copy rights in the same and in any arrangements and adaptations thereof, throughout the world, and any and all other rights that the Writer now has or to which he may be entitled or that he hereafter could or might secure with respect to the Composition, if these presents had not been made, throughout the World, and to have and to hold the same absolutely unto the Publisher and its successors and assigns.

(D) Writer's name again

(E) *Full* title of your song (If the title is "I Love You a Lot" don't write in "Love You a Lot")

(F) This is one of the paragraphs we discussed earlier which, at first glance, horrifies many writers—the right of the publisher to change words, music, and title, and the right to sell or assign, and world-wide rights of control sum up the paragraph. In reality, these rights are necessary for the publisher's legal protection. Some writers in the past have signed contracts with three or four publishers for the same song (usually to get a quick advance), thus necessitating world-wide copyright control. Since the right to publish is meant as an ownership of a portion or whole of a copyright, the publisher likes to have the same right to sell their portion or assign it as they choose. Established publishers rarely sell individual songs from their catalogue. This is almost unheard of. The only time they would be likely to sell your song is if they were selling their entire catalogue. Because no one can foresee the future value of a composition, publishers want to maintain the same rights of sale or transfer for their entire catalogue, or risk a great devaluation of that catalogue when a potential sale is in progress.

Rights of "assignment and transfer" refers to the right of the publisher to have affiliates such as subpublishers, print companies, etc., represent the copyright for their respective areas under agreements with the publishers. It is not a *sale* of the rights. As far as musical changes go, they're not as frequent as you might imagine. More often than not, it is a recording artist or record producer who wants some kind of musical or lyrical change. This paragraph gives the publisher the right to grant the producer the change. The new songwriter is usually reluctant to have his song reworked, but must realize the necessity for the publisher to have this authority. More often than not, a professional interested in your song will make a change (if they make any at all) for the commercial good of the song, not just for the sake of making a change. In reality, if a publisher did not have this authority, he might be considered liable to the writer for changes made for which he wasn't even aware, such as the artist himself changing, recording, and releasing the song on record, without the publisher ever hearing the recording until after it was released.

(G) The Writer hereby convenants, represents and warrants that the Composition hereby sold is an original work and that neither said work nor any part thereof infringes upon the title or the literary or musical property or the copyright in any other work, and that he is the sole writer and composer and the sole owner therefore and of all the rights therein, and has not sold, assigned, set over, transferred, hypothecated or mortgaged any right, title or interest in or to the Composition or any part thereof, or any of the rights herein conveyed and that he has not made or entered into any contract or contracts with any other person, firm or corporation whomsoever, affecting the Composition or any right, title or interest therein, or in the copyright thereof, and that no person, firm or corporation other than the Writer has or has had claims, or has claimed any right, title or interest in or to said work or any part thereof or any use thereof or any copyright therein, and that said work has never been published, and that the Writer has full right, power and authority to make this present instrument of sale and transfer.

(G) This material is fairly straightforward, and a further statement of the writer's claim to originality in the composition and sole legal ownership.

Royalty Payments to Writer

(H) Publisher shall pay or cause to be paid to Writer during the original and renewal terms of the copyright throughout the world the following sums that may accrue:

(1) A royalty of 10 cents per copy on all regular sheet music sold and paid for in the United States.

(2) A royalty of 10% of the net wholesale selling price of all other editions of each copy sold and paid for in the United States.

(3) If the Composition or any part thereof is included in any song book, song sheet, folio or similar publication issued by the Publisher in the United States, an amount determined by dividing 12.5% of the net wholesale selling price of the copies sold by the total number of copyrighted musical compositions.

(4) If, pursuant to a license granted by Publisher to a licensee not controlled by or affiliated with it, the Composition or any part thereof is included in any songbook, song sheet, folio or similar publication in the United States, that proportion of 50% of the gross amount received by Publisher from the licensee as the number of uses of the Composition under the license and during the license period bears to the total number of uses of the Publisher's copyrighted musical compositions (including the Composition) under the license and during the license period.

(5) An amount equal to 50% of all net receipts of the Publisher in respect of any license issued authorizing the manufacture of the parts of instruments serving to mechanically reproduce the Composition, or to use the Composition in synchronization with sound motion pictures, or to reproduce it upon so called "electrical transcriptions" for broadcasting purposes; and of any and all net receipts of the Publisher from any other source or right now known or which may hereafter come into existence.

(6) A royalty of 50% of all net sums received by the Publisher on regular piano copies and/or orchestrations thereof, and for the use of said Composition in any folio or composite work, sold and paid for in any foreign country.

(H1) Sheet music copies: The usual royalty payment to writers is between 8¢-10¢ per copy.

(H2) "Other editions" refers to marching band, concert or jazz arrangements, choral arrangements, instrumental collections, etc.

(H3) This refers to use of the song in songbooks and folios, etc., printed in the U.S. by the publisher. The usual royalty is 12 $1/2$%.

(H4) This refers to the use of the song in songbooks and folios printed in the U.S. by someone other than the publisher, such as a print publisher they may license to print all of their chart songs.

(H5) This refers to all records, tapes, film music, etc.

(H6) This means that one-half of all income derived by the publisher from foreign use of the song goes to the writer (50%).

(H7) In the event that the Composition shall not now have lyrics, and lyrics are added to the Composition, the above royalties shall be divided equally between the Writer and the other writers and composers.

(H7) This does not mean that the publisher *is* authorized to create lyrics, but it doesn't mean he *isn't*. Therefore, if this pops up in your contract, request specific wording as to whether you do or don't want the publisher to have that right. You may want to grant him that right based on your prior approval of the lyrics and/or lyricist.

(H8) It is agreed that no royalties are to be paid for professional copies, copies disposed of as new issues, copies distributed for advertising purposes, or lyrics or music separately printed in any folio, book, newspaper, song sheet, lyric folio or magazine, or any other periodical, except as above set forth. It is also distinctly understood that no royalties are payable on consigned copies unless paid for, and not until such time as an accounting therefor can be properly made.

(H8) The reasoning behind this clause is that since the publishers are not paid for any of these promotional copies, the writer does not receive income from a non-income source.

(H9) Writer shall receive his public performance royalties throughout the world directly from his own affiliated performing rights society and shall have no claim whatsoever against Publisher for any royalties received by Publisher from any performing rights society which makes payments directly to composers, authors and/or writers.

(H9) This is not to be confused with mechanical and other areas of income for which the publisher is always paid and is thereby responsible for payment to writer(s). The writer's share of performance income (airplay on radio and TV) is paid directly to writers by the licensing societies. (See chart on page 62.)

Royalty Advances

(I) In consideration of this Agreement, the Publisher agrees to pay the Writer(s) as follows: (a) The sum of $_____ paid to the Writer(s) (jointly in equal share) as a general advance against any royalties and other payments heretofore and hereafter payable to the Writer(s) by the Publisher, or any of its subsidiary or associated corporations, and to be recouped therefrom;

(I) This is self-explanatory, but remember, they are talking about advances against your own future royalties and an advance that they can recoup. When your royalties for song activity come due, all advances and expenses come off the top. So, the larger your advance, the less your royalty check will be at statement time. Then again to some, a bird in hand is definitely worth two in the bush.

Various Royalty Payment Schedules
From 3 Different Contracts

First variation:

(J1)   Royalty statements shall be rendered to Writer within forty-five (45) days following the close of each such semi-annual period. Each such statement shall be accompanied by a remittance of such amount as may be shown thereon to be due and payable.

Second variation:

(J2)   Within ninety (90) days after the end of each calendar semi-annual period, Publisher will render to Writer statements as to royalties for each period together with payment of accrued royalties then due, in excess of Ten Dollars ($10.00), if any. Publisher may deduct from such royalties payable any or all of any outstanding indebtedness then owing by Writer to Publisher under this or any other agreement. Writer shall be deemed to have consented to all such statements and accounts and same shall be binding upon Writer and not subject to objection for any reason unless specific objection in writing stating the basis thereof is made to Publisher within six (6) months after such statements and accounts are rendered, or, if objection is made and rejected by Publisher, suit has not been commenced against Publisher within six (6) months after such rejection is made.

Third variation:

(J3) The Publisher shall render the Writer(s), as above, on or before each August 15th covering the 6 months ending June 30th; each February 15th covering the 6 months ending December 31st, hereafter, so long as he shall continue publication or the licensing of any rights in the said Composition, royalty statements accompanied by remittance of the amount due, provided, however, that if it shall have heretofore been the custom of the Publisher to render royalty statements accompanied by remittance semi-annually, such custom may be continued.

(J)   As you can see from the above three variations of payment schedules, time periods may vary. Some publishers pay within 45 days, while others pay within 90 days of the semi-annual royalty period. It is also worthy of note that these statements are usually for a period of activity anywhere from the previous three to four months. You'll also notice that it is common practice (example J2) for a publisher to take his costs for publishing a song off the top of the writer's royalties. Furthermore, the writer has the opportunity in some cases (again example J2) to make a formal objection and/or inquiry within 6 months of receiving his statement from the publisher. Because of the time it takes for a majority of income to be accounted for on a specific recording, the writer should attempt to have any such clause amended to one year or eighteen months minimum for objection to statements.

RENEWALS

(K) The Writer hereby expressly grants and conveys to the Publisher the copyright of the Composition with renewals, and with the right to copyright and renew the same, and the right to secure all copyrights and renewals of copyrights and any and all rights therein that the Writer may at any time be entitled to, and agrees to sign any and all other papers which may be required to effectuate this Agreement. And the Writer does hereby irrevocably authorize and appoint the Publisher, its successors or assigns, his attorneys and representatives in their name or in his name to take and do such actions, deeds and things to make, sign, execute, acknowledge and deliver all such documents as may from time to time be necessary to secure the renewals ands extensions of the copyright in the Composition and to assign to the Publisher, its successors and assigns said renewal copyrights and all rights therein for the term of such renewals and extensions and the Writer agrees upon the expiration of the first term of any copyright in the Composition in this or in any contract, to do, make, execute, acknowledge and deliver to procure the due execution, acknowledgement and delivery to the Publisher, of all papers necessary to secure to it the renewals and extensions of all copyrights in the Composition and all rights therein for the terms of such renewals and extensions.

(K) This paragraph grants the right of renewals for the Publisher after the initial term of ownership and to continue all legal procedures involved in that copyright.

This paragraph is relatively obsolete (although some publishers, especially small lesser-known companies, might still be using pre-1978 song agreements containing this specific wording), since there is no renewal term in the life-plus-fifty year copyright law. A writer might be in a position to bargain this down to a specific number of years for renewal or return of copyright (see Chapter 6).

(L)   The Writer hereby authorizes the Publisher at its absolute discretion and at the Writer's sole expense to employ attorneys and to institute or defend any action or proceeding and to take any other proper steps to protect the right, title and interest of the Publisher in and to the Composition and every portion thereof acquired from the Writer pursuant to the terms hereof and in that connection to settle, compromise or in any other manner dispose of any matter, claim, action, or proceeding and to satisfy any judgment that may be rendered and all of the expense so incurred and other sums so paid by the Publisher, the Writer hereby agrees to pay the Publisher on demand, further authorizing the Publisher, whenever in its opinion its right, title or interest to any of the Writer's compositions are questioned or there is a breach of any of the covenants, warranties or representations contained in this contract or in any other similar contract heretofore or hereafter entered into between Publisher and Writer, to withhold any and all royalties that may be or become due to the Writer pursuant to all such contracts until such questions shall have been settled or such breach repaired, and to apply such royalties to the repayment of all sums due to the Publisher hereunder.

(L) This section has a number of variants. The basic meaning is that the writer is held financially responsible should someone sue him for copyright infringement, or should it be necessary for him and his publisher to sue someone else for the same thing. Sometimes this paragraph is broken up into two paragraphs—one dealing with the publisher and the writer's actions regarding the defense of a suit, and the other regarding the pursuit of a suit. Another variation is that, in many contracts, the writer and publisher split the costs of a copyright infringement suit *against* someone else. In the following paragraph, the publisher takes on the initial legal expense while earning 50% after legal fees if the suit is won. More often than not, however, this category is closer to the writing of (L) than of (M).

(M)   Any legal action brought by the Publisher against any alleged infringer of said Composition shall be initiated and prosecuted at his sole expense, and of any recovery made by him as a result thereof, after deduction of the expense of the litigation, a sum equal to Fifty Percent (50%) shall be divided as agreed among the Writer(s) of the said Composition.

(1) If a claim is presented against the Publisher alleging that the said Composition is an infringement upon some other, and because, thereof the Publisher is jeopardized, he shall thereupon serve written notice to the Writer(s), containing the full details of such claim, and thereafter until the claim has been adjudicated or settled shall pay any monies coming due the Writer(s) hereunder in escrow to any bank or trust company to be held pending the outcome of such claim; provided however, if no suit be filed within twelve months, after written notice to the Writer(s) by the Publishers of the adverse claim, the said bank or trust company shall release and pay to the Writer(s) all sums held in escrow, plus any interest which may have been earned thereupon. Such payments shall be with out prejudice to the rights of the Publisher in event of a subsequent adverse adjudication.

(2) From and after the service of summons in a suit for infringement filed against the Publisher in respect of the said Composition, any and all payments hereunder thereafter coming due the Writer(s) shall be paid by the Publisher in trust to any bank or trust company until the suit has been finally adjudicated and then be disbursed accordingly, unless the Writer(s) shall elect to file an acceptable bond in the sum of such payments, in which event the sum due shall be paid to him.

(N) The term Writer shall be understood to include all the authors and composers of the Composition above referred to. If there be more than one, the covenants herein contained shall be deemed to be both joint and several on the part of the writers and composers and the royalties hereinabove specified to be paid to the Writer shall, unless a different division of royalty be specified, be due to all the writers and composers collectively, to be paid by the Publisher in equal share to each. This agreement may be executed by writers and composers in several counterparts.

(N) This paragraph protects the writers (when there is more than one) from an inequitable breakdown of their rightfully due percentage of income. It is the writer's responsibility to inform the publisher regarding the correct split of income percentage that each writer should be paid by the publisher. That split should total 100%. For example, if there are three writers on a song and the publisher is not informed to the contrary, he will divide the shares equally, or 33-1/3% for each. In some cases, there is a main writer and one or two subordinate partners. The main writer (or biggest contributor) might feel entitled to 50%, thus leaving 25% for each of the two remaining partners. The publisher also holds all writers equally responsible regarding the terms of the agreement regardless of their income percentage. By signing, they are also legally protected regarding their claim to author participation, as well as any financial benefits from the exposure of the song.

> **(O)** This Agreement contains the entire understanding between the parties and all of its terms, conditions and covenants shall be binding upon and shall inure to the benefits of the respective parties and their heirs, successors and assigns. No modification or waiver hereunder shall be valid unless the same is in writing and is signed by the parties hereto.

(O) This means that any changes to the contract, mutually agreed upon after the signing, must be in writing.

> **(P)** The Publisher shall from time to time, upon written demand of the Writer or his representative, permit the Writer or his representative, through the services of an accountant only, to inspect at the place of business of the Publisher, all books, records, and documents relating to the Composition and all licenses granted, uses had and payments made therefor, such right of inspection to include but not by way of limitation, the right to examine all original accountings and records relating to uses and payments by manufacturers of commercial phonograph records, and the Writer or his representative may appoint a certified public accountant who shall at any time during usual business hours have access to all records of the Publisher relating to the Composition for the purpose of verifying royalty statements rendered or which are delinquent under the terms hereof.

(P) This clause, not found in all publishing contracts, relates to paragraph (J) regarding a writer's disagreement with his statements. The main reason you will not find it in all publishing contracts is because of the total chaos it can create if every writer who has one or two songs with a publisher desired to audit that publisher at almost any given time. In addition, unless a writer with one song published by a given publisher has had income and chart success with his one song, an audit isn't really worth the effort. However, the clause (or a similar statement) is always in the writer's best interest.

The above paragraph will also usually state that an audit may be made no more than once per calendar year and only upon a minimum of 30 days notice. By allowing only an authorized CPA to review the books, the publisher and writer are assured of a proper review without the possibility of tampering.

(Q) If the said Composition is not recorded within one year from the date hereof, the said Composition will be reassigned to the Writer.

(Q) This clause is strictly up to the publisher. If you represent yourself well and knowledgeably in your relationship, this clause will most likely be included, but don't expect it to be considered if you don't mention it. As you can imagine, there are also variations to this clause, such as "If said Composition is not recorded and *released*" or "...is not recorded by a major artist and released by a major label" within one year, etc. But these are variations you will have to bargain for. The advantage of this clause is obvious for the writer in that he is assured if the song is not worked, he can get it back to try somewhere else. However, the relationship with the publisher is also important, and if you feel he's doing all he can to get activity and he keeps up communication with you (even if it is just accepting your calls), you must be aware that some songs don't get recorded for quite a while. It's a publisher's persistence that gets each song its chance, so if you believe in the publisher and the song contract period is expiring, you may want to consider giving it to him for a second one-year term. He may work that much harder because of your faith in him.

These points are obviously not all of the possible ones that can crop up in a writer-publisher agreement, but they are the basic and most common ones. For example, demo costs are often a controversial issue. Some contracts require a 50-50 split of demo costs, with the writer's share coming out of future royalties due the writer on that song. Some publishers require a greater percentage of the costs payable from the writer's royalties.

Now that you have seen a single song contract as provided by a publisher, you'll find a single song contract on pages 152-168, created by the Songwriters Guild of America (SGA), formerly known as the AGAC contract (American Guild of Authors and Composers). By comparison to the publisher's contract, you will see that it is very "pro-songwriter." It also expands on areas that are not usually dealt with in publisher single song agreements, such as a sliding scale royalty on sheet music and band arrangements, licensing agent's charges, negotiations for new or unspecified uses, writer credits on sheet music, etc.

Where the SGA agreement may come in handy for you is by comparing it to the publisher's contract. You may see some areas of greater clarification and benefit *in compromise*; in compromise, because many publishing companies will not accept the SGA contract in its entirety from new writers and may refuse to accept your song if forced to accept the SGA agreement with it.

You do not have to become a member of the Songwriters Guild to use their contract, as they believe that educating new songwriters about their options (when these options exist by virtue of negotiation) is better than having them enter the unfamiliar world of publishing without a comparative frame of reference.

Many famous writers such as Johnny Mercer, Mitchell Parish, Bobby Troup, Jay Livingston, and Ray Evans have used the SGA agreement for years. Over 5,000 writers currently belong to the AGAC/ The Songwriters Guild (authors of the SGA agreement). It is important to note that the Guild is a voluntary association of songwriters, not a union. Therefore the SGA contract is not a negotiated contract between publishers and the Guild, but a songwriter agreement drafted by the Guild and its council representing what the Guild believes to be the best minimum songwriter contract available.

Their terms call for all royalty payments collected by publishers on behalf of members to be paid to them for disbursement to their writer members. There is an administration fee for this service. As to publishing companies who will accept the SGA contract, they are not necessarily better or more honest publishers than those who won't, but like anything else in a competitive society, your bargaining position is your guide. However, to get the full benefits of the Guild, a writer might want to consider membership.

The object of this chapter is to familiarize you with the basic information you'll need to understand a publishing contract, but not to make you an attorney. There is no substitute for a legal viewpoint; however, many clauses require just basic common sense, and the understanding that in any business or contract, both sides give something to get something. Whether it be services, contracts, or creativity, the publisher must protect himself as much as the writer.

The Songwriters Guild of America

NOTE TO SONGWRITERS: (A) DO NOT SIGN THIS CONTRACT IF IT HAS ANY CHANGES UNLESS YOU HAVE FIRST DISCUSSED SUCH CHANGES WITH THE GUILD; (B) FOR YOUR PROTECTION PLEASE SEND A FULLY EXECUTED COPY OF THIS CONTRACT TO THE GUILD.

POPULAR SONGWRITERS CONTRACT
© Copyright 1978 AGAC

AGREEMENT made this _____ day of _____ , 19____ between

_____

(hereinafter called "Publisher") and _____

_____

(Jointly and/or severally hereinafter collectively called "Writer");

WITNESSETH:

Composition

(Insert title of composition here) →

1. The Writer hereby assigns, transfers and delivers to the Publisher a certain heretofore unpublished original musical composition, written and/or composed by the above/named Writer now entitled_____

_____

(hereinafter referred to as "the composition"), including the title, words and music thereof, and the right to secure copyright therein throughout the entire world, and to have and to hold the said copyright and all rights of whatsoever nature thereunder existing, for

(Insert number of years here) →

_____ years from the date of this contract or

not more than 40

35 years from the date of the first release of a commercial sound recording of the composition, whichever term ends earlier, unless this contract is sooner terminated in accordance with the provisions hereof.

Paragraph 1

Writer assigns his song to the Publisher throughout the world for a designated number of years, not to exceed forty (40) (or thirty-five (35) years from the date of first release of a commercial sound recording). (The term reflects the provisions of the 1976 Copyright Revision Law.) The shorter the term, the better for the Writer, because if the song is successful, she can re-negotiate more favorable financial terms at an earlier time. The length of the term would depend on the bargaining strength and reputation of the Writer.

Performing Rights Affiliation

2. In all respects this contract shall be subject to any existing agreements between the parties hereto and the following small performing rights licensing organization with which Writer and Publisher are affiliated:

(Delete Two) → **(ASCAP, BMI, SESAC). Nothing contained herein shall, or shall be deemed to, alter, vary or modify the rights of Writer and Publisher to share in, receive and retain the proceeds distributed to them by such small performing rights licensing organization pursuant to their respective agreement with it.**

Paragraph 2

This recognizes that the Writer is a member of a particular performing rights society (either ASCAP, BMI, or SESAC) and that this Contract will not interfere with the Writer's collection of performing rights proceeds directly from his performing rights society. It is crucial that the Writer and Publisher are members of the same performing rights society.

Warranty   **3. The Writer hereby warrants that the composition is his sole, exclusive and original work, that he has full right and power to make this contract, and that there exists no adverse claim to or in the composition, except as aforesaid in Paragraph 3 hereof and except such rights as are specifically set forth in Paragraph 23 hereof.**

Paragraph 3

Writer warrants that the song was written by him, is original, and that Writer has the right to enter into the agreement.

Royalties   **4. In consideration of this contract, the Publisher agrees to pay the Writer as follows:**

(Insert amount of advance here) → **(a) $_____ as an advance against royalties, receipt of which is hereby acknowledged, which sum shall remain the property of the Writer and shall be deductible only from payments hereafter becoming due the Writer under this contract.**

Piano Copies   **(b) In respect of regular piano copies sold and paid for in the United States and Canada, the following royalties per copy:**

Sliding Scale   **_____% (in no case, however, less than 10%) of the wholesale selling price of the first 200,000 copies or less; plus**

(Insert percentage here)   **_____% (in no case, however, less than 12%) of the wholesale selling price of copies in excess of 200,000 and not exceeding 500,000; plus**

_____% (in no case, however, less than 15%) of the wholesale selling price of copies in excess of 500,000.

Foreign
Royalties

(Insert
percentage
here)

(c) _____% (in no case, however, less than 50%) of all net sums received by the Publisher in respect of regular piano copies, orchestrations, band arrangements, octavos, quartets, arrangements for combinations of voices and/or instruments, and/or other copies of the composition sold in any country other than the United States and Canada, provided, however, that if the Publisher should sell such copies through, or cause them to be sold by, a subsidiary or affiliate which is actually doing business in a foreign country, then in respect of such sales, the Publisher shall pay to the Writer not less than 5% of the marked retail selling price in respect of each such copy sold and paid for.

Orchestrations
and Other
Arrangements,
etc.

(Insert
percentage here)

(d) In respect of each copy sold and paid for in the United States and Canada, or for export from the United States, of orchestrations, band arrangements, octavos, quartets, arrangements for combinations of voices and/or instruments, and/or other copies of the composition (other than regular piano copies) the following royalties on the wholesale selling price (after trade discounts, if any):
_____% (in no case, however, less than 10%) on the first 200,000 copies or less; plus
_____% (in no case, however, less than 12%) on all copies in excess of 200,000 and not exceeding 500,000; plus
_____% (in no case, however, less than 15%) on all copies in excess of 500,000.

Publisher's
Song Book,
Folio, etc.

(e) (i) If the composition, or any part thereof, is included in any song book, folio or similar publication issued by the Publisher containing at least four, but not more than twenty-five musical compositions, the royalty to be paid by the Publisher to the Writer shall be an amount determined by dividing 10% of the wholesale selling price (after trade discounts, if any) of the copies sold, among the total number of the Publisher's copyrighted musical compositions included in such publication. If such publication contains more than twenty-five musical compositions, the said 10% shall be increased by an additional 1/2% for each additional musical composition.

Licensee's
Song Book,
Folio, etc.

(ii) If, pursuant to a license granted by the Publisher to a licensee not controlled by or affiliated with it, the composition, or any part thereof, is included in any song book, folio or similar publication, containing at least four musical compositions, the royalty to be paid by the Publisher to the Writer shall be that proportion of 50% of the gross amount received by it from the licensee, as the number of uses of the composition under the license and during the license period, bears to the total number of uses of the Publisher's copyrighted musical compositions under the license and during the license period.

(iii)   In computing the number of the Publisher's copyrighted musical compositions under subdivisions (i) and (ii) hereof, there shall be excluded musical compositions in the public domain and arrangements thereof and those with respect to which the Publisher does not currently publish and offer for sale regular piano copies.

(iv)   Royalties on publications containing less than four musical compositions shall be payable at regular piano copy rates.

Professional Material and Free Copies

(f)   As to "professional material" not sold or resold, no royalty shall be payable. Free copies of the lyrics of the composition shall not be distributed except under the following conditions: (i) with the Writer's written consent; or (ii) when printed without music in limited numbers for charitable, religious or governmental purposes, or for similar public purposes, if no profit is derived, directly or indirectly; or (iii) when authorized for printing in a book, magazine or periodical, where such use is incidental to a novel or story (as distinguished from use in a book of lyrics or a lyric magazine or folio), provided that any such use shall bear the Writer's name and the proper copyright notice; or (iv) when distributed solely for the purpose of exploiting the composition, provided, that such exploitation is restricted to the distribution of limited numbers of such copies for the purpose of influencing the sale of the composition, that the distribution is independent of the sale of any other musical compositions, services, goods, wares or merchandise, and that no profit is made, directly or indirectly, in connection therewith.

Mechanicals, Electrical Transcription, Synchronization, All Other Rights

(Insert percentage here)

(g)   _____% (in no case, however, less than 50%) of: All gross receipts of the Publisher in respect of any licenses (including statutory royalties) authorizing the manufacture of parts of instruments serving to mechanically reproduce the composition, or to use the composition in synchronization with sound motion pictures, or to reproduce it upon electrical transcription for broadcasting purposes; and of any and all gross receipts of the Publisher from any other source or right now known or which may hereafter come into existence, except as provided in paragraph 2.

Licensing Agent's Charges

(h)   If the Publisher administers licenses authorizing the manufacture of parts of instruments serving to mechanically reproduce said composition, or the use of said composition in synchronization or in timed relation with sound motion pictures or its reproduction upon electrical transcriptions, or any of them, through an agent, trustee or other administrator acting for a substantial part of the industry and not under the exclusive control of the Publisher (hereinafter sometimes referred to as licensing agent), the Publisher, in determining his receipts, shall be entitled to deduct from gross license fees paid by the Licensees, a sum equal to the charges paid by the Publisher to said licensing agent, provided, however, that in respect to synchronization or timed relation with sound motion pictures, said deduction shall in no event exceed $150.00 or 10% of said gross license fee, whichever is less; in connection with the manufacture of parts of instruments serving to mechanically reproduce said composition, said deductions shall not exceed 5% of said gross license fee; and in connection with electrical transcriptions, said deduction shall not exceed 10% of said gross license fee.

Block Licenses   (i)   The Publisher agrees that the use of the composition will not be included in any bulk or block license heretofore or hereafter granted, and that it will not grant any bulk or block license to include the same, without the written consent of the Writer in each instance, except (i) that the Publisher may grant such license with respect to electrical transcription for broadcasting purposes, but in such event, the Publisher shall pay to the Writer that proportion of 50% of the gross amount received by it under each such license as the number of uses of the composition under each such license during each such license period bears to the total number of uses of the Publisher's copyrighted musical compositions under each such license during each such license period; in computing the number of the Publisher's copyrighted musical compositions for this purpose, there shall be excluded musical compositions in the public domain and arrangements thereof and those with respect to which the Publisher does not currently publish and offer for sale regular piano copies; (ii) that the Publisher may appoint agents or representatives in countries outside of the United States and Canada to use and to grant license for the use of the composition on the customary royalty fee basis under which the Publisher shall receive not less than 10% of the marked retail selling price in respect of regular piano copies, and 50% of all other revenue; if, in connection with any such bulk or block license, the Publisher shall have received any advance, the Writer shall not be entitled to share therein, but no part of said advance shall be deducted in computing the composition's earnings under said bulk or block license. A bulk or block license shall be deemed to mean any license or agreement, domestic or foreign, whereby rights are granted in respect of two or more musical compositions.

Television and   (j)   Except to the extent that the Publisher and Writer have
New Uses   heretofore or may hereafter assign to or vest in the small performing rights licensing organization with which

Writer and Publisher are affiliated, the said rights or the right to grant licenses therefore, it is agreed that no licenses shall be granted without the written consent, in each instance, of the Writer for the use of the composition by means of television, or by any means, or for any purposes not commercially established, or for which licenses were not granted by the Publisher on musical compositions prior to June 1, 1937.

Writer's Consent to Licenses

(k) The Publisher shall not, without the written consent of the Writer in each case, give or grant any right or license (i) to use the title of the composition, or (ii) for the exclusive use of the composition in any form or for any purpose, or for any period of time, or for any territory, other than its customary arrangements with foreign publishers, or (iii) to give a dramatic representation of the composition or to dramatize the plot or story thereof, or (iv) for a vocal rendition of the composition in synchronization with sound motion pictures, or (v) for any synchronization use thereof, or (vi) for the use of the composition or a quotation or excerpt therefrom in any article, book, periodical, advertisement or other similar publication. If, however, the Publisher shall give to the Writer written notice by certified mail, return receipt requested, or telegram, specifying the right or license to be given or granted, the name of the licensee and the terms and conditions thereof, including the price or other compensation to be received therefor, then, unless the Writer (or any one or more of them) shall, within five business days after the delivery of such notice to the address of the Writer hereinafter designated, object thereto, the Publisher may grant such right or license in accordance with the said notice without first obtaining the consent of the Writer. Such notice shall be deemed sufficient if sent to the Writer at the address or addresses hereinafter designated or at the address or addresses last furnished to the Publisher in writing by the Writer.

Trust for Writer

(l) Any portion of the receipts which may become due to the Writer from license fees (in excess of offsets), whether received directly from the licensee or from any licensing agent of the Publisher, shall, if not paid immediately on the receipt thereof by the Publisher, belong to the Writer and shall be held in trust for the Writer until payment is made; the ownership of said trust fund by the Writer shall not be questioned whether the monies are physically segregated or not.

Writer Participation

(m) The Publisher agrees that it will not issue any license as a result of which it will receive any financial benefit in which the Writer does not participate.

Writer Credit

(n) On all regular piano copies, orchestrations, band or other arrangements, octavos, quartets, commercial sound recordings and other reproductions of the composition or parts thereof, in whatever form and however produced, Publisher shall include or cause to be included, in addition to the copyright notice, the name of the Writer, and Publisher shall include a similar requirement in every license or authorization issued by it with respect to the composition.

Paragraph 4

Sets forth royalties to be paid for various types of uses of the song. Note that the Contract sets forth *minimum* amounts that Writer must receive. Of course, Writer is free to attempt to negotiate for higher royalty rates. If no amounts are filled in, the minimum amounts apply (see Paragraph 20 of the initial contract). Paragraph 4 (k) provides that the initial publisher may not, without the Writer's written consent, grant certain licenses not specifically permitted by the contract (e.g. use of the title of the song; to give a dramatic represenation of the song; synchronization, licenses, etc.).

Writers'
Respective
Shares

5. Whenever the term "Writer" is used herein, it shall be deemed to mean all of the person herein defined as "Writer" and any and all royalties herein provided to be paid to the Writer shall be paid equally to such persons if there be more than one, unless otherwise provided in Paragraph 23.

Paragraph 5

This applies if there is more than one Writer. If so, each Writer will share royalties equally, unless specified otherwise in Paragraph 23.

Release of
Commercial
Sound
Recording

(Insert period
not exceeding
12 months)

6. (a) (i) The Publisher shall, within _____ months from the date of this contract (the "initial period"), cause a commercial sound recording of the composition to be made and released in the customary form and through the customary commercial channels. If at the end of such initial period a sound recording has not been made and released, as above provided, then, subject to the provisions of the next succeeding subdivision, this contract shall terminate.

(Insert amount
to be not less
than $250)

(Insert period
not exceeding
six months)

(ii) If, prior to the expiration of the initial period, Publisher pays the Writer the sum of $_____ (which shall not be charged against or recoupable out of any advances, royalties or other monies theretofor paid, then due, or which thereafter may become due the Writer from the Publisher pursuant to this contract or otherwise), Publisher shall have an additional _____ months (the "additional period") commencing with the end of the initial period, within which to cause such commercial sound recording to be made and released as provided in subdivision (i) above. If at the end of the

additional period a commercial sound recording has not been
made and released, as above provided, then this contract shall terminate.

(iii)   Upon termination pursuant to this Paragraph 6(a), all
rights of any and every nature in and to the composition and in and
to any and all copyrights secured thereon in the United States and
throughout the world shall automatically re-vest in and become the
property of the Writer and shall be reassigned to him by the
Publisher. The Writer shall not be obligated to return or pay to the
publisher any advance or indebtedness as a condition of such re-
assignment; the said re-assignment shall be in accordance with
and subject to the provisions of Paragraph 8 hereof, and, in addition, the Publisher shall pay to the Writer all gross sums which it has
theretofore or may thereafter receive in respect of the composition.

Writer's Copies   (b)   The publisher shall furnish, or cause to be furnished, to the
Writer six copies of the commercial sound recording referred to in
Paragraph 6(a).

Piano Copies,   (c)   The Publisher shall
Piano   ☐ (i)   Within 30 days after the initial release of a commer-
Arrangement   cial sound recording of the composition, make, publish and offer for
or Lead Sheet   sale regular piano copies of the composition in the form and
through the channels customarily employed by it for that purpose;
(Select (i) or (ii)   ☐ (ii)   Within 30 days after execution of this contract make
a piano arrangement or lead sheet of the composition and furnish
six copies thereof to the Writer.

In the event neither subdivision (i) nor (ii) of this subparagraph (c) is selected, the provisions of subdivision (ii) shall be automatically deemed to have been selected by the parties.

Paragraph 6

This required the Publisher to have a commercial sound recording of the song made and released within twelve (12) months from the
date of the Contract or to pay Writer a sum of not less than Two hundred
and Fifty ($250.00) Dollars for the right to extend this period for not
more than six (6) months. If Publisher does not comply, the Contract
terminates and all rights return to Writer.

When the sound recording is cut, Publisher is required to give
Writer six (6) copies of the sound recording.

Under Paragraph 6(c), Publisher must either (i) publish and
offer for sale regular piano copies of the song within thirty (30) days of
release of the sound recording; or (ii) make a piano arrangement or lead
sheet of the song within thirty (30) days of execution of the Contract
(with six (6) copies to be given to the Writer). The parties must select
which of the above alternatives will apply.

Foreign
Copyright

7. (a) Each copyright on the composition in countries other than the United States shall be secured only in the name of the Publisher, and the Publisher shall not at any time divest itself of said foreign copyright directly or indirectly.

Foreign
Publication

(b) No rights shall be granted by the Publisher in the composition to any foreign publisher or licensee inconsistent with the terms hereof, nor shall any foreign publication rights in the composition be given to a foreign publisher or licensee unless and until the Publisher shall have complied with the provisions of Paragraph 6 hereof.

Foreign
Advance

(c) If foreign rights in the composition are separately conveyed, otherwise than as a part of the publisher's current and/or future catalog, not less than 50% of any advance received in respect thereof shall be credited to the account of and paid to the Writer.

Foreign
Percentage

(d) The percentage of the Writer on monies received from foreign sources shall be computed on the publisher's net receipts, provided, however, that no deductions shall be made for offsets of monies due from the Publisher to said foreign sources; or for advances made by such foreign sources to the Publisher, unless the Writer shall have received at least 50% of said advances.

No Foreign
Allocations

(e) In computing the receipts of the Publisher from licenses granted in respect of synchronization with sound motion pictures, or in respect of any world-wide licenses, or in respect of licenses granted by the Publisher for use of the composition in countries other than the United States, no amount shall be deducted for payments or allocations to publishers or licensees in such countries.

Paragraph 7

Deals with the publisher's sub-licensing of the song in foreign countries. It guarantees that the Writer will receive no less than 50% of the revenue by the Publisher from rights licensed outside the U.S.

Termination
or Expiration
of Contract

8. Upon termination or expiration of this contract, all rights of any and every nature in and to the composition and in and to any and all copyrights secured thereon in the United States and throughout the world, shall re-vest in and become the property of the Writer, and shall be re-assigned to the Writer by the Publisher free of any and all encumbrances of any nature whatsoever, provided that:

(a) If the Publisher, prior to such termination or expiration, shall have granted a domestic license for the use of the composition, not inconsistent with the terms and provisions of this contract, the re-assignment may be subject to the terms of such license.

(b)   Publisher shall assign to the Writer all rights which it may have under any such agreement or license referred to in subdivision (a) in respect of the composition, including, but not limited to, the right to receive all royalties or other monies earned by the composition thereunder after the date of termination or expiration of this contract. Should the Publisher thereafter receive or be credited with any royalties or other monies so earned, it shall pay the same to the Writer.

(c)   The Writer shall not be obligated to return or pay to the Publisher any advance or indebtedness as a condition of the re-assignment provided for in this Paragraph 8, and shall be entitled to receive the plates and copies of the composition in the possession of the Publisher.

(d)   Publisher shall pay any and all royalties which may have accrued to the Writer prior to such termination or expiration.

(e)   The Publisher shall execute any and all documents and do any and all acts or things necessary to effect any and all re-assignments to the Writer herein provided for.

Paragraph 8

Explains what happens when the Contract terminates (i.e. all rights revert to Writer, subject to any outstanding licenses issued by the Publisher and the latter's duty to account for monies received after termination).

Negotiations for New or Unspecified Uses

9. If the Publisher desires to exercise a right in and to the composition now known or which may hereafter become known, but for which no specific provision has been made herein, the Publisher shall give written notice to the Writer thereof. Negotiations respecting all the terms and conditions of any such disposition shall thereupon be entered into between the Publisher and the Writer and no such right shall be exercised until specific agreement has been made.

Paragraph 9

Deals with exploitation of the song in a manner not yet contemplated and thus not specifically covered in the Contract. Any such exploitation must be mutually agreed upon by the Writer and the Publisher.

Royalty Statements and Payments

10. The Publisher shall render to the Writer, hereafter, royalty statements accompanied by remittance of the amount due at the times such statements and remittances are customarily rendered by the Publisher, provided, however, that such statements and

remittances shall be rendered either semi-annually or quarterly and not more than forty-five days after the end of each such semi-annual or quarterly period, as the case may be. The Writer may at any time, or from time to time, make written request for a detailed royalty statement, and the Publisher shall, within sixty days, comply therewith. Such royalty statements shall set forth in detail the various items, foreign and domestic, for which royalties are payable thereunder and the amounts thereof, including, but not limited to, the number of copies sold and the number of uses made in each royalty category. If a use is made in a publication of the character provided in Paragraph 4, subdivision (e) hereof, there shall be included in said royalty statement the title of said publication, the publisher or issuer thereof, the date of and number of uses, the gross license fee received in connection with each publication, the share thereto of all the writers under contract with the Publisher, and the Writer's share thereof. There shall likewise be included in said statement a description of every other use of the composition, and if by a licensee or licensees their name or names, and if said use is upon a part of an instrument serving to reproduce the composition mechanically, the type of mechanical reproduction, the title of the label thereon, the name or names of the artists performing the same, together with the gross license fees received, and the Writer's share thereof.

Examination of Books

11.(a) The Publisher shall from time to time, upon written demand of the Writer or his representative, permit the Writer or his representative to insepct at the place of business of the Publisher, all books, records and documents relating to the composition and all licenses granted, uses had and payments made therefor, such right of inspection to include, but not by way of limitation, the right to examine all original accountings and records relating to uses and payments by manufacturers of commercial sound recordings and music rolls; and the Writer or his representative may appoint an accountant who shall at any time during usual business hours have access to all records of the Publisher relating to the composition for the purpose of verifying royalty statements rendered or which are delinquent under the terms hereof.

(b) The Publisher shall, upon written demand of the Writer or his representative, cause any licensing agent in the United States and Canada to furnish to the Writer or his representative, statements showing in detail all licenses granted, uses had and payments made in conneciton with the composition, which licenses or permits were granted, or payments were received, by or through said licensing agent, and to permit the Writer or his representative to inspect at the place of business of such licensing agent, all books, records and documents of such licensing agent, relating thereto. Any and all agreements made by the Publisher with such licensing agent shall provide that any such licensing agent will comply with the terms and provisions hereof. In the event that the Publisher shall instruct such licensing agent to furnish to the Writer or his representative statements as provided for herein, and to permit the inspection of the books, records and documents as herein provided, then if such licensing agent should refuse to comply with the said instructions, or any of them, the Publisher agrees to institute and prosecute diligently and in good faith such action or proceedings as may be necessary to compel compliance with the said instructions.

(c) With respect to foreign licensing agents, the Publisher shall make available the books or records of said licensing agents in countries outside of the United States and Canada to the extent such books or records are available to the Publisher, except that the Publisher may in lieu thereof make available any accountants' reports and audits which the Publisher is able to obtain.

(d) If as a result of any examination of books, records or documents pursuant to Paragraph 11(a), 11(b) or 11(c) hereof, it is determined that, with respect to any royalty statement rendered by or on behalf of the Publisher to the Writer, the Writer is owed a sum equal to or greater than five percent of the sum shown on that royalty statement as being due to the Writer, then the Publisher shall pay to the Writer the entire cost of such examination, not to exceed 50% of the amount shown to be due the Writer.

(e) (i) In the event the Publisher administers its own licenses for the manufacture of parts of instruments serving to mechanically reproduce the composition rather than employing a licensing agent for that purpose, the Publisher shall include in each license agreement a provision permitting the Publisher, the Writer or their respective representatives to inspect, at the place of business of such licensee, all books, records and documents of such licensee relating to such license. Within 30 days after written demand by the Writer, the Publisher shall commence to inspect such licensee's books, records and documents and shall furnish a written report of such inspection to the Writer within 90 days following such demand. If the Publisher fails, after written demand by the Writer, to so inspect the licensee's books, records and documents, or fails to furnish such report, the Writer or his representative may inspect such licensee's books, records and documents at his own expense.

(ii) In the further event that the Publisher and the licensee referred to in subdivision (i) above are subsidiaries or affiliates of the same entity or one is a subsidiary or affiliate of the other, then, unless the Publisher employs a licensing agent to administer the licenses referred to in subdivision (i) above, the Writer shall have the right to make the inspection referred to in subdivision (i) above without the necessity of making written demand on the Publisher as provided in subdivision (i) above.

(iii) If as a result of any inspection by the Writer pursuant to subdivisions (i) and (ii) of this subparagraph (e) the Writer recovers additional monies from the licensee, the Publisher and the Writer shall share equally in the cost of such inspection.

Default in
Payment or
Prevention of
Examination

12. If the Publisher shall fail or refuse, within sixty days after written demand, to furnish or cause to be furnished, such statements, books, records or documents, or to permit inspection thereof, as provided for in Paragraphs 10 and 11 hereof, or within thirty days after written demand, to make the payment of any royalties due under this contract, then the Writer shall be entitled, upon ten days' written notice, to terminate this contract. However if the Publisher shall:

(a) Within the said ten-day period serve upon the Writer a written notice demanding arbitration; and

(b) Submit to arbitration its claim that is has complied with its obligation to furnish statements, books, records or documents, or permitted inspection thereof or to pay royalties, as the case may be, or both, and thereafter comply with any award of the arbitrator within ten days after such award or within such time as the arbitrator may specify;

then this contract shall continue in full force and effect as if the Writer had not sent such notice of termination. If the Pub-lisher shall fail to comply with the foregoing provisions, then this contract shall be deemed to have been terminated as of the date of the Writer's written notice of termination.

Paragraphs 10, 11 and 12

Deal with the method of payment of royalties to the Writer and the Writer's right to inspect Publisher's books.

Derivative
Works

13. No derivative work prepared under authority of Publisher during the term of this contract may be utilized by Publisher or any other party after termination or expiration of this contract.

Paragraph 13

Various uses of the song, such as sound recordings and arrangements, are considered "derivative works" under the Copyright Law. Often, such derivative works can have more financial value than the original sheet music. This provision provides that when the Contract terminates, the Publisher loses all rights in such derivative works, as well as in the original version of the song.

Notices

14. All written demands and notices provided for herein shall be sent by certified mail, return receipt requested.

Suits for
Infringement

15. Any legal action brought by the Publisher against any alleged infringer of the composition shall be initiated and prosecuted at its sole cost and expense, but if the Publisher should fail, within thirty days after written demand, to institute such action, the Writer shall be entitled to institute such suit at his cost and expense. All sums recovered as a result of any such action shall, after the deduction of the reasonable expense thereof, be divided equally between the Publisher and the Writer. No settlement of any such action may be made by either party without first notifying the other; in the event that either party should object to such settlement, then such settlement shall not be made if the party objecting assumes the prosecution of the action and all expenses thereof, except that any sums thereafter recovered shall be divided equally between the Publisher and the Writer after the deduction of the reasonable expenses thereof.

Infringement Claims

16.(a) If a claim is presented against the Publisher alleging that the composition is an infringement upon some other work or a violation of any other right of another, and because thereof the Publisher is jeopardized, it shall forthwith serve a written notice upon the Writer setting forth the full details of such claim. The pendency of said claim shall not relieve the Publisher of the obligation to make payment of the royalties to the Writer hereunder, unless the Publisher shall deposit said royalties as and when they would otherwise be payable, in an account in the joint names of the Publisher and the Writer in a bank or trust company in New York, New York, if the Writer on the date of execution of this contract resides East of the Mississippi River, or in Los Angeles, California, if the Writer on the date of execution of this contract resides West of the Mississippi River. If no suit be filed within nine months after said written notice from the Publisher to the Writer, all monies deposited in said joint account shall be paid over to the Writer plus any interest which may have been earned thereon.

(b) Should an action be instituted against the Publisher claiming that the composition is an infringement upon some other work or a violation of any other right of another, the Publisher shall forthwith serve written notice upon the Writer containing the full details of such claim. Notwithstanding the commencement of such action, the Publisher shall continue to pay the royalties hereunder to the Writer unless it shall, from and after the date of the service of the summons, deposit said royalties as and when they would otherwise be payable, in an account in the joint names of the Publisher and the Writer in a bank or trust company in New York, New York, if the Writer on the date of execution of this contract resides East of the Mississippi River, or in Los Angeles, California, if the Writer on the date of execution of this contract resides West of the Mississippi River. If the said suit shall be finally adjudicated in favor of the Publisher or shall be settled, there shall be released and paid to the Writer all of such sums held in escrow less any amount paid out of the Writer's share with the Writer's written consent in settlement of said action. Should the said suit finally result adversely to the Publisher, the said amount on deposit shall be released to the Publisher to the extent of any expense or damage it incurs and the balance shall be paid over to the Writer.

(c) In any of the foregoing events, however, the Writer shall be entitled to payment of said royalties or the money so deposited at and after such time as he files with the Publisher a surety company bond, or a bond in other form acceptable to the Publisher, in the sum of such payments to secure the return thereof to the extent that the Publisher may be entitled to such return. The foregoing payments or deposits or the filing of a bond shall be without prejudice to the rights of the Publisher or Writer in the premises.

Paragraphs 15 and 16

Deal with bringing lawsuits against infringers and defending lawsuits in the event someone claims that the Writer's song infringed a copyright.

Arbitration   17. Any and all differences, disputes or controversies arising out of or in connection with this contract shall be submitted to arbitration before a sole arbitrator under the then prevailing rules of the American Arbiration Association. The location of the arbitration shall be New York, New York, if the Writer on the date of execution of this contract resides East of the Mississippi River, or Los Angeles, California, if the Writer on the date of execution of this contract resides West of the Mississippi River. The parties hereby individually and jointly agree to abide by and perform any award rendered in such arbitration. Judgment upon any such award rendered may be entered in any court having jurisdiction thereof.

Paragraph 17

In the event there is a dispute between the Writer and the Publisher and they cannot resolve it, such dispute is to be settled by arbitration (generally considered a more expeditious and inexpensive means of settling claims).

Assignment   18. Except to the extent herein otherwise expressly provided, the Publisher shall not sell, transfer, assign, convey, encumber or otherwise dispose of the composition or the copyright or copyrights secured thereon without the prior written consent of the Writer. The Writer has been induced to enter into this contract in reliance upon the value to him of the personal service and ability of the Publisher in the exploitation of the composition, and by reason thereof it is the intention of the parties and the essence of the relationship between them that the rights herein granted to the Publisher shall remain with the Publisher and that the same shall not pass to any other person, including, without limitations, successors to or receivers or trustees of the property of the Publisher, either by act or deed of the Publisher or by operation of law, and in the event of the voluntary or involuntary bankruptcy of the Publisher, this contract shall terminate, provided, however, that the composition may be included by the Publisher in a bona fide voluntary sale of its music business or its entire catalog of musical compositions, or in a merger or consolidation of the Publisher with another corporation, in which event the Publisher shall immediately give written notice thereof to the Writer; and provided further that the composition and the copyright therein may be assigned by the Publisher to a subsidiary or affiliated company generally engaged in the music publishing business. If the Publisher is an individual, the composition may pass to a legatee or distributee as part of the inheritance of the Publisher's music business and entire catalog of musical compositions. Any such transfer or assignment shall, however, be conditioned upon the execution and delivery by the transferee or assignee to the Writer of an agreement to be bound by and to perform all of the terms and conditions of this contract to be performed on the part of the Publisher.

Paragraph 18

This places restrictions on Publisher's rights to sell the Writer's song to another publisher other than as part of the Publisher's entire catalogue.

Subsidiary Defined

19. A subsidiary, affiliate, or any person, firm or corporation controlled by the Publisher or by such subsidiary or affiliate, as used in this contract, shall be deemed to include any person, firm or corporation, under common control with, or the majority of whose stock or capital contribution is owned or controlled by the Publisher or by any of its officers, directors, partners or associates, or whose policies and actions are subject to domination or control by the Publisher or any of its officers, directors, partners or associates.

Amounts

20. The amounts and percentages specified in this contract shall be deemed to be the amounts and percentages agreed upon by the parties hereto, unless other amounts or percentages are inserted in the blank spaces provided therefor.

Modifications

21. This contract is binding upon and shall enure to the benefit of the parties hereto and their respective successors in interest (as hereinbefore limited). If the Writer (or one or more of them) shall not be living, any notices may be given to, or consents given by, his or their successors in interest. No change or modification of this contract shall be effective unless reduced to writing and signed by the parties hereto.

The words in this contract shall be so construed that the singular shall include the plural and the plural shall include the singular where the context so requires and the masculine shall include the feminine and the feminine shall include the masculine where the context so requires.

Paragraph Headings

22. The paragraph headings are inserted only as a matter of convenience and for reference, and in no way define, limit or describe the scope or intent of this contract nor in any way affect this contract.

Special Provisions

23.

Witness:

_____

Witness:

_____

Witness:

_____

Witness:

_____

Publisher:_____

By _____

Address_____

Writer_____(L.S.)

Address:_____

Soc. Sec. #_____

Writer_____(L.S.)

Address_____

Soc. Sec. # _____

Writer_____(L.S.)

Address_____

Soc. Sec. # _____

Different Types of Publishing Deals

THERE ARE BASICALLY FOUR different publishing deals most commonly used in the music industry. These do not include the song-by-song agreements discussed in Chapter 3. Song-by-song deals (or "single song agreements" as they are often called) are usually used by publishers in their relations with new and upcoming writers. This is not to say that the four types of publishing deals to be discussed in this chapter are not ever negotiated with new or upcoming writers, but a clear distinction should first be made between the two types of new and upcoming writers.

The first group consists of the majority of writers—those who have had limited musical or writing experience, with few or no contacts for exposure of their songs. The second group usually consists of professional or semi-professionals involved in one or more areas of the music business who are also writers. Such people as demo singers and studio musicians who meet many music industry people, music arrangers, and artist managers, as well as record producers who also write, often interest publishers, even though they may have no track record of writing success. Long-term publishing deals are not always made with writers or writer/artists who have great track records. They are often made with people who have potential, as well as their own outlets for the use of their music. This is not to say they'll be successful as writers just because they are involved in one or more aspects of the business. The four deals we will discuss here are:

1. Staff writing deals
2. Split publishing deals
3. Administration deals
4. Subpublishing deals.

The Staff Writing Deal

The staff writing deal is relatively simple. In the '40s, '50s and early '60s, publishers had many professional writers on staff who were always professional music writers and lyricists. Their job was to turn out songs for everyone, because very few of the pop singers wrote. By the middle '60s, the advent of a self-contained group (artists who wrote their own songs) made it necessary for publishers to change their thinking. It was no longer profitable for publishers to keep a staff of writers on salary (some publishers had as many as 10 or 15 writers), and they began looking for writers who could do more in the industry than just write. A writer who could sing and record her own songs was certainly a more valuable investment. The same held true for a writer/producer who would record other people with his songs, which gave a publisher a greater possibility of at least some of the writer's material reaching the marketplace.

Of course, a publisher paid for these advantages, and that's what is discussed here. A staff writing deal is simply a "writer for hire" agreement. Most of the clauses in a "single song agreement" will be found in a "staff writing agreement." What is different is the following:

a. The writer is writing exclusively for the publisher for a fixed period of time (usually 2-3 years).
b. She must submit a specific number of songs to the publisher as she writes them. The number of songs varies depending on how prolific the writer is, and could be anywhere from ten to thirty or more songs per year. Some contracts require that each song must be acceptable to the publisher before he includes it against the

number of songs the writer owes on her commitment. Otherwise, many publishers believe that the writer could write only junk to fulfill her commitment and the publisher would have to accept it. This can happen when a writer is near the end of her contract with a publisher and the writer is not intending to renew her agreement. (Be aware that these agreements require 100% of an agreed upon number of songs. What do you do if you have co-written some of your compositions with one or two other writers? The publisher will usually not try to discourage you from co-writing [especially if it is with other successful or talented writers], but they will protect their investment as follows: If your song commitment is ten songs a year and you have written four songs with one other writer, those four will count as one-half song each. Therefore, your remaining obligation is eight 100% written or controlled songs [four songs equals two songs plus eight more solely-written songs]).

c. The writer is given a salary either weekly or monthly, which may or may not include an advance. As in single-song agreements, any advances (including salary) are recoupable by the publisher from any income derived by any of the songs in the writer's catalogue. That means that publishers can and will recoup from a writer's share paid to them as well as publisher's share. This is called "cross collateralization."

d. A staff writing deal is usually made wherein the publisher receives all (100%) of the publisher's share of the copyright per song (writer's share is considered a separate 100% total) for all the songs the writer writes while under contract. This may also include any past catalogue the writer may have owned, although more often than not, 100% of the past catalogue is either not available or the writer has no percentage of ownership at the time (often because of a prior staff-writing deal or catalogue sale).

Split Publishing Deal

Split publishing deals are usually deals between an established publishing company (or an affiliate of a record company) and a small writer-owned company. The writer (who is often an artist or producer) wants greater exploitation on his copyrights, which the bigger company can usually provide. He also relinquishes the headache of administration to the bigger company, leaving himself more time to spend on the creative end and less on the business end. The publisher gets the opportunity to administer and share in the income he creates on copyrights that he feels have potential, with the knowledge that the co-publisher (the writer) will be using his own outlet for recordings of the songs.

Occasionally, an interesting type of split publishing deal will arise when a staff writer with one publisher writes with a staff writer of another publisher. Although this situation requires no separate contract, since each writer is already under contract for his exclusive services to his publisher, the two publishing companies involved wind up splitting the copyright. Split publishing deals are always worked out with the use of a co-administration agreement between the two publishers. The person who originally owns or acquires the copyright (usually the writer) has already assigned his rights to his publisher via his publishing contract.

Split publishing deals are almost always done with writers who have at least some degree of track record. They cover everything a writer writes (or acquires for his publishing company) within a one-year period, with the publisher having two one-year options to renew the agreement. Because these writers can range from those having one song on a successful LP to an established producer or artist, part of their incentive to co-publish is the advance a publisher will pay them to "buy" into their already successful composition. They are also speculating that the combined activities of the publisher and writer will create even greater success in the near future. Established writers have been known to get $100,000 a year and more in their co-publishing agreements. These monies are always advances, not purchases, and are recoupable by the publisher.

The value of a co-publishing deal to a publisher is usually far less than the figures mentioned above, since there are realistic limitation and guidelines that can give a publisher a fair evaluation of the income potential of a writer. For example, a publisher does a co-publishing deal with a writer who is neither an artist on a label nor a producer with an active track record. However, the artist did have an LP cut or record selling 300,000 records last year, but that song is owned by a previous publisher. Therefore, the publisher signing the writer is, from a standpoint of catalogue and income, starting from scratch. In order for the writer to equal last year's success, she must have another LP cut with a reasonably successful artist.

Here are the step-by-step thoughts a publisher may follow: If the record sells 300,000 LPs, CDs, cassettes, etc., at the statutory rate, and the writer is sole writer, then the total income (which would take up to two years for the publisher to receive) is $15,000. So, if the writer was asking for $60,000 a year, the publisher may feel this is much too high based on the calculations, and although he may believe in the talent of the writer, he might not want to risk such a sum on factors neither he nor the writer controls. The writer could have six or seven songs recorded, but this doesn't mean they will be released. If they are released, that doesn't mean they would sell anywhere near the equivalent of her first record. With these factors in mind, the publisher will usually make an offer that can be recouped realistically based on a combination of the writer's talent and the publisher's outlets. *In a copublishing deal, the publisher receives 25% of the income after recoupment of advances, even though he owns 50% of the publishing rights.* That is due to the fact that, in just about all areas of income splits (as opposed to percentages referred to in copyright ownership page 171, paragraph d), the writer's share is designated as 50% of the total royalties received. Therefore, the remaining 50% (which is called "publisher's share") is split between the publisher and the "writer turned co-publisher."

Administration Deals

Administration deals are usually worked out between an established writer or writer/artist and a well-organized, highly visible publishing company.

These deals are often compromises of necessity by star artist/ writers, or just individually active and successful writers who want their own publishing, but similar to the split publishing situation, need competent administration of their music. Some writers, because of representation by attorneys, have been convinced to allow their legal advisors to administer their publishing. Since attorneys do not provide any creative services to writers (such as promoting cover records, film projects, TV projects for the writer's songs, etc.), a writer's compositions are at the mercy of the knowledge (or lack thereof) of a secretary who is assigned the actual job of doing the administration for the attorney. Giving your catalogue to a legal entity for administration, especially since there's no creative promotion, is committing your catalogue to anonymity.

The publisher's function in an administration deal is to handle the day-to-day collections of money, the necessary filing of copyright forms, the making of lead sheets, the dealings with BMI and ASCAP for collecting royalties in the U.S. and foreign countries, and the general paperwork associated with maintaining up-to-date files on the writer's catalogue, along with proper licensing for TV shows, films, etc. (see Chapter 10, "How A Publishing Company Works"). The administrator's income from such activities is between 10-20% of the publisher's share of the income (the publisher in this case being the writer).

It's important to understand that in an administration deal, the administering publisher is not the copyright owner. He is only an exclusive representative of the actual publisher, who is often the writer or one of the writers associated with the administered catalogue. This means the administrator has the exclusive right to handle all of the business affairs related to the catalogue. The administrator is often given administration rights because of what the copyright owner feels the administrator can do to get cover records on his catalogue, as well as to administer the catalogue. In this case, a usual arrangement would be for both parties to split 50-50 on the income from cover records secured by the administrator.

Since the creative aspects of these deals are speculative, the more established the catalogue and the associated writers are, the better the opportunity for cover records. Therefore, it is unlikely that this deal would be available to new writers. Since the administrator is the collector for royalties, he would deduct his income percentage from sales of cover records and turn the remaining publisher's income and writer's shares over to their respective recipients. Basic administration deals are all-encompassing; unless there is a specific clause in the agreement to the contrary, all sources of income from the catalogue are subject to the administrating company's 10-20% fee. Even if the writer (catalogue owner) records an album of her own songs, she must still expect that the administration fee will be deducted from her royalties on those copyrights. The same effort, time, and paperwork go into the administering of these songs as they would for a song from the same catalogue that the administrator got a cover record on.

In today's ever-growing music market, another incentive for writers who secure administrative deals with active publishing companies is the opportunity for exposure of their copyrights in films, video, television, and commercials. Since the income splits are often treated the same as in cover records, the publisher has an incentive to do more than just administer the copyright.

It must be stressed that the creative areas mentioned above are negotiable points, and should the publisher be successful in utilizing particular copyrights, he may negotiate an ownership interest in those copyrights as well.

Subpublishing Deals

A subpublishing deal is a deal between a publisher who owns the copyright to certain songs or a certain catalogue, and a publisher in a foreign country, chosen by the original publisher to represent him in that country. For example, a publisher in the U.S. may have songs he feels would do well in England, but he does not have an office there and is not interested in opening one. He would contact publishers in England until he finds one he feels would be interested in and capable of handling some or all of his songs there.

On the other hand, a British publisher may have the same idea in mind in reverse—having representation in the U.S., thus making the American publisher the subpublisher. Generally, a subpublisher only represents the catalogue for the country his company is located in, unless the deal is with a large international publishing company.

Writers don't often get involved in sub-publishing deals unless they are publisher/writers or established producer/writers with a publishing company, but a successful subpublishing deal can have a great effect on the writer. Many times a writer with a fair amount of income and popularity in his home country can also have huge hits in a foreign country, often because of the subpublisher affiliation.

The percentage a subpublisher receives from the publisher for the average subpublishing deal basically covers the subpublisher's costs for bookkeeping, label copy information, lead sheets, tapes, mailings, and correspondence involving the catalogue. If the income from record activity in that country is not due directly to the subpublisher, he may get only 10-25% for representation, paperwork, and collection of income. This could be a situation where a British producer had heard a hit in America and went back to England and recorded it there with a British act. If the British subpublisher had played it for the British producer and it subsequently was recorded by him and earned income, the subpublishing deal would be a percentage of the income based on a prior written agreement with the domestic publisher (which usually is 50% of mechanical and performance royalties). It is important to note that the subpublisher never *owns* the copyrights involved, or any piece thereof, in a subpublishing deal. He only represents the songs exclusively for that country or group of countries, usually for a 2-3 year period with ample renewal clause possibilities, if both parties agree.

Because of the incredible income "potential" for a foreign song in the American market (if the song hits), a double standard of sorts has developed over a number of years. Since America is considered to be about 51% of the world market, foreign publishers usually make a subpublishing deal for their songs in America for little or no advance monies. The reverse is true for American songs in foreign countries. Foreign publishers want the opportunity to represent successful American publishers in their countries, and therefore they will advance monies (sometimes very large sums) to the stateside publishers. Although enormous advances to American publishers seemed to have peaked in 1973, large advances are still being made. The reasoning is based on simple facts. American songs are more often hits and cover records in foreign countries than foreign songs are hits here. This is reflected in the American Top 40, R&B and Country charts. The Top 40 charts are usually 95-98% American and British songs, with the great majority being American copyrights. The R&B and Country charts are even more one-sided, varying from 98-100% American songs. A great percentage of foreign songs are not "big sellers" here, partially because of the language barrier and partially because many countries still turn out a great percentage of ethnic, rather than contemporary, music.

Another type subpublishing deal is where a subpublisher will collect 10-25% income for songs where there is no local cover recording, and a higher percentage after a local cover is established. This could range up to 50% of all income for the subpublisher, or might only concern that 50% for the local cover recording. Subpublishers also usually collect 10% of the retail price on the sheet music, and a percentage of the 10% pro-rated against the number of songs in a folio (should one of the songs be in a folio).

At this point, it is worth summarizing where the new writer stands in regard to the previous types of publishing deals:

A. **Staff-writing deals**—Unless you have a good track record or are a multi-faceted individual (such as a singer/writer), your chances are slim regarding staff-writing until you can build such a track record.

B. **Split publishing deals**—They are more likely once you establish some kind of rapport with publishers. Again, it is more likely if you're a writer/artist and have your own semi-active and legitimate publishing company (see Chapter 12). Remember, split publishing deals can be made on a *song-by-song* basis if a publisher feels you have enough going for you to justify retaining a piece of your own copyright. Split publishing deals for a writer *and* his catalogue are much harder to come by, because a publisher is often making a large financial and time-consuming investment in what could be a lot of songs. So, if the writer *and* catalogue have proven themselves on occasion (such as having some album cuts and single releases), the publisher feels more comfortable about his speculation regarding the prospects for such a deal. After all, if a writer owns 100% of the writer's share and 50% of the publisher's share, the active publisher only owns the remaining 50% of the publisher's share, or $1/4$ of the total income.

C. **Administration deals**—This deal totally rules out possibilities for *new* writers.

D. **Subpublishing deals**—Also rule out *new* writers.

The above-mentioned deals show you the choices a new writer has. Although these deals are common situations, they are only common, for the most part, with *established* writers. The new writer must continue to plug away on a song-by-song basis.

The Foreign Market and Your Songs

SONGWRITERS LIVING IN the United States tend to ignore the foreign markets—there is enough to do here just trying to be a success! The U.S. is approximately 51% of the world record market, and learning how to adapt and compete in the American market is still a lifetime process. So why think of other countries? With the technological advances of the '80s and '90s like FAX machines (that can send a piece of paper across the world in minutes), supersonic jets, optical scanners, modems, telexes and telephones, the world is simply shrinking, and music has become more international. England, West Germany, Japan, and France are major record markets. Australia, Holland, Belgium, Scandinavia, South Africa, Canada, Italy, Brazil, and Spain are long established markets for sales, and countries like Hong Kong, Korea, Singapore, Indonesia, the Philippines, Turkey, Greece, and Thailand are growing markets.

The international pop music market has been a strong part of our American market ever since the Beatles hit our shore with "I Want To Hold Your Hand" in 1964. Many songwriters have been getting inspiration from music played here that comes from all over the world. Aside from the countless British groups, acts from Australia to Japan, Spain to Sweden, and a plethora of Canadian acts have influenced our music and given us a glimpse of what they created in their own countries.

With the ease and speed of air travel today, songwriters, like any other Americans, often have the opportunity to go abroad, and what you hear can't help but give you a broader knowledge of music from other countries. Often, it is a combination of local or ethnic music with vintage American rock and roll, but the combination will somehow sound new. (Elvis was new because he combined country with R&B to make his own brand of rock and roll.)

The point is, thirty years of American pop and rock and roll shipped abroad has been slowly but surely coming back to us in various forms from various countries. This makes it easier than ever before for you to study what is happening in these countries musically and incorporate elements you like into your own music. TV shows like Top Of The Pops, MTV and the international music awards shows have given us a firsthand glimpse into what is successful in other countries.

When competing in the U.S. marketplace, it is sometimes beneficial to the American writer to add some elements from other places when you are looking for that competitive edge (i.e., the South African influence in Paul Simon's "Graceland" LP). You may find one particular type of music from another nation that blends well with your own writing style, and this can lead to your songs having greater viability in that country as well as in the U.S. You may, in fact, find that writing for or with a certain country's artists and writers may be more to your liking.

Obviously, other countries have different sets of laws, music business structure, promotional techniques, record sale standards and a slew of things the U.S. doesn't have. All of the above can affect the ability to promote your writing for or in a foreign market, so it is best to learn as much as you can about that market.

In general, co-writing with a foreign writer is the quickest way to learn a foreign market, and often you don't even have to leave the U.S. to find one. Many talented musician/writers are lured to America from all over the world (England and Australia in particular) and usually head for the music capitals, L.A., New York, and to some extent, Nashville. Licensing societies' creative coordinators or publishers might also be able to direct you to someone. If you are going abroad, ask the societies or the National Music Publishers Association for references of English-speaking publishers overseas. Having a track record is helpful, of course, but you would be surprised how many foreign acts are looking for great American-sounding original songs they can incorporate into their own style, and with that knowledge, foreign publishers might give your song a listen.

Writer and Publisher Industry Problems and Challenges

The Berne Convention... To Join Or Not To Join— Is There A Question?

As discussed briefly in Chapter 3, the Berne Convention is one of four major treaties established to protect copyrights on an international basis. The U.S. belongs to the Universal Copyright Convention (among several smaller conventions, see Chapter 3) which is more in line with our own copyright laws. Unfortunately, the UCC carries less clout in the international community than the Berne Convention, especially in the areas of protection against record and tape piracy and counterfeiting. The Berne Convention, encompassing 76 nations, is the most comprehensive international copyright treaty. Along with the U.S., only the U.S.S.R. and the Peoples Republic of China are the major non-signatories.

The U.S. drew closer to the Berne Convention acceptance with the advent of the 1976 copyright revisions, since one of the foremost qualifications for Berne membership is a country's copyright law including a "life plus 50 year" protection for copyrights. Three bills have been introduced in Congress since 1986, and the tide toward joining Berne is swelling in the country.

The main problems with Berne membership are the unresolved positions: 1) Eliminating the jukebox compulsory license as required by Berne, and 2) music groups want it made clear to U.S. legislators and to Berne that situations regarding Berne's so-called "moral rights provisions" of integrity (that is, mutilation and distortion protection for copyrights) can be handled through our already-existing laws.

The lineup in favor of Berne membership includes ASCAP, BMI, SESAC, the National Music Publishers' Association (NMPA), the Recording Industry Association of America (RIAA) and the U.S. copyright office. Although there seems to be overwhelming support for joining Berne, some groups have expressed fear of literary author lawsuits following Berne compliance and have made for some interesting opponents to the joining of the convention. Most notable is a coalition of twelve major book publishers called the Coalition to Preserve the American Copyright Tradition. The book publishers claim that unless Congress specifies that only U.S. law can be used to handle morality questions, joining the Berne Convention would prompt an unprecedented increase in lawsuits from authors and other copyright owners charging mutilation and distortion of their works. Without that guarantee, the book publishers claim that an author could sue a magazine charging that a three-page story has been mutilated when it was edited to one page. Balancing the fears of these book publishers is the fact that the 100 year old Berne Convention has witnessed no such rush to sue by creative people in the countries where it is the law.

Songwriters will benefit from greater royalties because greater protection against piracy and counterfeiting will increase legitimate sales. It is likely that the jukebox problems will be resolved between the performing rights societies and the jukebox industry by negotiations to decide on a rate that could then be approved officially and set by the copyright royalty tribunal.

Both ASCAP and BMI point out that there are more than two dozen countries in which we do not have a clear right of protection. With so many threats to the system, the push to get all the protection and help we can is a wise move.

Record and Tape Piracy—Finally Turning The Tide

The next time you buy a record or tape at a ridiculously low price, take it home, and find that the packaging, artwork, and/or recording quality are very shoddy, keep in mind that you don't feel half as bad as the songwriters whose compositions are on that record. You've bought a pirated copy. The songwriters are not getting any royalties and the public is not getting any quality, but the pirate and bootleggers are reaping a fortune!

An estimated $1.2 billion is lost to pirates each year. If that number seems hard to relate to, try this number: One of every four LPs or tapes sold around the world is a pirate copy. Over one-third of all recorded music piracy emanates from Southeast Asia, and much of that winds up in Arab countries where copyright protection is nonexistent.

Due, however, in part to the IFPA's (the International Federation of Phonogram and Videogram Producers) constant vigilance and Congress's threat to take away certain countries' preferential trade status with the U.S., copyright protection consciousness is developing. Territories like Malaysia, Thailand, and Singapore have recently amended their copyright laws to protect foreign recordings, and progress is being made in Taiwan, Korea, and Hong Kong. In Turkey, new legislation has been passed to deal with piracy. In Egypt, the government ratified the Phonogram Convention and set up a special police force to defeat pirates. Indonesia, a country that's rarely noticed in U.S. headlines, has the fifth largest population in the world (150,000,000) and was the leading culprit in piracy before October 1987, when it, too, amended its copyright laws, providing protection to foreign works for the first time. True, it took threats of restricting Indonesian imports and curtailing private investment in Indonesia by the U.S. government to do it.

How much effect all this is having will only be known in years to come, but some of the results are already encouraging. For example, the Hong Kong market in 1970 was made up of more than 90% pirated material. By 1986, the territory was 95% legitimate. In Greece, where piracy was rampant, IFPA anti-piracy raids put enough of a dent in the business to allow a 36% increase of legitimate product in one year.

In Singapore in 1980, about 120,000,000 pirated units per year were going to the Middle East and South America. By 1986, pirate exports were down to 15,000,000. That last figure, although only 12% of the 1980's total, shows there is still much to do about pirating. The virtual obliteration of piracy is possible if all remaining territories amend their copyright laws to protect foreign copyrights and then enforce those laws with judicious use of the police. Countries that have amended the laws can put a further nail in the pirate's coffin by joining the Berne Convention.

Then, of course, we can do our share by encouraging and advising others not to buy tapes and records we know or suspect are pirated. After all, most legitimate distributors do not sell to flea market sellers, and certainly not at absurdly low prices.

Illegal Copying—"Thou Shalt Not Steal... But God Didn't Say Anything About Copying."

Ever since the mass availability of copying machines, the nation's conscience has been repeatedly tested. Why buy 150 copies of a band arrangement for your school when you can simply buy one and copy 149? Why buy 94 choral arrangements for your Sunday services, when you can buy one and copy 93?

During the 1960s and 1970s, two of the nation's most trusted and relied upon institutions, the educational system and church groups, became the most flagrant violators of copyright law provisions as they relate to illegal copying of printed music. Many people in our industry were justifiably alarmed that institutions entrusted with the country's moral, spiritual, and educational teachings were violating the rights of a segment of the population they were responsible for educating.

Trying to put things in perspective (and avoid the panic that comes with the knowledge they were losing millions of dollars to illegal copying), the music publishing community decided to take action in the form of educating the educators. They concluded that a 15-year old musician who buys a copy of a song to rehearse with his band may copy it two or three times and not understand the ramifications of illegal copying, even if informed. However, educators should be made aware that they were not only depriving many of a legitimate income, but were also breaking the law as well. The publishers felt the educators would put two simultaneous objectives of the law into effect voluntarily: 1) They would stop copying and provide budgets for their musical needs, just as they provide budgets for everything else, and 2) they would educate their students and congregations to respect this area of the law, as they would teach those who come before them respect for all other areas of the law. To this end, the music business spent huge sums of money for pamphlets, newspaper and magazine articles, lecturers to attend schools and churches, but all seemingly to no avail.

Although lawsuits have been won against church groups who had been copying illegally, no amount of explanations, cajoling, lectures, lawsuits, or educational materials have slowed the tide of blatant disregard for the rights of songwriters and publishers alike. In 1976, for example, a survey of Chicago-area Catholic churches showed that there was a 55% infringement rate of the printed music used. In April of 1984, a music publisher won a judgment against the Archdiocese of Chicago for copyright infringement. Incredibly, evidence was discovered that of the 447 churches in the Archdiocese, over 230 had made extensive, unlicensed photocopies of music to the tune of 225,000 unauthorized hymnals containing 1,418,123 illicit copies of hymns over a three-year period. At the time the action was filed, the copyright owner offered an annual copyright license of $100 a year for unlimited use as long as all photocopies were destroyed at the end of each year and a new license was purchased. Because the Archdiocese would not comply with this $100 per year license fee, it ultimately cost the Archdiocese over $3 million in a judgment that was awarded to the publisher.

Another direction taken recently by the industry may have a better effect. The NMPA has been approaching the leadership of these "user" groups and making them aware that their institutions' disregard for this very fragile area of music creation could lead to the gradual disappearance of a great deal of printed music they now assume will be around forever. These groups are being encouraged to study the market conditions and see for themselves, rather than just take the word of the publishers. They are also being warned that they must consider the effects of unrestricted illegal copying on the future of American composers who would be forced to turn to other careers to ensure a livelihood.

If fear of legal reprisals doesn't work, perhaps the common sense notion that "you can't misuse your resources or they will dry up like drained riverbeds" will. Music is a natural resource, only as abundant as the composers and songwriters that remain a part of it.

Those interested in knowing more of what is happening in illegal copying should contact the National Music Publishers' Association (NMPA) at 205 E. 42nd Street, New York, New York 10017, (212) 370-5330.

The 7" Single...More Than A Nostalgic Loss

For a number of years, a debate has been ensuing between record companies and retailers as to the value of 7" singles in the marketplace. Many believe they should serve only as a promotion tool to sell LPs, while others feel they should be out there to make a profit. Although most consumers seem to prefer long-playing releases, particularly for adult-oriented music, there is still a market for the 45s, especially among teens and jukebox operators. There are also people who only want the song they've heard on the radio, or perhaps can't afford an LP.

The reason the future of the 45 single is of importance to songwriters is the potential loss in record sales, not only in less royalties from mechanical sales, but *reduced performance income* as well. Many records earn more for writers in royalties from airplay than they do for record sales, and this is especially true for the so-called "turntable hit," a record that is played often but doesn't sell too well. True, a broader base of airplay might prevail with more LP cuts getting more play, but the long-established financial incentive and goal of songwriters to have that big hit would be gone.

It is hard to believe that a competitive society like America would no longer have a list of favorites in the form of the charts, but without singles, that might just be what happens. Singles are also important at their price level as a vehicle to introduce new artists to the marketplace.

The advent of the cassette single in June of 1987 marked the first new single configuration since the 12" was adopted in the '70s, and also the first totally different single's format from vinyl since the advent of the 78 rpm record. Indications are that it's likely cassette singles are bolstering the singles market. In fact, this format will replace vinyl singles in the future. A question arises with cassette singles as to the record companies' policies toward that bastion of songwriter income for eight decades—the "B" side. Cassettes certainly won't look stark without it, as a blank "B" side on a record would! The record industry has been putting a second side on most cassette singles, since the public is accustomed to having a "B" side. Hopefully, this practice will con-tinue on cassettes as well. There is no greater equalizer than the voice of the public.

You can also be sure that publishers will be making it known to record companies that they won't accept elimination of the "B" side easily, nor will recording artists, producers, and songwriters. More than one format can exist and prosper if the public wants it to.

Home Taping—
"Rights Of The Consumer vs. Intellectual Property Rights"

A major problem for songwriters of today and the future began in the early 1970s with the advent of sophisticated home cassette recorders and blank cassette tapes, followed soon after by portable home duplicating cassette machines containing two cassette decks in one. These machines were usually wired directly to built-in AM-FM radios and now are standard equipment with record decks, the afore-mentioned AM-FM receivers, and tape-to-tape capabilities.

This equipment, and the blank tape it uses, have tremendously encouraged home taping of songs. The manufacturers of blank tape and cassette equipment should support the creation of music, since without music, what good is most of their tape and machines?

Home taping is already a huge drain on the U.S. music industry. It eliminates approximately $1.5 billion in sales, equal to almost one-third of the industry's income. You don't have to be a rocket scientist to figure out that this equals one-third less income to songwriters, since what is being taped are copyrighted works. This is also a major reason why new recording releases are down over 40% since 1977. In July of 1987, the International Tape/Disc Association released its sales figures for 1986 showing a whopping 25% increase in blank audio cassettes sold over 1985! This added up to 368,488,000 blank tapes. If only 20% of the blank tapes were used to record music from radios or records (and a lot more than 20% is estimated to be used), writers and publishers would have lost income in the area of $44,000,000 for 1986 alone (assuming the same amount of recordings were sold instead of home-taped).

What seemed to be the most logical solution to this problem was introduced in the form of a Home Taping Bill in 1985 (S.1739). Simply stated, it would've required a royalty on blank tape, standard cassette equipment, and dual deck cassette recorders. In February 1987, the Japanese licensing society (JASRAC) went on record favoring this form of protection, and their position was a welcome endorsement given the fact that most of the "duplicating" equipment was being manufactured in Japan. At the same time, well-meaning technologists came up with the decoder technology that could be installed in machines to stop home taping, making certain machines only usable as players. These machines would have been less expensive than player/ recorders, and would provide the consumer, who had no intentions of using the equipment to record, with a more economical means of playing their pre-recorded cassette tapes.

The technology only served to distract certain key members of the Senate as S.1739, the home audio taping act, was drafted, and the complex problems of home video taping also began to over-shadow the "royalty on cassettes" bill. By 1986, S.1739 had lost its "royalty on blank tape" provisions, but still had a royalty on home taping equipment.

In May of 1986, the Senate Judiciary Subcommittee approved a bill that would have imposed a 5% royalty on the wholesale price of cassette machines and a 25% royalty for dual machines to compensate copyright owners. In mid-August, however, the Reagan Administration shot down the bill, calling the royalty system "arbitrary" and potentially burdensome to government agencies. As an alternative, the Administration proposed further study of electronic devices that would thwart home taping.

In the meantime, millions of dollars of income are being lost because consumers are not being properly educated as to the damage that is being done to the creative community because of home taping. More than 200 years ago, Dr. Samuel Johnson, a philosopher and author, said, "No man but a blockhead ever wrote except for money." Home taping makes you wonder if the writing community isn't being forced to wear the mantle of "blockhead" without choice. As to the question of whether home taping is even legal based on the copyright law, keep in mind that technology has always been ahead of the law since 1909 when experts said that the penny arcade machine was a mere toy and didn't require granting copyright owners protection from music used in conjunction with such machines. Before you knew it, along came the jukebox with a big fat exemption for the jukebox owners and another loss of income for the creative community due to lack of foresight.

The current problem isn't even justified by an exemption to the copyright law. As a matter of fact, the only court decision relating to home taping was the Sony Betamax case that "video" taping in the home for personal use was not a copyright infringement, but it explicitly did not embrace audio taping in its decision. Furthermore, the court's video decision concentrated only on the "time shifting" (which is not relevant to audio taping), and the failure of the film industry in the early days of videotaping to show any great economic loss due to home recordings. This is quite the opposite of the audio industry, which is made up of record companies, publishers, and writers who have proved gigantic losses and harm year after year.

However, it seems that no one wants to address the issue, especially to the public, that home audio taping might be illegal under certain copyright law interpretations. In all of this confusion, simplicity and logic seem to be the only propositions around which to rally. Since we have gone from the pursuit of a blank tape royalty to an equipment royalty to a computer chip to block taping, etc., perhaps it is time to go full circle and come back to pursuing a blank tape royalty, along with the constant commitment that everyone in the music business, even new songwriters, need to educate their associates and voice their opinions to their Congresspersons on the issues. You can be sure that the tape manufacturers are doing it.

Note: For more up-to-date information about what you can do, contact the Coalition to Save America's Music, 1200 New Hampshire Avenue, N.W., Suite 480, Washington, D.C. 20036, (202) 872-3667, contact: Margie Berman.

Radio—"We're Not In The Record Business."
It is fair to question why radio would be included in a chapter on problems of the music industry. Radio became the major user of music from almost the day it was invented, and true, radio has become a partner to the music industry. The problem is that radio does not consider itself a "partner," and from this attitude comes the situation that hurts songwriters and all the music of the time. Ask many broadcasters their opinion on the radio business in conjunction with the music business, and you will find a curious point of view: "We're not in the record-selling business." Technically they're right, but why continually bite the hand that helps feed you?

This seems to be a very narrow-minded approach, and almost ludicrous when you consider that audiences tune in to hear music, not commercials, and most records are sold *after* being exposed by radio. Broadcasters are smart enough to know that if something other than music could sell advertising better on radio, all of the stations in America would be talk shows.

The point is, this kind of thinking allows some disc jockeys and radio station managers to feel like they don't have any responsibility to the people who supply them with the music, namely the songwriters, publishers, and record companies. Radio stations don't even pay for records; they get them free, and no royalties are paid on free records.

However, of perhaps even greater concern is the fact that some broadcasters have encouraged "home tapers" to tape away. Some disc jockeys even announce in advance when a hot new LP by a superstar act is going to be played in its entirety, with the reminder, "Don't forget to get your cassette machines ready."

The "we are not in the record business" attitude hurts the consumer, as well, since most people like to know who and what they are hearing (ever try to find a record in a store by singing a few bars to the manager?), but some stations' DJs think it is hip to play a record and not even mention the artist or title.

Then there is the station format that plays fifteen songs in a row and *maybe* they will mention the first and last song titles and artists. Again, there's a lack of responsibility to the music, the creators, the owners of the music, and the public, since fifteen in a row means there is no need for the "taper" to edit out commercials or DJ chatter. This is an unspoken invitation to tape. It is also a coincidence of sorts, but it seems that the DJs who play fifteen in a row or don't mention titles after playing songs also don't talk over the intros or endings of records. This time-honored practice by DJs, says (at least silently), "...If you want the beginning and end without patter, buy the record."

Some jocks and stations still care and have taken a greater responsibility in the partnership. The ones who don't care should realize they are hurting a business that feeds them and who they, willingly or not, help feed. It is hard to believe radio has forgotten that record companies are advertisers too, and short-sighted, ill treatment of the record business can not help station revenues. If the public lets the stations know of their concerns, then the stations are sure to take heed. After all, you are not only their listener, you are their consumer, and there are other stations you could be listening to.

The Controlled Composition Clause

Probably the most important element in the new copyright law of 1976 as far as songwriters were concerned was the increase in the mechanical royalty rate from 2¢ to 2 ³/4 ¢ per cut. When the law took effect in January 1978, the record companies had prospered through sixty-nine years of low royalty payments to writers, while continuing to increase prices on their LPs and singles. So, all of a sudden the record industry claimed the increases would sharply raise record prices.

There is a point to all of this. In 1978, for the first time, the record companies found a way that they could cut a cost, a cost that they could *control*. That cost reduction manifested itself in the "controlled composition clause." Simply put, this is a clause inserted in an artist's contract stating that the record company will pay a *reduced* percentage of the statutory rate on songs, rather than the full statutory rate as had always been the case on new record releases. This reduced rate usually averages out to three quarters of the full rate.

Since the copyright law provides for a maximum royalty but no minimum royalty (what were the legislators thinking at the time?), the record companies were seemingly within their rights. They took their position one step further, however, and they not only imposed such a clause on songwriter/artists, but also on artists who used outside songs. It is one thing if a writer/artist, paid to record and put out an LP of her own songs, grants the right to reduce the royalties paid to her as a writer and publisher (though under duress, as the record companies make it a deal point), but it is another thing when an artist who wants to record outside songs has to ask someone not involved with her record deal to take a reduced rate!

Think about all of the artist/writers who co-write. You might quite possibly be a co-writer. The alternative is that your song may not make that LP. Why can't you just say no? You can, but the record companies have cleverly made the artists the "bad guys," since any song on the LP at statutory forces the artist to take less royalty on the total number of songs (for example, an LP containing ten songs worth $5^{1}/4¢$ in publisher and writer share at statutory [1988 rates]). Under the controlled composition clause, however, the artist can only receive three quarters of that rate, or .39375¢ (less than 40¢). Therefore, that one song receiving statutory, which is approximately a penny and a fourth more, reduces the artist's royalty by approximately the same amount to .354¢.

This doesn't sound like a big deal, does it? By penalizing the artist for taking your statutory rate song, the artist loses out about $6,562 on a gold LP; and by forcing three-quarter rates on the artist, the record companies save $62,500 in publisher and writer royalties on every gold LP (500,000 units sold).

What this means to songwriters is that recording artists with controlled composition clauses are often going to be less interested in considering outside songs for their records. If they do take an outside song but the writer is not with an established publishing company, they will try to proceed with the reduced rate scenario. They usually won't do this to an established publisher, because they know the policy of most companies is to say "no," and then the artist will have to make up the difference. However, if your song is great, they will usually want it, no matter what.

The long-range effect of the controlled composition clause creates a danger in that the best available songs may not always be recorded. A possible alternative for the copyright holder would be to negotiate a reduced rate until the record recoups to its breakeven point, at which time full statutory rate would take effect.

Record companies must be reminded that *it all starts with the song*, and discounting the product before it even reaches the public is going to eventually create less-than-quality product. Potential loss to the public and writers would seem to justify some kind of amendment to the copyright law (there is no reduced royalty in Europe, for example). No one seems to want to take up this cause presently. Maybe if more voices were heard, it would become more of a major issue.

"We Won't Practice Law If You Won't Practice Publishing"

A disturbing practice that has crept into the music publishing business has been the development of certain attorneys who assume the role of publisher. Some attorneys can provide legitimate administrative services (certain major firms have a professionally trained in-house administration staff), but more often than not in small law firms (and in large ones, too), the actual work performed for writers and their catalogues is not performed by the attorney, but by a secretary. Secretaries are rarely trained in the areas of publishing administration or the complexities inherent in publishing. Many attorneys, even those specializing in music, are not generally qualified to handle the day-to-day activities of a publishing company, even if they are knowledgeable in copyright law and contract negotiations.

There is a distinct difference between providing *administrative services* and providing the services of a fully qualified and *active publishing company*. I have never known one attorney who has ever gotten a song recorded for a writer, yet by administering the writer's music, the attorney is denying the writer the opportunity to seek out a reputable publisher who could provide a variety of services, such as writer collaborations, film projects, TV projects, song exploitation, foreign representation, administrative services, and just plain song-plugging. If an attorney with whom you are working wishes to handle your publishing, don't be afraid to find out specifically what he can and can't do. You would ask the same thing of a publisher. Analyze whether his services fit your needs. You will probably find that publishers do not like to practice law, but some lawyers like to practice publishing. Remember, they could be practicing with your career, and in that case, "practice does not make perfect."

PMRC = "Intimidating Reminder of McCarthyism"

The biggest fear of creative people has always been censorship. In 1985, the PMRC (Parents Music Recourse Center) took it upon itself to be the conscience of the nation as it relates to lyrics in rock music, and declared war on the record industry, and quite possibly, the First Amendment. With threats ranging from picketing of record dealers to the pursuit of legislation against what they claimed to be pornographic lyrics, the PMRC extracted compromises from various record companies whereby they would sticker LPs containing controversial lyrics— the objective, it seemed, being to have such lyrics banned.

On one hand, this might be dismissed as a collection of overly concerned individuals letting off some steam. However, these individuals happened to be the wives of various powerful politicians giving overwhelming clout and publicity to their demands, whether those demands were justifiable or not.

The real question, however, was a much broader problem that could affect every songwriter (not to mention every creator of anything) in the country. The question is, does any group have the right to force, or threaten to force, censorship upon the music industry, and consequently, the American people? The problem with the rating system for records with explicit lyrics (as the PMRC opted for) is that lyrics by their very nature are often impressionistic, vague, poetic, and highly subject to interpretation. A church in Texas condemned Simon and Garfunkel's "Bridge Over Troubled Water" since they interpreted the lyric to be drug-related.

The nature of the popular music business is to expose talent, not hide it. Record covers, song titles, and promotional photos make it clear as to what is being sold, and parents can react accordingly. It is interesting to note that only a small percentage of heavy metal acts' recordings contain obscenities, and if the rebellious and violent lyric of youth that is not considered obscene in heavy metal or rap still irks some people, what must they think of opera, which often deals with sexual and violent themes? Censorship aimed at only one segment of music that supposedly fills the criteria looks suspiciously like prejudice, as if this particular segment of music is purposely being singled out for publicity's sake and not for the principal supposedly behind the PMRC's attacks.

Since we have a free press that constantly reviews recordings, and press information abounds on performers' activities, there is no need to pressure record stores, record manufacturers, and songwriters with threats of censorship. One potentially worthwhile aspect of the PMRC crusade may have been their educational campaign via slide show presentations stressing their "porn rock" convictions that were available to consumer groups. Like any information dissemination, whatever helps the parents decide what is appropriate, such as the PMRC's slide show and speeches, is the American way of awareness. Censorship or threat of censorship is not. The infamous blacklisting of writers in the '50s was accomplished by intimidating people, much like what we are seeing here, as groups try to impose their values by pressure when they cannot reach their ends within the guidelines of the Constitution.

Although it is true that people in the public eye have always had a responsibility to be aware of their influence on children, most songwriters are already aware and carry the burden willingly, as attested to by years and years of great music emanating from our shores. Songwriters and writer/artists who created "We Are The World," Live-Aid, Farm-Aid, Band-Aid and many other humanitarian creations, may be in the same catchall the censors look to ostracize .

This world may have locked us into only two types of societies; those with freedom of expression and those without. Russian parents don't worry about questionable lyric in music, but I doubt if most Americans would like to be in their shoes. Even though most of you probably don't write heavy metal lyric, freedom means that the heavy metal writer is as free as the country or the R&B writer. If the work of heavy metal writers could be threatened by censorship, is your work far behind? Questionable taste on the part of a small segment of the songwriting community is not justification for censorship.

DAT: The Beginning Or The End

When music historians look back on the '80s, one technological advancement will loom over the rest. DAT (not a way of saying "that" with a New York accent), meaning "digital audiotape," is the tape version of compact disc technology. These machines revolutionized existing taping technologies, and they made possible, for the first time, digital to digital copying, and vastly improved the quality of analog-to-digital home taping.

DAT machines capture and preserve recordings with perfect fidelity. The combination of DAT and CD machines will give home tapers a perfect master and a copying medium that permits infinite duplication of perfect copies. The buyer is in for a technological treat.

However, while the public is celebrating this treat, the music community is playing catch-up again. If home taping is a coffin to creativity, DAT provides the nails in the coffin. Until a technology is invented for the manufacture of pre-recorded DAT cassettes and music is licensed for that format, the only possible use for DAT machines is home taping.

Recording sales in all formats, and consequently, publishing revenues, could drop if DAT machines take hold as audio cassette machines did. Record and publishing execs have expressed concern about DAT since its prototype was introduced in June of 1986, and feel its capability to produce "master quality" recordings would be a greater inducement to home taping.

All segments of the U.S. music community agree that DAT is a threat. Some want legislation for upward of a 35% levy on imported DAT machines not equipped with home taping protection (such as a copy code scanner). Others want a law that requires anti-copying chips in all DAT machines. Perhaps the best approach is to revise the copyright law so that all new hardware technology is referenced in some way as to compensate writers, publishers, and record companies, *and* a royalty, mandated by law, on all software products (i.e. audio cassettes, video cassettes, DAT cassettes) payable to creators and copyright owners, possibly through licensing societies or the Harry Fox Agency.

Since it is unrealistic to deny the right of the consumer to buy a product and use it, a large portion of the industry believes that the above is a realistic and workable solution.

Nothing will diminish home taping faster than higher blank tape prices as they compare to lower prerecorded tape and record prices.

The recordable compact disc machine is not far off. Revised copyright laws giving rights' owners their justifiable authority to license in any and all medium can head off the threat our industry faces every few years as a new and more sophisticated technology makes our more-than-a-decade-old revised copyright law look outdated. Our representatives in Congress (who love it when our music is their overseas ambassador) should purposely put creative legislation ahead of the typical wait-and-see approach. With this technology, playing catch-up and never being caught up, could be the music business' epitaph.

Source Licensing—
"The Broadcaster's Balloon Is Full Of Hot Air"

This is one of the worst situations affecting songwriters and publishers. The minute the new copyright law of 1978 was enacted, a coalition of local TV broadcasters attempted to dismantle the blanket licensing system by dragging their cause into court in what is now known as the Buffalo Broadcasting Case. Their chief opponents were the songwriters of America and their supporters, and the licensing societies ASCAP, BMI, and SESAC. For seven years, the broadcasting "Goliaths" threw everything but TV sets at the societies' "Davids," and finally in 1985, the judgment came: The courts reaffirmed that blanket licensing was lawful, and most reasonable people believed the broadcasters would have learned to coexist with the music community after their expensive legal lesson. Unfortunately, that has not been the case.

After what seemed like a ten-second pause, the broadcasting moguls came back with an obvious ploy geared toward reversing the court's decision. In 1986, their goal was to win through legislation what they had been unable to win either in court or in negotiations with songwriters' representatives—unlimited use of copyrighted music for little or no cost. The legislation (S.1980 in the Senate and HR.3521 in the House of Representatives) was an attempt by corporate giants to revise the copyright laws so that royalty payments to composers and lyricists would be reduced enormously. It would increase profits for the already wealthy owners of 800 local TV stations who gross over $12 billion a year.

Since TV started in the 1940s, a system has existed whereby TV stations pay for the use of music under what are called "blanket licenses." It is relatively impossible for each individual songwriter, composer, and lyricist to keep track of when her music is played, how often, and by whom, so the blanket license system has proven to be the most effective and balanced way of ensuring an income and recognition for their efforts.

The blanket license works like this: Fees are negotiated with broadcasters by the representatives of the writers—ASCAP, BMI, and SESAC. The concept of continued payment for continuing use of music is protected. The more frequently a piece of music or a song is played on a TV show, the more money the writer receives.

The broadcasters are attempting to abolish this system by shifting the licensing of music used on syndicated programs and local TV from the broadcasters to the program producers (or syndicators). Under such a system, the producers would have to obtain the performing rights together with the one-time synchronization right, absorbing the cost that should rightfully fall to the broadcasters. The stations, therefore, would no longer need licenses from ASCAP, BMI, and SESAC.

The effect of this legislation would be disastrous. It would eliminate the right of continuing payment for continuing use of one's musical work. Payment would be made only once, before the value of the work in the marketplace could be determined. Millions and millions of dollars would be lost annually, and few composers of music for TV would be able to earn a decent living. Of course, the ultimate loser would be the public, who would be deprived of the great variety of music programming now available, as well as great music that would never be written.

Only the broadcasters stand to gain, and to that end, the broadcasting lobby shifted its focus to Congress, increasing its honorariums and contributions and warning Congressional members that their faces may not appear on local TV news quite as often if they didn't support the law that the owner of their local TV station wanted. A prime example of that strategy became known when one of the co-sponsors of Representative Fredrick Boucher's (D-VA) source licensing bill, Representative Marvin Leaths' (D-TX), interest in the legislation became known after several examples of his notes to colleagues concerning the bill popped up in the December 6, 1985 newsletter, *Communications Daily*. The notes quoted Leaths as advising fellow House members that, "...Pleasing station managers now on this issue could prove important plus during the next year's Congressional elections," and urging them, "Get on this, then call your station managers and tell them—it should help in your campaign."

In their effort to convince Congress to pass the source licensing legislation, the local television broadcasters have made certain arguments based on erroneous statements. The broadcasters are claiming that they are being squeezed financially by the current system of blanket licensing. How can that possibly be when they gross about $12 billion, and the percentage of revenues paid as license fees for music is only about one percent?

Another argument broadcasters put forward is that the blanket license robs them of their clout in the marketplace. If that were so, how do they explain the fact that the one percent license fee in current use dropped from its two percent level in the '50s?...Hardly evidence of the composers' great market power?

In another curious anomaly, broadcasters claim that the blanket license has been "forced" on them. If that were so, how do they explain why they have always had alternatives available to them, such as direct licensing with the composer and source licensing negotiated by a program producer? In addition, they may also exercise the option of a "per program" agreement.

Historically, broadcasters have always chosen to use the blanket license. They could have used source licensing, but never tried to obtain source licenses by any bonafide means. Specifically, they never offered to pay—they wanted free source licenses.

Broadcasters also claim that the blanket license system is unfair. However, the facts state that the President of the National Association of Broadcasters praised the fairness of the blanket license and advocated its use for cable television. Just before these bills were introduced, he told a Congressional subcommittee that the blanket license is an equitable way to "negotiate a price that correctly reflects the value of the work in the marketplace..."

It should also be pointed out that the broadcasters benefit from considerable judicial protection. For example, all rates negotiated between ASCAP and the broadcasters are subject to Federal Court review, with the burden on music to show the fees to be reasonable.

What protection do the songwriters have? Their income is never automatic. When a program is produced, composers and lyricists receive relatively little compensation "up front" in the hopes that the program will succeed. That is why it is so important for writers to be compensated through a royalty system that recognizes the value of *performances.*

One of the most unjust broadcaster claims is that there is no logical reason for music performance rights to be conveyed separately from all other rights in a syndicated TV show. They claim that composers can negotiate residuals in the same way as scriptwriters. The reality is that the logic is right in the copyright act. That act grants two separate rights—to record or synchronize, and to perform. Producers synchronize; broadcasters perform. Each groups now gets the license they need. Composers are not scriptwriters. For their own union-based reasons, scriptwriters accept residuals (along with large upfront payments, vacations, and health and welfare benefits) in lieu of performance fees. Songwriters have always been treated differently from scriptwriters. First, unlike music creators, TV scriptwriters and other non-music creators are represented by unions. Under a recent National Labor Relations Board ruling, composers cannot form a union to obtain "residuals" on their works. They depend on the separate performance rights payments that the proposed bills would largely abolish. Second, the scriptwriters always write for a particular program. Much of the music used in syndicated programs is existing music—music not specifically created for the program.

Third, the broadcasters paint an erroneous picture of television music—as if all of it were background and theme music created specifically for a program. In fact, there are a great many pre-existing standards and other kinds of music incorporated in television programs and films. This music is usually owned by publishers who license users on behalf of themselves and their writers. As to the mass of music now included in programs and films, this bill would destroy existing rights and disappoint all of the parties' reasonable expectations—the writers, publishers, and producers—for the sole benefit of the broadcasters. For example, the film *Casablanca* includes some fifteen standard songs, nearly all of which are not owned by the film's producer. How would the composers (or their estates) be compensated under the proposed legislation? The broadcasters have not addressed that question except to suggest that the producers should now go back and buy the necessary rights for the stations from each owner or his estate.

The next broadcaster argument is one that smacks of hypocrisy. They claim that some Hollywood production studios, who are also music publishers and copyright proprietors, are being paid twice for the same music on a TV show they syndicate. The facts are, publishers affiliated with major studios receive under ten percent of ASCAP's payment for local TV performances, and much of that ten percent is earned for pre-existing songs, not for works written specifically for television programs. However, about five percent of ASCAP's payments for local TV performances goes to music publishers owned by broadcasters!! Wouldn't it be interesting to watch them license themselves? They have even tried to justify their argument by announcing that the same set of rules that apply to movies shown in theatres should apply to movies shown on television. This is an interesting concept, since songs in films are licensed from anywhere from $5,000-$100,000, which is then to be split with the writers. For TV, most publishers are lucky when they get $500-$600, which is then split with writers.

Movies have special treatment because of an anti-trust case won in 1948. The court found ASCAP in violation of the anti-trust law and ordered source licensing for movie theatres only. Recently, broadcasters tried to prove they were entitled to the same anti-trust relief, and they lost in court. The courts have emphatically upheld the blanket license system for broadcasters. Movie exhibitors, unlike broadcasters, pay movie producers a percentage of their box office gross. The two industries are governed by separate and very different business practices.

The broadcasters say that source licensing is needed to stimulate competition among composers of television music. But the facts say that music composers and publishers have always competed vigorously to have their music included in television programs and films that may be televised. This competition occurs at the producer level. Composers want assignments; they and their publishers want their music used. Only the quality music that the producer feels will add to the success of the show wins out. The source licensing bill would not increase that kind of competition. By reducing incentives, they would diminish competition.

The broadcaster, apparently liking the way the previous argument sounded, took it a step further to claim that source licensing would bring more good music to TV. The facts say, however, that the present system encourages producers to use music because the initial cost is minimal—perhaps $3,000 for the music in a one-hour program. If the source licensing bill were enacted, there would be less copyrighted music used; the producers are risk-takers who succeed in getting only three percent of their programs into syndication. With such odds, the risk-takers simply could not afford to gamble more than they do now, and will be driven to use public domain, or "library" music, or to avoid music altogether. To the degree composers were hired at all, they would be in a poor bargaining position and would end up with fewer assignments and less money.

The next broadcaster claim was that 85% of the members of ASCAP do not get one cent for local television performance. The facts are that more than 4,000 ASCAP writer members received some local television royalty distribution in 1985 and 1986. ASCAP payments are made only to members whose music is played. Nothing could be more equitable. Those who receive payments for television performances are a minority of the members, but it is a constantly changing minority based on the ever-changing selection of music used. Therefore, the argument is misleading and ignores a fact well-known to broadcasters: ASCAP and BMI membership is open to all writers who have had just one work published or recorded. Four thousand writers is a very respectable figure, considering the nature and size of the societies' membership and the limited opportunities available to writers to have their music included in television programs.

The broadcasters' final claim is that local composers will benefit as a result of this legislation, because local TV broadcasters who are not paying a blanket license fee will have the monetary incentive to pay local composers for locally-produced programs. In actuality, most local programming consists of non-musical programs— news, sports, and weather. Even if the broadcasters intended to start "jobbing out" musical production at the local level, the number of assignments created for local composers would be minimal, and local composers would have no bargaining power with the station. Broadcasters would use library music, as they do now on occasion. The owners of music libraries generally do not pay any royalties to writers. Nothing in this legislation offers any guarantee to the local composer. Instead, it would take away the guarantees that composers enjoy under the current system.

The blanket license system works and has remained free of scandal and rip-off of the creator. To replace a system that echoes these common sense principals with one that forbids payment for continuing performance would destroy the incentive to create. Armed with this knowledge and the facts, songwriters, lyricists, and composers both known and unknown have written to their Senators and Congresspersons and have visited in Washington with legislators to present the creative community's position.

It is interesting to note that songwriters, music publishers (American and foreign), TV and movie producers, the advertising industry, music lovers and performers, in addition to the Register of Copyrights, Commissioner of Patents, the Bar Associations specializing in copyright law, leaders of the Congressional Arts Caucus, the Administration and European economic community, *all* went on record opposing source licensing legislation in 1986. Not surprisingly, the only ones endorsing the broadcasters' bill are the local broadcasters.

Despite their obvious shortcoming and aura of favoritism, the source licensing bills have powerful friends and allies in the two most powerful groups in America—government and broadcasting. Boucher's allies want to "reform" the long-maintained, carefully established, fine-tuned system that has made American music the standard of the world. If they succeed and their bill passes, the owners of radio stations may be next in line to try to further erode the copyright protection of songwriters, and after that, more than likely, the TV networks.

An ax is set to fall on the songwriters, and if it does, the entire intellectual property rights community of this nation is bound to be crushed along with them. It is easy to see the imperative nature of protecting intellectual works, which affect not only songwriters but also novelists, poets, and playwrights. It is even more important to recognize that the issue of broadcasters vs songwriters is not only a direct attack on copyright protection, but really one more example of the powerful ripping-off of the economically powerless.

For more information on this situation, contact BMI or ASCAP (addresses in Appendices). You can also write your Congressperson or Senator and tell them how you feel.

This chapter's intent is not only to point up the problems you face as writers, but also to enlighten you to the challenges faced by the creative community of which you have willingly chosen to be a part. One of the most positive aspects of songwriting is that no one does it because they have to or just because it is a job. It is because we love it and we want to do it. In knowing some of the problems and challenges you face with other writers, known and unknown, rich and poor, you will develop a sense (that is, if this is really your career) of belonging to a noble and respected group, and with that feeling of belonging comes an obligation to protect it and help it grow. To that end, this chapter is dedicated to making you aware of what you need to *do* as a person in order to be what you want to *be* as a songwriter.

(Special thanks to ASCAP and Congressman Howard Berman (D-CA) for making their information available, as well as to Hal David for his informative eloquence.)

New Technologies and Their Effects On The Songwriter

IT WAS NOT AN ACCIDENT or coincidence that many of the songwriters' challenges discussed in Chapter 16 relate to new technology. Therefore, this chapter deals with the positive effects of such technlogical advancements on creators and copyright owners. New technologies are spawning more diversified ways of getting the same product to the public; that same product being the *recording* and the *song*.

The 45 rpm 7" single, for example, having been around since the 1950s, has in the last ten years given birth to the 12" single, the dance mix single, and the club mix single. These new configurations have two benefits for songwriters: First, they diversify the marketplace for your song. Giving a recording a different "mix" or rearrangement of instrumentation, and often an enlarged rhythm section, can provide a record with new life or open up an area of sales that it would never have penetrated before. The single that a pop DJ plays and the one you dance to at a club are usually different. Someone who hears the record at a dance club and subsequently buys it will probably get the 12"dance version and may have never heard or liked the version played on the radio.

The second benefit is that almost all 12" singles, dance mixes, etc., are more than six minutes long. This means an increased mechanical royalty to songwriters who often forget that they are paid one of two ways, either $5\frac{1}{4}$ ¢ per song or 1¢ per minute of music, whichever is greater. An eight-minute dance recording is worth 8¢ instead of $5\frac{1}{4}$¢ per song. If that doesn't sound like much, remember at statutory rate, 100,000 records sold is $5,250, but at 8 ¢, 100,000 records is $8,000, or $2,750 more.

A cassette single and cassette EP is just another configuration of the 45 rpm single, but it is grabbing a share of sales that surveys have shown would normally have been lost. In October 1987, Arista Records conducted a survey and found over 42% of those who purchased a cassette single had not purchased a vinyl single in the past year. A similar share, 41.5%, said they would not have bought a single if it had been available on vinyl only. Further to the Arista poll, over 98% said they intended to continue buying cassette singles, and over 92% said that the availability of the cassette single is encouraging them to increase their singles collections. So the cassette single not only serves as an important income earner for writers, it continues a tradition enabling record companies to bring new talent to the marketplace, and new talent always needs new songs. *Billboard* Magazine, always reflecting the times in its charts and reports, includes sales of cassette singles in both the Top 100 Singles and Top Black Singles charts.

Music videos are still another format by which music is exposed. The new areas of income opened up by music videos are *performances on TV* and, to a lesser degree, *sales through retail stores*. Video sales are also not a major income earner unless your song is on a video by, for example, Bruce Springsteen or Michael Jackson.

Typical video sales are 5-10,000 units. However, the real benefit to writers is not music video performance income or sales—it is simply in the visibility of the video used regularly on TV. This visibility has proven video's ability to help sell records, so that writers and artists are not strictly at the mercy of radio to expose their product.

MTV, the first of the successful music video shows, opened up a vast panorama for songwriters. Now a writer often creates a song not only with the image of the artist singing it, but with an idea of how it would look in a video.

Music videos' effect on songwriters in the future will go much deeper than just visualizing a lyric. Writers will have to become even more atuned on an international level due to MTV in conjunction with Viacom's expansion into Europe. Effective August 1, 1987, MTV started transmitting to 14 European nations. Although Europe already had Sky Channel (which covered 92% of Europe and 44% of the population watch it) and Super Channel's Music Box Video Clip Show (74% of Europe and 27% watching it), MTV is the first 24-hour, all-music channel. Initially, they have been programming a lot of British and European acts, but the U.S. influence is sure to be felt in the coming years, and hopefully on a scale close to record sales (70% of the records sold in Europe are by U.S. and British acts). MTV Europe has been launched with 1.6 million subscriber households (coincidentally, the same number MTV started with in the U.S., MTV U.S. now claims 35 million households). But with 14 million Europeans now watching satellite-delivered TV programs on cable, MTV has plenty of room to grow, and American songwriters have another greater area of exposure for their music.

One of the reasons for the growth of television music was another of the technological hardware advances—stereo TV. It simply sounds better, and even teenagers who had been watching TV since they were infants heard a new dimension from an old friend and noticed the difference it made so notably in music. Dialogue in stereo is still dialogue, but now watching music shows isn't sacrificing sound quality. With stereo TV as the foundation, the exposure mediums for music (like MTV) can continue to provide songwriters with an additional promotional tool for their music for many years to come.

An additional hardware marvel that came about in the 80s was another configuration player for the recording buyer—the CD player and its software companion, the compact disc. They entered the marketplace to augment, and in a sense, compete with the already existing LP. Since CDs are more expensive than LPs, and since there are well over one hundred million record players already in use in this country, both systems will probably compete for some years. CDs' main advantage for the songwriter (other than the better sound quality) is the fact that CDs can hold more music than LPs. This will hopefully lead back to the days of 10, 11, 12, and even 13 songs on an album (*I believe several record company executives turned blue at that last statement*). Reduced costs in product manufacturing for future CDs, and the obvious capability of CDs to give the customer quality sound and a longer format, offer more chances for more songwriters to get on more LPs.

With the advent of CD singles, CD jukeboxes are an additional area for song exposure, and several big name jukebox companies (Rowe International, Rockola, etc.) are making 45/CD combo players. With approximately 46 million singles sold annually to the American jukebox industry, this market for both sales and exposure is an important one for the songwriter. There are over 250,000 jukeboxes in the U.S., able to hold an average of 100 records at one time, therefore keeping 25 million records at a time before the public. And who knows how many different songs?! Long live the jukebox, in any configuration.

Technological advancements in music that have been made since the turn of the century are graphically illustrated on the following page in the form of "The Technology Tree."

The "Technology Tree"

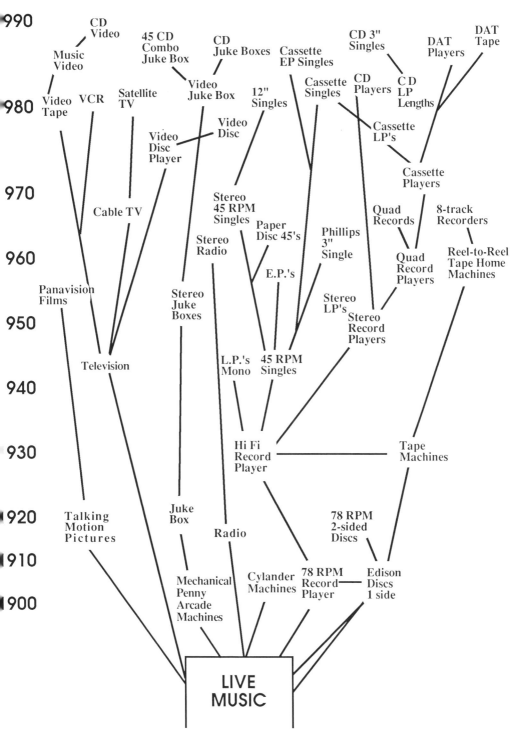

990

CD Video

Music Video

45 CD Combo Juke Box

CD Juke Boxes

Cassette EP Singles

CD 3" Singles

DAT Players

DAT Tape

980

Video Tape

VCR

Satellite TV

Video Juke Box

12" Singles

Cassette Singles

CD Players

CD LP Lengths

Video Disc Player

Video Disc

Cassette LP's

Cassette Players

970

Cable TV

Stereo 45 RPM Singles

Quad Records

8-track Recorders

960

Panavision Films

Stereo Radio

Paper Disc 45's

Phillips 3" Single

Quad Record Players

Reel-to-Reel Tape Home Machines

950

Stereo Juke Boxes

E.P.'s

Stereo LP's

Stereo Record Players

Television

L.P.'s Mono

45 RPM Singles

940

930

Hi Fi Record Player

Tape Machines

920

Talking Motion Pictures

Juke Box

Radio

78 RPM 2-sided Discs

910

Mechanical Penny Arcade Machines

Cylander Machines

78 RPM Record Player

Edison Discs 1 side

900

LIVE MUSIC

A
Final
Note

MY PURPOSE IN WRITING THIS BOOK was to help you to have a better understanding of the writer/publisher relationship, as well as the music publishing business as a whole. Naturally, my greatest hope is that the information in the book will enlighten you, but I hope it will motivate you as well.

The music of tomorrow is in the hands of new writers and would-be writers of today. Good publishers are looking for you as hard as you are looking for them. If you can build those relationships, then you, the writers, the industry, and the public will surely benefit.

U.S. SONGWRITER ORGANIZATIONS

Akron Composers and Musicians Exchange
625 Hillsdale Avenue
Akron, OH 44303

American Guild of Authors and Composers
6430 Sunset Boulevard
Hollywood, CA 90028

Arizona Songwriters Association
P.O. Box 678
Phoenix, Arizona 85001

Atlanta Songwriters Association
2091 Faulkner Road
Atlanta, GA 30324

Baltimore-Washington Songwriters Assoc.
5507 Stuart Avenue
Baltimore, MD 21215

Columbus Songwriters Association
3312 Petzinger Road
Columbus, OH 43227

Composers Workshop Hawaii
P.O. Box 22368
Honolulu, HI 96822

Connecticut Songwriters Association
P.O. Box 2995
New Haven, CT 06515

Kansas City Songwriters Association
9210 W. 81st Terrace
Overland Park, KS 66204

Kansas Songwriters Association
117 West 8th Street
Hays, KS 67601

Los Angeles Songwriters Showcase
P.O. Box 93759
Hollywood, CA 90093

Memphis Songwriters Association
P.O. Box 41365
Memphis, TN 38104

Middle Atlantic Songwriters Association
444 Rocky Run Road
Midway Park, NC 28544

Minnesota Songwriters Association
3806 6th Street, North
Minneapolis, MN 55412

Missouri Songwriters Association
693 Green Forest Drive
Fenton, MO 63026

Muscle Shoals Music Association
P.O. Box 551
Sheffield, AL 35660

Nashville Songwriters Assoc., International
803 18th Avenue South
Nashville, TN 37203

National Academy of Songwriters
6381 Hollywood Boulevard
Hollywood, CA 90028

New Mexico Songwriters and Musicians
Association
P.O. Box 7187
Albuquerque, NM 87120

New Orleans Songwriters Association
2643 DeSoto Street
New Orleans, LA 70119

North Bay Songwriters Association
P.O. Box 6023
Santa Rosa, CA 95406

Northern California Songwriters Assoc.
855 Oak Grove Avenue
Menlo Park, CA 94025

Northwest Songwriters Network
E. Crestwood CT
Port Orchard, WA 98366

Open Door Music Society
1921 West 4th Avenue
Vancouver, British Columbia
Canada V6J 1M7

Pacific Northwest Songwriters Association
P.O. Box 98324
Seattle, WA 98188

Pennsylvania Association of Songwriters,
Composers and Lyricists
244 N. Ninth Street
Allentown, PA 18102

Portland Music Association
P.O. Box 6723
Portland, OR 97228

RASCAL—Rochester Association of
Songwriters, Composers and Lyricists
47 Maplehurst Road
Rochester, NY 14617

Rocky Mountain Music Association
231 Harrison Street
Denver, CO 80206

Sacramento Songwriters Showcase
4632 U Street
Sacramento, CA 95817

San Diego Songwriters Association
P.O. Box 270026
San Diego, CA 92128-0976

San Francisco Folk Music Center
885 Clayton Street
San Francisco, CA 94117

San Gabriel Valley Music Association
P.O. Box 396
West Covina, CA 91790

Santa Barbara Songwriters Guild
P.O. Box 2238
3 West Carrillo Street, Suite 8
Santa Barbara, CA 93120

Santa Cruz Songwriters Guild
P.O. Box 76
Ben Lomond, CA 95005

Songwriters Association of Jacksonville
P.O. Box 10394
Jacksonville Beach, FL 32247

Songwriters Assoc. of Washington, D.C.
1377 K Street, N.W., #632
Washington, D.C. 20005

Songwriters of San Diego
7972 Mission Center Court
San Diego, CA 92108

Songwriters Association of Philadelphia
515 Burnham Road
Philadelphia, PA 19119

Songwriters Guild of America
6430 Sunset Boulevard, Suite 317
Hollywood, CA 90028

Songwriters Guild of America
276 5th Avenue, Suite 306
New York, NY 10001

Songwriters Guild of America
50 Music Square West, Suite 702
Nashville, TN 37203

Songwriters Workshop of Cleveland
2777 Lancashire Road, Suite 4
Cleveland Heights, OH 44106

Songstage
23 Hartwood Street
Albany, NY 12205

South Bay Songwriters Association
P.O. Box 50443
Pal Alto, CA 94303

Southern California Songwriters Guild
P.O. Box 723
Cypress, CA 90630

Tucson Songwriters Association
620 N. 6th Avenue
Tucson, AZ 85705

Utah Songwriters Association
1875 East Casino Way
Salt Lake City, UT 84121

LICENSING SOCIETIES

ASCAP
ASCAP Building
1 Lincoln Plaza
New York, NY 10023
(212) 595-3050

ASCAP
Los Angeles
6430 Sunset Boulevard
Los Angeles, CA 90028
(213) 466-7681

ASCAP
London
52 Haymarket, Suite 9
London SWIY4RP England
011-44-1-930-1121

ASCAP
Nashville
2 Music Square West
Nashville, TN 37203
(615) 244-3936

ASCAP
Puerto Rico
Office 505
First Federal Savings Condominium
1519 Ponce de Leon Avenue
Santurce, Puerto Rico 00910
(809) 725-1688

BMI
320 West 57th Street
New York, NY 10019
(212) 586-2000

BMI
Shovel Shop Square 3A
North Easton, MA 02356
(617) 238-0174

BMI
5105 Tollview Road, Suite 240
Rolling Meadows, IL 60008
(312) 870-8060

BMI
14-8500 SW 117th Road, Suite 116
Miami, FL 33183
(305) 271-8220

BMI
8730 Sunset Boulevard, 3rd Floor West
Los Angeles, CA 90069
(213) 659-9109

BMI
1325 South Diary Ashford, Suite 260
Houston, TX 77077
(713) 558-3500

BMI
230 Half Mile Road
Redbank, NJ 07701
(201) 758-0700

BMI
10 Music Square East
Nashville, TN 37203
(615) 259-3625

BMI
Edif. Pan Am 905 Hato Rey
San Juan, Puerto Rico 00917
(809) 754-6490

BMI (San Francisco Area)
111 Bayhill Drive
San Bruno, CA 94066
(415) 583-8355

BMI
727 N. 1st Street
St. Louis, MO 63102
(314) 621-3100

BMI
79 Harley House
Marylebone
London NW5HN England
935-8517

SESAC
55 Music Square East
Nashville, TN 37203
(615) 320-0055

RECORD LABELS

A & M Records, Inc.
595 Madison Avenue
New York, NY 10022
(212) 826-0477

A & M Records, Inc.
1416 North LaBrea Avenue
Hollywood, CA 90028
(213) 469-2411

Amherst Records
1800 Main Street
Buffalo, NY 14208
(716) 883-9520

Arista Records, Inc.
6 West 57th Street
New York, NY 10019
(212) 489-7400

Arista Records, Inc.
8370 Wilshire Boulevard
Los Angeles, CA 90211
(213) 655-9222

Atlantic Recording Corp.
75 Rockefeller Plaza
New York, NY 10019
(212) 484-6000

Atlantic Recording Corp.
9229 Sunset Boulevard
West Hollywood, CA 90069
(213) 205-7450

Capitol Records, Inc.
1370 Avenue of the Americas
New York, NY 10019
(212) 757-7470

Capitol Records, Inc.
1750 North Vine Street
Los Angeles, CA 90028
(213) 462-6252

Capitol Records, Inc.
1111 16th Avenue South
Nashville, TN 37212
(615) 320-5009

Chameleon Records
3355 West El Segundo Boulevard
Hawthorne, CA 90250
(213) 973-8282

Chrysalis Records
645 Madison Avenue
New York, NY 10022
(212) 758-3555

Chrysalis Records
9255 Sunset Boulevard
West Hollywood, CA 90069
(213) 550-0171

CBS Records, Inc.
51 West 52nd Street
New York, NY 10019
(212) 975-4321

CBS Records, Inc.
1801 Century Park West
Century City, CA 90067
(213) 556-4700

CBS Records, Inc.
34 Music Square East
Nashville, TN 37203
(615) 742-4321

Elektra/Asylum/Nonesuch Records
75 Rockefeller Plaza
New York, NY 10019
(212) 484-7200

Elektra/Asylum/Nonesuch Records
9229 Sunset Boulevard
West Hollywood, CA 90069
(213) 205-7400

EMI America/Liberty Records
(div. of Capital Records, Inc.)
1370 Avenue of the Americas
New York, NY 10019
(212) 757-7470

EMI America/Liberty Records
(div. of Capital Records, Inc.)
6920 Sunset Boulevard
Hollywood, CA 90028
(213) 461-9141

EMI America/Liberty Records
(div. of Capital Records, Inc.)
1111 16th Avenue South
Nashville, TN 37212
(615) 320-5009

Enigma Records
1750 E. Holly Avenue
El Segundo, CA 90245
(213) 640-6869

Epic Records
(subs. of CBS Records, Inc.)
51 W. 52nd Street
New York, NY 10019
(212) 975-4321

Epic Records
(subs. of CBS Records, Inc.)
1801 Century Park West
Los Angeles, CA 90067
(213) 556-4700

Epic Records
(subs. of CBS Records, Inc.)
34 Music Square East
Nashville, TN 37203
(615) 742-4321

Fantasy/Prestige/Milestone/Stax
2600 10th Street
Berkeley, CA 94710
(415) 549-2500

Geffen Records
9126 Sunset Boulevard
West Hollywood, CA 90069
(213) 278-9010

Geffen Records
75 Rockefeller Plaza, Suite 1804A
New York, NY 10019
(212) 484-7170

International Record Syndicate (IRS)
Building 422
100 Universal City Plaza
Universal City, CA 91608
(818) 777-4730

Island Records
14 East 4th Street, 3rd Floor
New York, NY 10012
(212) 477-8000

Island Records
6525 Sunset Boulevard, 2nd Floor
Hollywood, CA 90028
(213) 469-1285

K-TEL International, Inc.
15535 Medina Road
Plymouth, NM 55447-1480
(800) 328-6640

MCA Records, Inc.
70 Universal City Plaza
Universal City, CA 91608
(818) 777-4000

MCA Records, Inc.
445 Park Avenue
New York, NY 10022
(212) 605-0665

MCA Records, Inc.
1701 West End Avenue
Nashville, TN 37203
(615) 244-8944

Mercury Records
(div. of PolyGram Records, Inc.)
810 Seventh Avenue
New York, NY 10019
(212) 333-8000

Mercury Records
(div. of PolyGram Records, Inc.)
8335 Sunset Boulevard
Los Angeles, CA 90069
(213) 656-3003

Motown Record Corp.
6255 Sunset Boulevard
Hollywood, CA 90028
(213) 468-3500

MTM Music Group
21 Music Square East
Nashville, TN 37203
(615) 242-1931

Polydor
(div. of PolyGram Records, Inc.)
810 Seventh Avenue
New York, NY 10019
(212) 333-8000

Polydor
(div. of PolyGram Records, Inc.)
3800 Alameda, Suite 1500
Burbank, CA 91505
(818) 955-5200

Profile Records
740 Broadway, 7th Floor
New York, NY 10003
(212) 529-2600

QWEST Records
7250 Beverly Boulevard, Suite 207
Los Angeles, CA 90036
(213) 934-4711

RCA
1133 Avenue of the Americas
New York, NY 10036
(212) 930-4000

RCA
6363 Sunset Boulevard
Hollywood, CA 90028
(213) 468-4000

RCA-Ariola International
30 Muisc Square West
Nashville, TN 37203
(615) 664-1200

Reprise Records
3300 Warner Boulevard
Burbank, CA 91505
(818) 846-9090

Scotti Bros. Records
2114 Pico Boulevard
Santa Monica, CA 90405
(213) 450-3193

Sire Records Co.
c/o Warner Bros.
75 Rockefeller Plaza
New York, NY 10019
(212) 484-6800

Solar Records
1635 North Cahuenga Boulevard
Hollywood, CA 90028
(213) 461-0390

T.C. Records
121 Meadowbrook Drive
Summerville, NJ 08876
(201) 359-5110

Virgin
(div. of CBS Records, Inc.)
30 West 23rd Street, 11th Floor
New York, NY 10010
(212) 463-0980

Virgin
(div. of CBS Records, Inc.)
9247 Alden Drive
Beverly Hills, CA 90210
(213) 278-1181

Warner Bros. Records, Inc.
3300 Warner Boulevard
Burbank, CA 91505
(818) 846-9090

Warner Bros. Records, Inc.
75 Rockefeller Plaza, 20th Floor
New York, NY 10019
(212) 484-6800

Warner Bros. Records, Inc.
P.O. Box 120897
Nashville, TN 37212
(615) 320-7525

ARTISTS AND THEIR MANAGERS

Anita Baker
B & B Associates
604 North Crescent Drive
Beverly Hills, CA 90212
(213) 275-7020

Beach Boys
Management III
9744 Wilshire Boulevard, 4th Floor
Beverly Hills, CA 90212
(213) 550-7100

Bee Gees
Borman Sternberg Entertainment
9220 Sunset Boulevard, Suite 320
West Hollywood, CA 90069
(213) 859-9292

Regina Belle
Worldwide Entertainment Complex
641 Lexington Avenue, 14th Floor
New York, NY 10022
(212) 759-1693

George Benson
Fritz-Turner Management
648 North Robertson
Los Angeles, CA 90069
(213) 854-6488

T. Graham Brown
Starbound Management
1516 16th Avenue, S.
Nashville, TN 10022
(615) 298-1501

Peabo Bryson
David Franklin
Omni International, Suite 1290
Atlanta, GA 30303
(404) 688-2233

Belinda Carlisle
Gold Space Management
Suite 470
3575 Cahuenga Boulevard West
Los Angeles, CA 90068
(213) 850-5660

Belinda Carlisle
Gold Space Management
120 W. 44th Street, Suite 608
New York, NY 10036
212-840-6011

Lane Caudell
Nelson Larkin Productions
1233 17th Avenue
S. Nashville, TN 37212
(615) 255-7744

Ray Charles
Ray Charles Enterprises
2107 W. Washington Boulevard
Los Angeles, CA 90018
(213) 737-8000

Rosanne Cash
Side One Management
1775 Broadway
New York, NY 10019
(212) 307-1015

Kim Carnes
Kragen Management
1112 North Shearborn Drive
West Hollywood, CA 90069
(213) 854-4400

Stanley Clarke
Carolyn Clark Management
8817 Rangeley
Los Angeles, CA 90048
(213) 273-5687

Natalie Cole
B & B Associates
604 North Crescent Drive
Beverly Hills, CA 90212
(213) 275-7020

Sheena Easton
Harriet Wasserman Management
Suite 490
3575 Cahuenga Blvd. West
Los Angeles, CA 90068
(213) 850-5660

Samantha Fox
Zomba Productions, Ltd.
Zomba House, 185-187
Willesden, London NW10 England
(01) 459-8899

Aretha Franklin
Cecil Franklin
16919 Stansbury
Detroit, MI 48231
(313) 341-3743

Glenn Frey
Fitzgerald-Hartley
7250 Beverly Blvd., Suite 200
Los Angeles, CA 90036
(213) 934-8002

Janie Fricke
Jackson & Co.
P.O. Box 798
Lancaster, TX 75146
(214) 223-2441

Crystal Gayle
Gayle Enterprises
51 Music Square East
Nashville, TN 37203
(615) 324-2651

Terri Gibbs
Progressive Management
947 Wingrove Drive
Nashville, TN 37203
(615) 321-0586

Gary Glenn
Henry Marx Management
c/o Grand Trine
9229 Sunset Blvd., Suite 720
Los Angeles, CA 90069
(213) 650-7579

Emmy Lou Harris
Mark Rothbaum Associates
P.O. Box 2689
Danbury, CT 06813
(203) 792-2400

Nona Hendryx
Vickie Wickham
130 West 47th Street
New York, NY 10019
(212) 977-3170

Howard Hewett
Shankman-DeBlasio
2434 Main Street, Suite 202
Santa Monica, CA 90405
(213) 399-7744

Whitney Houston
Galaxy Artist Management
410 E. 50th Street
New York, NY 10022
(212) 319-3880

Englebert Humperdinck
John Smythe
555 N. Broadway, #105
Jericho, NY 11753
(516) 938-1333

Billy Idol
Demann Entertainment
9200 Sunset Boulevard
West Hollywood, CA 90069
(213) 550-8200

Freddie Jackson
Hush Productions
231 West 58th Street, 2nd Floor
New York, NY 10019
(212) 582-1095

Al Jarreau
Pat Raines and Associates
9034 Sunset Boulevard, Suite 250
Los Angeles, CA 90069
(213) 550-6132

Waylon Jennings
Mark Rothbaum Associates
P.O. Box 2689
Danbury, CT 06813
(203) 792-2400

Ricki Lee Jones
Pat Raines and Associates
9034 Sunset Boulevard, Suite 250
West Hollywood, CA 90069
(213) 550-6132

The Judds
Ken Stilts Co.
P.O. Box 17087
Nashville, TN 37217
(615) 754-6100

The Kendalls
World Class Talent, Inc.
1522 Demonbreun Street
Nashville, TN 37203
(615) 244-1964

Chaka Khan
Burt Zell Management
17251 Avenida de la Herradura
Pacific Palisades, CA 90222
(213) 459-8107

Evelyn 'Champagne' King
Bob Schwaid
119 W. 57th Street
New York, NY 10019
(212) 541-5580

Kiss
Glickman/Marks Management
655 Madison Avenue
New York, NY 10021
(212) 752-7455

Patti LaBelle
Gallin-Morey Associates
8730 Sunset Blvd., Penthouse West
West Hollywood, CA 90069
(213) 659-5593

Stacy Lattisaw
Buddy Allen Management, Inc.
65 West 55th Street, Suite 6C
New York, NY 10019
(212) 581-8988

Cyndi Lauper
Dave Wolff
65 West 55th Street, Suite 4G
New York, NY 10019
(212) 977-9340

Levert
Harry J. Coombs
110-112 Lantoga Road, Apt. D
Wayne, PA 19087
(215) 254-0152

Huey Lewis & The News
Bob Brown
P.O. Box 779
Mill Valley, CA 94942
(415) 381-0181

Gloria Loring
The Craig Co.
8485 Melrose Place, Suite E
West Hollywood, CA 90069
(213) 655-0236

Loretta Lynn
Buckskin Management
7 Music Circle North
Nashville, TN 37203
(615) 259-2599

Madonna
Demann Entertainment
9200 Sunset Boulevard
West Hollywood, CA 90069
(213) 550-8200

Manhattan Transfer
Avnet Management
3805 West Magnolia
Burbank, CA 91505
(818) 841-2500

The Manhattans
Worldwide Entertainment Complex
641 Lexington Avenue, 14th Floor
New York, NY 10022
(212) 759-1693

Barry Manilow
Stilleto, Ltd.
P.O. Box 69180
West Hollywood, CA 90069
(213) 650-8560

Reba McEntire
Bill Carter Management
1114 17th Avenue South, Suite 101
Nashville, TN 37212
(615) 327-1270

Charly McClain
John Lentz
P.O. Box 2757
Nashville, TN 37219
(615) 244-4994

Glenn Medeiros
Carefree Management
1800 Main Street
Buffalo, NY 14208
(716) 883-9520

George Michael
Lippman Kahane Enterprises
9669 Oakpass Road
Beverly Hills, CA 90210
(213) 858-0585

Stephanie Mills
Starlight Management
5807 Topanga Canyon Blvd., #D105
Woodland Hills, CA 91367
(818) 716-1377

Eddie Money
Bill Graham Productions
P.O. Box 1994
San Francisco, CA 94101
(415) 884-0815

Eddie Money
Bill Graham Productions
34 East 64th Street
New York, NY 10021
(212) 371-8770

Anne Murray
Balmur, Ltd.
4881 Yonge Street, #412
Toronto, Ontario M2N 5XS Canada
(416) 223-7700

New Edition
Guardian Productions
161 West 54th Street
New York, NY 10019
(212) 581-5398

Olivia Newton-John
Roger Davies Management
3575 Cahuenga Blvd. West, Suite 580
Los Angeles, CA 90068
(213) 850-0662

Stevie Nicks
Frontline Management
80 Universal City Plaza, 4th Floor
Universal City, CA 91608
(818) 777-6000

The Nylons
Headquarters Entertainment Corporation
157 Princess Street, Suite 300
Toronto, Ontario M5A 4M4
Canada
(416) 363-7363

Dolly Parton
Gallin-Morey Associates
8730 Sunset Blvd., Penthouse West
Los Angeles, CA 90069
(213) 659-5593

Pointer Sisters
Gallin-Morey Associates
8730 Sunset Blvd., Penthouse West
Los Angeles, CA 90069
(213) 659-5593

Prince
Cavallo-Ruffalo-Fragnou
11355 W. Olympic Blvd., Suite 555
Los Angeles, CA 90064
(213) 473-1564

Kenny Rogers
Kragen & Co.
112 North Sherbourne Drive
West Hollywood, CA 90069
(213) 854-4400

Diana Ross
RTC Management
780 3rd Avenue, Suite 3003
New York, NY 10017
(212) 758-6655

Schuyler/Knobloch & Bickhardt
Tangerine Music Group
1101 17th Avenue South
Nashville, TN 37212
(615) 329-0436

T.G. Sheppard
Scotti Bros.
2114 Pico Boulevard
Santa Monica, CA 90405
(213) 450-9797

Lynyrd Skynyrd
Boyland Management
Box 50853
Nashville, TN 37505
(615) 386-9626

Starship
Grunt Records
2400 Fulton Street
San Francisco, CA 94118
(415) 668-2326

38 Special
Mark Spector
850 Seventh Avenue, Suite 105
New York, NY 10019
(212) 315-1410

B.J. Thomas
Rainsong Productions
P.O. Box 120003
Arlington, TX 76012
(817) 261-3021

Randy Travis
Elizabeth Hatcher
1610 18th Avenue South
Nashville, TN 37212
(615) 885-1540

Tanya Tucker
Joe Tucker
P.O. Box 816
Brentwood, TN 37027
(615) 373-3087

Tina Turner
Roger Davies Management
3575 Cahuenga Blvd West, Suite 580
Los Angeles, CA 90068
(213) 850-0662

Luther Vandross
Alive Entertainment
1775 Broadway, Suite 2120
New York, NY 10019
(212) 977-8780

Gino Vanelli
Pat Raines & Associates
9034 Sunset Blvd., Suite 250
West Hollywood, CA 90069
(213) 550-8132

Suzanne Vega
A.G.F. Entertainment
1500 Broadway, Suite 2805
New York, NY 10036
(212) 221-2400

Billy Vera & The Beaters
Gallin-Morey Associates
8730 Sunset Boulevard
Penthouse West
Los Angeles, CA 90069
(213) 659-5593

John Waite
Frontline Management
80 Universal City Plaza
Universal City, CA 91608
(818) 777-6006

Jennifer Warnes
Gary George Management
8370 Wilshire Blvd., Suite 310
Beverly Hills, CA 90211
(213) 658-5786

Deniece Williams
D.W. Enterprises
P.O. Box 3853
Beverly Hills, CA 90212
(213) 476-6471

Shanice Wilson
Bill Dern
8455 Fountain Avenue
Los Angeles, CA 90069
(213) 650-5369

Tom Wopat
Brokaw Co.
9255 Sunset Boulevard, Suite 706
West Hollywood, CA 90069
(213) 273-2060

Tammy Wynette
Tammy Wynette Enterprises
1800 Grand Avenue
Nashville, TN 37212
(615) 321-5308

RECORD PRODUCERS

Brian Ahern
Happysack Productions
5102 Vineland Avenue
North Hollywood, CA 91601
(818) 761-0511

Ron and Howard Albert
Fat Albert Productions
1735 Northeast 149th Street
Miami, FL 33161
(305) 947-5611

Ray Baker
49 Music Square East
Nashville, TN 37203
(615) 329-1323

Steve Barri
Starsong Productions
4545 Dempsey Avenue
Encino, CA 91536
(818) 906-2257

Barry Beckett
c/o Warner Bros. Records
P.O. Box 120897
Nashville, TN 37212
(615) 320-7525

Tony Bongiovi
Power Station Studios
441 West 53rd Street
New York, NY 10019
(212) 246-2900

Jim Bowen
c/o MCA Recaords
1514 South Street
Nashville, TN 37212
(615) 244-8944

Steve Buckingham
c/o CBS Records
34 Music Square East
Nashville, TN 37203
(615) 742-4321

Peter Bunetta
c/o Ripe Productions
4121 Wilshire Boulevard, Suite 215
Los Angeles, CA 90010
(213) 385-0882

Tony Camillo Productions
121 Meadowbrook Drive
Summerville, NJ 08876
(201) 359-5110

Boomer Castleman
Box 120723
Nashville, TN 37212
(615) 776-2343

Ron Chancey
824 19th Avenue South
Nashville, TN 37203
(615) 329-0331

Mike Chapman c/o Dreamland Records
8920 West Olympic Boulevard
Beverly Hills, CA 90211
(213) 550-3980

Rick Chertoff
c/o CBS Records
51 West 52nd Street
New York, NY 10019
(212) 975-4321

Jerry Crutchfield
1114 17th Avenue South
Nashville, TN 37212
(615) 327-4622

Rick Chudacoff
c/o RIPE PROD'NS.
4121 Wilshire Boulevard, Suite 215
Los Angeles, CA 90010
(213) 385-0882

George Duke
c/o Herb Cohen
5831 Sunset Boulevard
West Hollywood, CA 90028
(213) 461-3277

Keith Diamond
c/o Steven R. Rand, Esq.
1180 Avenue of the Americas, 12th Floor
New York, NY 10036
(212) 944-7575

Tom Dowd
c/o Tom Dowd Productions
2000 S. Bayshore Drive
Coconut Grove, FL 33133
(305) 285-0252

Keith Forsey
c/o Stuart Silfen, P.C.
485 Madison Avenue, 17th Floor
New York, NY 10022
(212) 980-0145

Rob Galbraith
c/o Headline Int'l. Talent
12 Music Circle South
Nashville, TN 37203
(615) 256-7585

Kenneth Gamble
309 South Broad Street
Philadelphia, PA 19107
(215) 548-3510

Val Garay
c/o Record One Studios
13849 Ventura Boulevard
Sherman Oaks, CA 91423
(818) 907-6381

Quincy Jones
c/o Qwest Records
7250 Beverly Boulevard, Suite 207
Los Angeles, CA 90036
(213) 934-4508

Kashif
c/o Raymond Kate Ent.
9255 Sunset Boulevard
Los Angeles, CA 90069
(213) 273-4211

Jerry Kennedy
54 Music Square East
Nashville, TN 37203
(615) 256-7648

Richard Landis
6856 Los Altos Place
Los Angeles, CA 90028
(213) 876-3820

Kyle Lehning
c/o Morning Star Studios
155 Saunders Ferry Road
Hendersonville, TN 37075
(615) 824-9439

Brent Maher
Creative Workshop
2804 Azalea Place
Nashville, TN 37204
(615) 385-0670

Arif Mardin
c/o Atlantic Records
75 Rockefeller Plaza
New York, NY 10019
(212) 484-6000

Nick Martinelli
c/o GFA
218 South 16th Street, Suite 300
Box 50
Philadelphia, PA 19103
(215) 735-2800

Michael Masser
c/o Devonshire Sound
10729 Magonlia
North Hollywood, CA 91601
(818) 985-1945

Eddie Money
c/o Bill Graham Prod'ns.
201 11th Street
San Francisco, CA 94103
(415) 864-0815

Bob Montgomery
c/o Tree Publishing
P.O. Box 1273
Nashville, TN 37212
(615) 726-0890

James Mtume
c/o Ifland/Mtume, Inc.
50 Park Place, Suite 1419
Newark, NJ 07102
(201) 642-3818

Ron Nevison
c/o Michael Lippman
9669 Oak Pass Road
Beverly Hills, CA 90210
(213) 858-0585

Richard Perry
5505 Melrose Avenue
Los Angeles, CA 90038
(213) 464-4757

Don Powell
708 N. First Street, Suite 135
Minneapolis, MN 55401
(612) 339-9880

Turley Richards
Tur-Rich Prod'ns.
707 Brightwood Place
Louisville, KY 40207
(502) 893-6023

Marti Sharron
c/o Richard Leher, Esq.
11377 W. Olympic Blvd., Suite 900
Los Angeles, CA 90064
(213) 312-3167

Billy Sherill
1022B 18th Avenue South
Nashville, TN 37212
(615) 321-4544

George Tobin
Studio Sound Recorders
11337 Burbank Boulevard
N. Hollywood, CA 91608
(818) 506-4487

Narada Michael Walden
c/o Perfection Light Prod'ns.
1925 Francisco Boulevard
San Rafael, CA 94901
(415) 459-1111

John Waite
c/o Frontline Management
80 Universal City Plaza
Universal City, CA 91608
(818) 777-6006

Tom Waits
c/o Ellen Smith
Island Records
14 E. 4th Street, 3rd Floor
New York, NY 10012
(212) 477-8000

Richie Zito
c/o Lippman Kahane Ent.
9669 Oak Pass Road
Beverly Hills, CA 90210
(213) 858-0585

MUSIC PUBLISHERS

Acuff-Rose Publications, Inc.
c/o Opryland Music Group
P.O. Box 40427
Nashville, TN 37204
(615) 385-3031

Fred Ahlert Music Corporation
8150 Beverly Boulevard, Suite 202
Los Angeles, CA 90048
(213) 652-5131

Almo Music Corporation
1358 North LaBrea Avenue
Hollywood, CA 90028
(213) 469-2411

Almo Music Corporation
c/o Rondor Group
1904 Adelcia Street
Nashville, TN 37212
(615) 321-0820

Arista Music Publishing Group
8370 Wilshire Boulevard
Beverly Hills, CA 90211
(213) 655-9222

Irving Berlin Music Corporation
1290 Avenue of the Americas
New York, NY 10019
(212) 247-4200

The Bicycle Music Company
8075 West Third Street, Suite 400
Los Angeles, CA 90048
(213) 659-6361

Bourne Company
437 Fifth Avenue
New York, NY 10016
(212) 575-1800

Boyland Music Group
Box 50853
Nashville, TN 37205
(615) 386-9626

Buckhorn Music Publishing Co.
1007 17th Avenue South
Nashville, TN 37212
(615) 327-4590

Bug Music
6777 Hollywood Boulevard
Hollywood, CA 90028
(213) 466-4352

CBS Music
51 West 52nd Street
New York, NY 10019
(212) 975-4321

Cedarwood Publishing Co., Inc.
39 Music Square East
Nashville, TN 37203
(615) 255-6535

Chrysalis Music
9255 Sunset Boulevard
West Hollywood, CA 90069
(213) 550-0171

Chrysalis Music
645 Madison Avenue
New York, NY 10022
(212) 758-3555

Col Gems—EMI (ASCAP)
(see Screen Gems)

Cookhouse Music
1204 16th Avenue South
Nashville, TN 37203
(615) 320-0307

Collins Court Music
P.O. Box 121407
25 Music Square West
Nashville, TN 37212
(615) 255-5550

Cotillion Music, Inc., Walden Music
75 Rockefeller Plaza
New York, NY 10019
(212) 484-6000

Creative Entertainment (BMI)
6290 Sunset Boulevard, #1700
Hollywood, CA 90028
(213) 463-5661

Criterion Music Corporation
6124 Selma Avenue
Hollywood, CA 90029
(213) 469-2296

Criterion Music Corporation
1025 17th Avenue South
Nashville, TN 37212
(615) 327-2146

Dejamus
63 Music Square East
Nashville, TN 37203
(615) 320-7870

Dewalden Music
6255 Sunset Boulevard, Suite 1911
Hollywood, CA 90028
(213) 462-1922

Fame (BMI)
603 East Avalon Avenue
P.O. Box 2527
Muscle Shoals, AL 35662
(205) 381-0801

Famous Music Corporation
1 Gulf & Western Plaza
New York, NY 10023
(212) 333-3433

Famous Music Corporation
6430 Sunset Boulevard
Hollywood, CA 90028
(213) 461-3091

Famous Music Corporation
1233 17th Avenue South
Nashville, TN 37212
(615) 329-0500

The Fricon Entertainment Co., Inc.
1048 S. Ogden Street
Los Angeles, CA 90019
(213) 931-7323

House of Cash
700 Johnny Cash Highway
Henderson, TN 38340
(615) 824-5110

Geffen Music
9130 Sunset Boulevard
West Hollywood, CA 90069
(213) 278-9010

Island Music
6525 Sunset Boulevard, 2nd Floor
Hollywood, CA 90028
(213) 469-1285

Jack Music, Inc.
P.O. Box 120477
Nashville, TN 37212
(615) 383-0330

Jobete Music Co., Inc.
6255 Sunset Boulevard
Hollywood, CA 90028
(213) 468-3400

Katrina Music Publishing Company
1 Commerce Square, Suite 1590
Memphis, TN 38103
(901) 523-0533

Paul Leka Music
Connecticut Recording
1122 Main Street
Bridgeport, CT 06604
(203) 366-9168

Lowery Music Company, Inc.
3051 Clairmont Road, N.E.
Atlanta, GA 30359
(404) 325-0832

Marsaint Music
3809 Clematis Avenue
New Orleans, LA 70122
(504) 949-8386

MCA Music
1755 Broadway
New York, NY 10019
(212) 841-8000

MCA Music
70 Universal City Plaza
Universal City, CA 91608
(818) 777-1000

MCA Music
1114 17th Avenue South, Suite 205
Nashville, TN 37212
(615) 327-4622

Merit Music
P.O. Box 121524
Nashville, TN 37212
(615) 297-0900

Mighty Three Music
309 South Broad Street
Philadelphia, PA 19107
(215) 546-3510

Ivan Mogull Music Corporation
721 5th Avenue
New York, NY 10022
(212) 355-5636

MTM Music Group
21 Music Square East
Nashville, TN 37203
(615) 242-1931

National League Music
3575 Cahuenga Blvd. West, Suite 650
Los Angeles, CA 90068
(213) 969-8133

Michael O'Connor Music
P.O. Box 1869
Studio City, CA 91604
(213) 762-7551

Peer International Corporation
8159 Hollywood Boulevard
Los Angeles, CA 90069
(213) 656-0364

Peer International Corporation
810 7th Avenue
New York, NY 10019
(212) 265-3910

George Pincus & Sons Music Corporation
1650 Broadway
New York, NY 10019
(212) 245-0110

Polygram Music Publishing
3800 Alameda
Burbank, CA 91505
(818) 955-5200

Polygram Music Publishing
810 7th Avenue
New York, NY 10019
(212) 333-8000

Dave Rubinson and Friends
1734 Fell Street
San Francisco, CA 94117
(415) 777-2930

SBK Songs (formerly CBS Songs)
49 E. 52nd Street
New York, NY 10022
(212) 975-4886

SBK Songs
8800 Sunset Boulevard
Los Angeles, CA 90069
(213) 652-8078

SBK Songs
35 Music Square East
Nashville, TN 37203
(615) 742-8081

Screen Gems—EMI Music, Inc.
1370 Avenue of the Americas
New York, NY 10019
(212) 489-6740

Screen Gems—EMI Music, Inc.
6920 Sunset Boulevard
Hollywood, CA 90028
(213) 469-8371

Screen Gems—EMI Music, Inc.
1207 16th Avenue South
Nashville, TN 37212
(615) 320-7700

Scotti Brothers Music
2114 Pico Boulevard
Santa Monica, CA 90405
(213) 450-3193

September Music Corporation
250 West 57th Street
New York, NY 10022
(212) 581-1338

Shapiro, Bernstein & Co., Inc.
10 East 53rd Street
New York, NY 10022
(212) 751-3395

Shelby Singleton Music, Inc.
3106 Belmont Boulevard
Nashville, TN 37212
(615) 385-1960

Southern Writers Group
2804 Azelea Place
P.O. Box 40764
Nashville, TN 37204
(615) 383-8682

Tree Publishing (BMI)
P.O. Box 1273
Nashville, TN 37202
(615) 726-0890

Warner/Chappell Music, Inc.
9000 Sunset Boulevard, Penthouse
Los Angeles, CA 90069
(213) 273-3323

Warner/Chappell Music, Inc.
810 7th Avenue
New York, NY 10019
(212) 399-6910

Warner/Chappell Music, Inc.
44 Music Square West
Nashville, TN 37203
(615) 254-8777

Welk Music Group
1299 Ocean Avenue, Suite 800
Santa Monica, CA 90401
(213) 451-5727

Welk Music Group
54 Music Square East
Nashville, TN 37203
(615) 256-7648

Window Music Publishing Co., Inc.
809 18th Avenue South
Nashville, TN 37203
(615) 327-3211

The Writers Group
P.O. Box 120555
Nashville, TN 37212
(615) 327-9299

COMMONLY USED FORMS OF THE
PERFORMING RIGHTS SOCIETIES

APPLICATION FOR PUBLISHER-MEMBERSHIP
IN THE
AMERICAN SOCIETY of COMPOSERS, AUTHORS and PUBLISHERS
One Lincoln Plaza, New York, N.Y. 10023

I(we) hereby apply for membership, as a ☐ Standard/☐ Popular Production Music Publisher, in the American Society of Composers, Authors and Publishers. If elected I(we) agree to be bound by the Society's Articles of Association as now is effect, and as they may be amended, and I(we) agree to execute agreements in such form and for such periods as the Board of Directors shall have approved or shall hereafter approve for all members.

The following information is submitted in support of this application:

1. Firm Name _____

2. Business address _____

_____
City   State   Zip Code

Telephone Number (   ) _____

3. Check and complete one of the following to indicate organization of company:

A. CORPORATION ☐ Corporate I.D. No. _____
State of Incorporation _____ Date of Charter _____

Name	Stockholders (list all stockholders)	Soc. Sec. No.	Home Address & Zip Code	Percentage of Ownership

Name	Officers (list all officers)	Soc. Sec. No.	Home Address & Zip Code	Office Held

B. PARTNERSHIP ☐ (list all partners) Year Business Established _____

Name		Soc. Sec. No.	Home Address & Zip Code	Percentage of Ownership

C. INDIVIDUAL OWNERSHIP ☐ Year Business Established _____

Name _____ Soc. Sec. No. _____

Home Address _____
Street Address   City   State   Zip Code

If owner is or has been a member or affiliate of ASCAP, BMI or SESAC, or of a foreign performing right licensing organization please state the name of the organization with which owner is affiliated and relationship _____

If publishing company, please indicate firm name _____

4. Cities in Which Branch Offices Are Maintained

City	State	Street Address	Area Code & Telephone #

5. If any owner, stockholder, officer, or employee with any executive responsibilities, has been or is now connected with any publishing company, songwriter's agency, recording company, performance rights licensing organization (as an employee), or any other organization engaged in the solicitation, publication or exploitation of music, please fill in the information requested below:

Name of Individual	Telephone	Name of Company	If Publishing Company Indicate Performance Rights Affiliation	Position Held	Years of Association

6. If you have made, or intend to make, any charge to an author (lyricist), or composer in connection with the examination, publication, recording or exploitation of any composition published or to be published by you, please state the nature of the charge and the service to be performed.

_____

7. I (we) have read ASCAP's Articles of Association and make this application with full knowledge of their contents. I (we) understand that any agreement entered into between ASCAP and me (us) will be in reliance upon the information contained in this application and attached schedules I (we) understand that the agreement will be subject to cancellation if any information contained in this application is not fully and correctly provided or if the true name of each owner, stockholder and officer is not provided as requested.

_____
Firm Name

_____
By

_____
Title

Date _____ _____ _____
     month day year

DO NOT FILL IN BELOW
_____

Received: _____

DESIGNATION OF PUBLISHER REPRESENTATIVE

Section 11 of Article III of the Society's Articles of Association provides that:

"Each publisher member, if a co-partnership, firm, association or corporation shall file with the secretary of the Society, from time to time, the name of a person who shall be deemed to be its representative in the Society for all purposes, and wherever in these Articles of Association there shall be reference to publisher members relating to election as directors, holding other office or serving in any other capacities, the same shall have reference to such representatives. If a co-partnership or firm, such representative shall be a member thereof and if an association or corporation, such representative shall be an officer thereof. No such co-partnership, firm, association or corporation shall have more than one representative at any one time. Such designation may be revoked at any time by notice in writing given to the Society provided that a new representative shall be named, subject to the restrictions above contained."

In accordance with the above, if you are a co-partnership, firm, association or corporation, please indicate below the name of your representative, whose signature must also appear on the line indicated.

_____

Publisher *(Please Print)*

_____

Name of Representative *(Please Print)*
and Title

_____

Signature of Representative

_____

Date

WARRANTY LETTER

American Society of Composers,
    Authors and Publishers
One Lincoln Plaza
New York, New York 10023

Gentlemen:

I (we) make the following representations:

1. Schedule A attached is a true and correct list of the domestic copyrighted musical compositions owned by me (us) as of this date.

2. Schedule B attached is a true and correct list of the foreign copyrights of which performing rights for the United States are owned by me (us) (showing in each case the countries represented by me (us)).

I (we) hereby represent that there are no existing assignments or licenses, direct or indirect, of non-dramatic performing rights in or to any of the works listed on Schedules A and B except for the assignments or licenses of which I (we) have attached true copies.

_____

Firm Name

_____

By

_____

Title

SCHEDULE A

List of Domestic Copyrighted Musical Compositions Owned by the Applicant

TITLE	YEAR OF COPYRIGHT	COMPOSER	AUTHOR	PUBLISHER*

Note: — For works based on compositions in the public domain, the title, author and composer of the public domain source must be indicated.

*To be filled out only if the work was not originally published by applicant, but by another publisher from whom applicant has obtained the copyright by assignment, purchase or otherwise. A copy of the assignment, sales contract or similar document also should be forwarded to the Society.

SCHEDULE B

List of Foreign Copyrights of which Performing Rights for the United States are owned by Applicant.

(Please indicate in each case the countries represented by applicant.)

TITLE	COUNTRY REPRESENTED*	COMPOSER	AUTHOR

*For instance, if applicant sub-publishes the work for the United States and Canada, then those countries should be indicated in this column. Do not list the country of the original publisher.

Clearance Form

Broadcast Music, Inc., 320 West 57th Street, New York, N.Y. 10019
Att. Clearance Department

COMPLETE FORM IN ACCORDANCE WITH INSTRUCTIONS ON THE
REVERSE SIDE AND RETURN BOTH COPIES TO BMI. DO NOT USE
THIS FORM TO CORRECT OR REVISE INFORMATION ON A PRE-
VIOUSLY CLEARED WORK. SEND DETAILS IN A LETTER.

**FOR BMI USE
DO NOT WRITE BELOW**

ENTERED VIA SCOPE

DATE: _____

BY: _____

TITLE — ONE WORK PER FORM

	Credit Rate	Mulpt Credit	Clear-ance	BMI	Log U.S./Can.

IF BASED ON PUBLIC DOMAIN - GIVE ORIGINAL TITLE, WRITER AND SOURCE

CHECK IF WORK IS FROM:
☐ MOTION PICTURE OR TV FILM
☐ BROADWAY SHOW
☐ OFF-BROADWAY SHOW

GIVE TITLE OF PICTURE, FILM OR SHOW
(SEE REVERSE SIDE)

WRITER(S) NAME(S)			WRITER(S) ADDRESS(ES)	Perf. Rts. Orgn.	Percentage Share	Mode of Pay-ment	WR
LAST	FIRST	MIDDLE					
SOC. SEC. NO.							
SOC. SEC. NO.							
SOC. SEC. NO.							
SOC. SEC. NO.							
SOC. SEC. NO.							

PUBLISHER(S) NAME(S)

☐ CHECK HERE IF NO RIGHTS GRANTED BY WRITER(S) TO ANY PUBLISHER.
☐ CHECK HERE IF PUBLISHER IS ADMINISTRATOR ONLY. DO NOT CHECK THIS BOX IF
PUBLISHER OWNS PART OR ALL OF COPYRIGHT AND/OR PERFORMING RIGHTS.
NAME(S) OF U.S. ORIGINAL PUBLISHER(S):

	Perf. Rts. Orgn.	Percentage Share	Credit U.S.	Can.	Orig. Pub.	World Rights

IF WORK IS OF FOREIGN ORIGIN, COMPLETE BELOW AND ATTACH AN ADDITIONAL
COPY OF THIS FORM:
U.S. SUB–PUBLISHER(S): (PLEASE GIVE TERRITORIES)

FULL NAME OF FOREIGN ORIGINAL PUBLISHER:

PLEASE DO NOT SUBMIT NON-MUSICAL WORKS. THEY CANNOT
BE CLEARED BY BMI. FOR SPOKEN WORD MATERIAL WITH A
MUSICAL BACKGROUND, SEE INSTRUCTIONS ON REVERSE SIDE.

TYPE OR PRINT NAME AND ADDRESS OF SUBMITTING BMI AFFILIATE.

MAIL
CONFIRM-
ATION
TO:

RECORD LABEL & NO. OF 1ST RECORD RELEASE

ARTIST   RELEASE DATE

DATE SUBMITTED TO BMI

AUTHORIZED SIGNATURE

CLEARED   IN   ACCORDANCE   WITH   TERMS   ON   REVERSE   SIDE

APPLICATION FOR PUBLISHER AFFILIATION

| **BROADCAST MUSIC, INC.**
Publisher Administration
10 Music Square East
Nashville, TN 37203
615-259-3625 | **BROADCAST MUSIC, INC.**
Performing Rights Administration
320 West 57th Street
New York, NY 10019
212-586-2000 | **BROADCAST MUSIC, INC.**
Publisher Administration
8730 Sunset Blvd., 3rd Fl. W.
Los Angeles, CA 90069-2211
213-659-9109 |

NOTE:

ALL QUESTIONS MUST BE ANSWERED.
APPLICATION MUST BE SIGNED ON LAST PAGE AND RETURNED TO
THE BMI OFFICE FROM WHICH IT WAS RECEIVED WITH A $25.00
CHECK OR MONEY ORDER FOR ADMINISTRATION FEE. (NOTE:
THIS AMOUNT IS NOT REFUNDABLE.)

FEE (for BMI use)

☐ CHECK

☐ MONEY ORDER

REC'D _____

1. NAME OF YOUR PROPOSED PUBLISHING COMPANY:

(In order to eliminate confusion it is necessary to reject any name identical with, or similar to, that of
an established publishing company. Also, any name using INITIALS as part of your company name
cannot be accepted.)

1st Choice: _____

2nd Choice: _____

3rd Choice: _____

4th Choice: _____

5th Choice: _____

2. BUSINESS ADDRESS:

_____

_____

Zip Code

☐☐☐ - ☐☐☐☐☐☐☐

AREA CODE   TELEPHONE NO.

3. LIST <u>ONE COMPOSITION</u> OWNED BY YOUR PUBLISHING COMPANY WHICH HAS BEEN COMMERCIALLY
RECORDED OR IS LIKELY TO BE BROADCAST OR PERFORMED IN CONCERTS OR OTHERWISE PUBLICLY
PERFORMED.

TITLE	FULL NAME(S) OF WRITER(S)	WRITER(S) PERF. RIGHTS AFFILIATION BMI, ASCAP, SESAC OR OTHER	COMMERCIAL RECORDING NAME OF LABEL	RELEASE DATE

IF CUE SHEETS ARE NECESSARY, PLEASE SUBMIT.

10/85

4. COMPLETE A, B OR C TO INDICATE HOW YOUR COMPANY IS ORGANIZED:

A. <u>INDIVIDUALLY OWNED</u>:

Name of Individual _____ Date of Birth _____

Home Address _____ Soc. Sec. No. __ __ __   __ __   __ __ __ __

_____ Zip Code _____

Are you now or have you ever been a writer-member or writer-affiliate of BMI, ASCAP, SESAC, or of any foreign performing rights licensing organization? If so, state name of organization and the period during which you were a member or affiliate.

_____

B. <u>PARTNERSHIP</u>

<u>List all Partners</u>   *If not available, request form S.S.#4 from I.R.S.   *Fed. Tax Acct. No. __ __   __ __ __ __ __ __

NAME	HOME ADDRESS & ZIP CODE	SOC. SEC. NO.	PERCENTAGE OF OWNERSHIP
_____	_____	___ __ ____	_____
	_____		
_____	_____	___ __ ____	_____
	_____		
_____	_____	___ __ ____	_____
	_____		

C. <u>FORMALLY ORGANIZED CORPORATION</u>:   *Fed. Tax Acct. No __ __   __ __ __ __ __ __

*If not available, request form S.S.#4 from I.R.S.

(Complete only if corporation is now in existence)

State in which incorporated _____

PHOTOCOPY OF CERTIFICATE OF INCORPORATION MUST BE SUBMITTED WITH THIS APPLICATION

<u>List All Stockholders</u>

Name	Home Address & Zip Code	Percentage of Ownership
_____	_____	_____
_____	_____	_____
_____	_____	_____

<u>List all Officers</u>

Name	Home Address & Zip Code	Office Held
_____	_____	_____
_____	_____	_____
_____	_____	_____

5. LIST ALL EXECUTIVE EMPLOYEES, FOR EXAMPLE:
   professional manager, contact man, etc.

NAME	HOME ADDRESS & ZIP CODE	POSITION HELD

6. If any owner, stockholder, officer or executive employee has been or is connected with any record company, publishing company, songwriters agency, or any other organization engaged in the solicitation, publication or exploitation of music, please give the following information:

NAME OF INDIVIDUAL	NAME OF COMPANY	IF PUBLISHING CO., IS IT BMI?	POSITION HELD	YEARS OF ASSOCIATION FROM	TO

N O T I C E

IT IS ACKNOWLEDGED THAT ANY CONTRACT CONSUMMATED BETWEEN APPLICANT AND BMI WILL BE ENTERED INTO IN RELIANCE UPON THE REPRESENTATIONS CONTAINED IN THIS APPLICATION AND THE REPRESENTATION THAT ALL OWNERS, INCLUDING PARTNERS, ARE OVER THE AGE OF EIGHTEEN. THE CONTRACT WILL BE SUBJECT TO CANCELLATION IF ANY QUESTION HEREIN CONTAINED IS NOT ANSWERED FULLY AND ACCURATELY OR IF THE TRUE NAME OF EACH OWNER, STOCKHOLDER, OFFICER AND/OR EXECUTIVE EMPLOYEE IS NOT REPORTED IN QUESTIONS 4, 5 and 6 HEREOF.

DATE _____   SIGNATURE _____
                                                          SIGN IN INK

_____
(PLEASE PRINT NAME OF PERSON SIGNING)

242 ∎

BMI

AGREEMENT made on .... between BROADCAST MUSIC, INC.
("BMI"), a New York corporation, whose address is 320 West 57th Street, New York, N.Y. 10019 and

.... doing business as ....

a ....

.... ("Publisher"), whose address is...

....

W I T N E S S E T H :

FIRST: The term of this agreement shall be the period from ....

to ...., and continuing thereafter for additional periods of five (5) years each unless
terminated by either party at the end of such initial period, or any such additional five (5) year period, upon notice
by registered or certified mail not more than six (6) months or less than three (3) months prior to the end of any
such term.

SECOND: As used in this agreement, the word "works" shall mean:

A. All musical compositions (including the musical segments and individual compositions
written for a dramatic or dramatico-musical work) whether published or unpublished, now owned or copyrighted
by Publisher or in which Publisher owns or controls performing rights, and

B. All musical compositions (including the musical segments and individual compositions
written for a dramatic or dramatico-musical work) whether published or unpublished, in which hereafter during
the term Publisher acquires ownership or copyright or ownership or control of the performing rights, from and
after the date of the acquisition by Publisher of such ownership or control.

THIRD: Except as otherwise provided herein, Publisher hereby sells, assigns and transfers to BMI,
its successors or assigns, for the term of this agreement:

A. All the rights which Publisher owns or acquires publicly to perform, and to license others
to perform, anywhere in the world, any part or all of the works.

B. The non-exclusive right to record, and to license others to record, any part or all of any of
the works on electrical transcriptions, wire, tape, film or otherwise, but only for the purpose of performing such
work publicly by means of radio and television or for archive or audition purposes and not for sale to the public or
for synchronization (1) with motion pictures intended primarily for theatrical exhibition or (2) with programs
distributed by means of syndication to broadcasting stations.

C. The non-exclusive right to adapt or arrange any part or all of any of the works for performance purposes, and to license others to do so.

FOURTH:

A. The rights granted to BMI by subparagraph A of paragraph THIRD hereof shall not include
the right to perform or license the performance of more than one song or aria from a dramatic or dramatico-

musical work which is an opera, operetta, or musical show or more than five (5) minutes from a dramatic or dramatico-musical work which is a ballet if such performance is accompanied by the dramatic action, costumes or scenery of that dramatic or dramatico-musical work.

B. Publisher, together with all the writers and co-publishers, if any, shall have the right jointly, by written notice to BMI, to exclude from the grant made by subparagraph A of paragraph THIRD hereof performances of works comprising more than thirty (30) minutes of a dramatic or dramatico-musical work, but this right shall not apply to such performances from (1) a score originally written for and performed as part of a theatrical or television film, (2) a score originally written for and performed as part of a radio or television program, or (3) the original cast, sound track or similar album of a dramatic or dramatico-musical work.

C. Publisher retains the right to issue non-exclusive licenses for performances of a work or works (other than to another performing rights licensing organization), provided that within ten (10) days of the issuance of such license BMI is given written notice of the titles of the works and the nature of the performances so licensed by Publisher.

FIFTH:

A. As full consideration for all rights granted to BMI hereunder and as security therefor, BMI agrees to make the following payments to Publisher with respect to each of the works in which BMI has performing rights:

(1) For performances of works on broadcasting stations in the United States, its territories and possessions BMI will pay amounts calculated pursuant to BMI's then standard practices upon the basis of the then current performance rates generally paid by BMI to its affiliated publishers for similar performances of similar compositions. The number of performances for which Publisher shall be entitled to payment shall be estimated by BMI in accordance with its then current system of computing the number of such performances.

It is acknowledged that BMI licenses the works of its affiliates for performance by non-broadcasting means, but that unless and until such time as feasible methods can be devised for tabulation of and payment for such performances, payment will be based solely on broadcast performances. In the event that during the term of this agreement BMI shall establish a system of separate payment for non-broadcasting performances, BMI shall pay Publisher upon the basis of the then current performance rates generally paid by BMI to its other affiliated publishers for similar performances of similar compositions.

(2) For performances of works outside of the United States, its territories and possessions BMI will pay to Publisher all monies received by BMI in the United States from any performing rights licensing organization which are designated by such organization as the publisher's share of foreign performance royalties earned by any of the works after the deduction of BMI's then current handling charge applicable to its affiliated publishers.

(3) In the case of works which, or rights in which, are owned by Publisher jointly with one or more other publishers who have granted performing rights therein to BMI, the sum payable to Publisher under this subparagraph A shall be a pro rata share determined on the basis of the number of publishers, unless BMI shall have received from Publisher a copy of an agreement or other document signed by all of the publishers providing for a different division of payment.

B. Notwithstanding the foregoing provisions of this paragraph FIFTH, BMI shall have no obligation to make payment hereunder with respect to (1) any performance of a work which occurs prior to the date on which BMI shall have received from Publisher all of the material with respect to such work referred to in subparagraph A of paragraph TENTH hereof, and in the case of foreign performances, the information referred to in subparagraph B of paragraph FOURTEENTH hereof, or (2) any performance as to which a direct license as described in subparagraph C of paragraph FOURTH hereof has been granted by Publisher, its co-publisher or the writer.

SIXTH:. BMI will furnish statements to Publisher at least twice during each year of the term showing the number of performances of the works as computed pursuant to subparagraph A(1) of paragraph FIFTH hereof, and at least once during each year of the term showing the monies received by BMI referred to in subparagraph A(2) of paragraph FIFTH hereof. Each such statement shall be accompanied by payment of the sum thereby shown to be due to Publisher, subject to all proper deductions, if any, for advances or amounts due to BMI from Publisher.

SEVENTH:

A. Nothing in this agreement requires BMI to continue to license the works subsequent to the termination of this agreement. In the event that BMI continues to license any or all of the works, however, BMI shall continue to make payments to Publisher for so long as Publisher does not make or purport to make directly or indirectly any grant of performing rights in such works to any other licensing organization. The amounts of such payments shall be calculated pursuant to BMI's then current standard practices upon the basis of the then current performance rates generally paid by BMI to its affiliated publishers for similar performances of similar compositions. Publisher agrees to notify BMI by registered or certified mail of any grant or purported grant by Publisher directly or indirectly of performing rights to any other performing rights organization within ten (10) days from the making of such grant or purported grant and if Publisher fails so to inform BMI thereof and BMI makes payments to Publisher for any period after the making of any such grant or purported grant, Publisher agrees to repay to BMI all amounts so paid by BMI promptly on demand. In addition, if BMI inquires of Publisher by registered or certified mail, addressed to Publisher's last known address, whether Publisher has made any such grant or purported grant and Publisher fails to confirm to BMI by registered or certified mail within thirty (30) days of the mailing of such inquiry that Publisher has not made any such grant or purported grant, BMI may, from and after such date, discontinue making any payments to Publisher.

B. BMI's obligation to continue payment to Publisher after the termination of this agreement for performances outside of the United States, its territories and possessions shall be dependent upon BMI's receipt in the United States of payments designated by foreign performing rights licensing organizations as the publisher's share of foreign performance royalties earned by any of the works. Payment of such foreign royalties shall be subject to deduction of BMI's then current handling charge applicable to its affiliated publishers.

C. In the event that BMI has reason to believe that Publisher will receive or is receiving payment from a performing rights licensing organization other than BMI for or based on United States performances of one or more of the works during a period when such works were licensed by BMI pursuant to this agreement, BMI shall have the right to withhold payment for such performances from Publisher until receipt of evidence satisfactory to BMI of the amount so paid to Publisher by such other organization or that Publisher has not been so paid. In the event that Publisher has been so paid, the monies payable by BMI to Publisher for such performances during such period shall be reduced by the amount of the payment from such other organization. In the event that Publisher does not supply such evidence within eighteen (18) months from the date of BMI's request therefor, BMI shall be under no obligation to make any payment to Publisher for performances of such works during such period.

EIGHTH: In the event that this agreement shall terminate at a time when, after crediting all earnings reflected by statements rendered to Publisher prior to the effective date of such termination, there remains an unearned balance of advances paid to Publisher by BMI, such termination shall not be effective until the close of the calendar quarterly period during which (A) Publisher shall repay such unearned balance of advances, or (B) Publisher shall notify BMI by registered or certified mail that Publisher has received a statement rendered by BMI at its normal accounting time showing that such unearned balance of advances has been fully recouped by BMI.

NINTH:

A. BMI shall have the right, upon written notice to Publisher, to exclude from this agreement, at any time, any work which in BMI's opinion (1) is similar to a previously existing composition and might constitute a copyright infringement, or (2) has a title or music or lyric similar to that of a previously existing composition and might lead to a claim of unfair competition, or (3) is offensive, in bad taste or against public morals, or (4) is not reasonably suitable for performance.

B. In the case of works which in the opinion of BMI are based on compositions in the public domain, BMI shall have the right, at any time, upon written notice to Publisher, either (1) to exclude any such work from this agreement, or (2) to classify any such work as entitled to receive only a stated fraction of the full credit that would otherwise be given for performances thereof.

C. In the event that any work is excluded from this agreement pursuant to subparagraph A or B of this paragraph NINTH, or pursuant to subparagraph C of paragraph TWELFTH hereof, all rights of BMI in such work shall automatically revert to Publisher ten (10) days after the date of the notice of such exclusion given by BMI to Publisher. In the event that a work is classified for less than full credit under subparagraph B(2) of this paragraph NINTH, Publisher shall have the right, by giving notice to BMI within ten (10) days after the date of BMI's notice to Publisher of the credit allocated to such work, to terminate all rights in such work granted to BMI herein and all such rights of BMI in such work shall revert to Publisher thirty (30) days after the date of such notice from Publisher to BMI.

TENTH:

A. With respect to each of the works which has been or shall be published or recorded commercially or synchronized with motion picture or television film or tape or which Publisher considers likely to be performed, Publisher agrees to furnish to BMI:

(1) Two copies of a completed clearance sheet in the form supplied by BMI, unless a cue sheet with respect to such work is furnished pursuant to subparagraph A(3) of this paragraph TENTH.

(2) If such work is based on a composition in the public domain, a legible lead sheet or other written or printed copy of such work setting forth the lyrics, if any, and music correctly metered; provided that with respect to all other works, such copy need be furnished only if requested by BMI pursuant to subsection (c) of subparagraph D(2) of this paragraph TENTH.

(3) If such work has been or shall be synchronized with or otherwise used in connection with motion picture or television film or tape, a cue sheet showing the title, composers, publisher and nature and duration of the use of the work in such film or tape.

B. Publisher shall submit the material described in subparagraph A of this paragraph TENTH with respect to works heretofore published, recorded or synchronized within ten (10) days after the execution of this agreement and with respect to any of the works hereafter so published, recorded, synchronized or likely to be performed prior to the date of publication or release of the recording, film or tape or anticipated performance.

C. The submission of each clearance sheet or cue sheet shall constitute a warranty by Publisher that all of the information contained thereon is true and correct and that no performing rights in any of the works listed therein has been granted to or reserved by others except as specifically set forth therein.

D. Publisher agrees:

(1) To secure and maintain copyright protection of the works pursuant to the Copyright Law of the United States and pursuant to the laws of such other nations of the world where such protection is

afforded; and to give BMI prompt written notice of the date and number of copyright registration and/or renewal of each work registered in the United States Copyright Office.

(2) At BMI's request:

(a) To register each unpublished and published work in the United States Copyright Office pursuant to the Copyright Law of the United States.

(b) To record in the United States Copyright Office in accordance with the Copyright Law of the United States any agreements, assignments, instruments or documents of any kind by which Publisher obtained the right to publicly perform and/or the right to publish, co-publish or sub-publish any of the works.

(c) To obtain and deliver to BMI copies of: unpublished and published works; copyright registration and/or renewal certificates issued by the United States Copyright Office; any of the documents referred to in sub-section (b) above.

E. Publisher agrees to give BMI prompt notice by registered or certified mail in each instance when, pursuant to the Copyright Law of the United States, (1) the rights granted to BMI by Publisher in any work shall revert to the writer or the writer's representative, or (2) copyright protection of any work shall terminate.

ELEVENTH: Publisher warrants and represents that:

A. Publisher has the right to enter into this agreement; Publisher is not bound by any prior commitments which conflict with its undertakings herein; the rights granted by Publisher to BMI herein are the sole and exclusive property of Publisher and are free from all encumbrances and claims; and exercise of such rights will not constitute infringement of copyright or violation of any right of, or unfair competition with, any person, firm, corporation or association.

B. Except with respect to works in which the possession of performing rights by another person, firm, corporation or association is specifically set forth on a clearance sheet or cue sheet submitted to BMI pursuant to subparagraph A of paragraph TENTH hereof, Publisher has exclusive performing rights in each of the works by virtue of written grants thereof to Publisher signed by all the authors and composers or other owners of such work.

TWELFTH:

A. Publisher agrees to defend, indemnify, save and hold BMI, its licensees, the advertisers of its licensees and their respective agents, servants and employees, free and harmless from and against any and all demands, loss, damage, suits, judgments, recoveries and costs, including counsel fees, resulting from any claim of whatever nature arising from or in connection with the exercise of any of the rights granted by Publisher in this agreement; provided, however, that the obligations of Publisher under this paragraph TWELFTH shall not apply to any matter added to, or changes made in, any work by BMI or its licensees.

B. Upon the receipt by any of the parties herein indemnified of any notice, demand, process, papers, writ or pleading, by which any such claim, demand, suit or proceeding is made or commenced against them, or any of them, which Publisher shall be obliged to defend hereunder, BMI shall, as soon as may be practicable, give Publisher notice thereof and deliver to Publisher such papers or true copies thereof, and BMI shall have the right to participate by counsel of its own choice, at its own expense. Publisher agrees to cooperate with BMI in all such matters.

C. In the event of such notification of claim or service of process on any of the parties herein indemnified, BMI shall have the right, from the date thereof, to exclude the work with respect to which a claim is made from this agreement and/or to withhold payment of all sums which may become due pursuant to this agreement or any modification thereof until receipt of satisfactory written evidence that such claim has been withdrawn, settled or adjudicated.

THIRTEENTH: Publisher makes, constitutes and appoints BMI, or its nominee, Publisher's true and lawful attorney, irrevocably during the term hereof, in the name of BMI or that of its nominee, or in Publisher's name, or otherwise, to do all acts, take all proceedings, and execute, acknowledge and deliver any and all instruments, papers, documents, process or pleadings that may be necessary, proper or expedient to restrain infringement of and/or to enforce and protect the rights granted by Publisher hereunder, and to recover damages in respect of or for the infringement or other violation of the said rights, and in BMI's sole judgment to join Publisher and/or others in whose names the copyrights to any of the works may stand, and to discontinue, compromise or refer to arbitration, any such actions or proceedings or to make any other disposition of the disputes in relation to the works; provided that any action or proceeding commenced by BMI pursuant to the provisions of this paragraph THIRTEENTH shall be at its sole expense and for its sole benefit.

FOURTEENTH:

A. It is acknowledged that BMI has heretofore entered into, and may during the term of this agreement enter into, contracts with performing rights licensing organizations for the licensing of public performing rights controlled by BMI in territories outside of the United States, its territories and possessions (hereinafter called "foreign territories"). Upon Publisher's written request, BMI agrees to permit Publisher to grant performing rights in any or all of the works for any foreign territory for which, at the time such request is received, BMI has not entered into any such contract with a performing rights licensing organization; provided, however, that any such grant of performing rights by Publisher shall terminate at such time when BMI shall have entered into such a contract with a performing rights licensing organization covering such foreign territory and shall have notified Publisher thereof. Nothing herein contained, however, shall be deemed to restrict Publisher from assigning to its foreign publisher or representative the right to collect a part or all of the publishers' performance royalties earned by any or all of the works in any foreign territory as part of an agreement for the publication, exploitation or representation of such works in such territory, whether or not BMI has entered into such a contract with a performing rights licensing organization covering such territory.

B. Publisher agrees to notify BMI promptly in writing in each instance when publication, exploitation or other rights in any or all of the works are granted for any foreign territory. Such notice shall set forth the title of the work, the country or countries involved, the period of such grant, the name of the person, firm, corporation or association entitled to collect performance royalties earned in the foreign territory and the amount of such share. Within ten (10) days after the execution of this agreement Publisher agrees to submit to BMI, in writing, a list of all works as to which Publisher has, prior to the effective date of this agreement, granted to any person, firm, corporation or association performing rights and/or the right to collect publisher performance royalties earned in any foreign territory.

C. In the event that BMI transmits to Publisher performance royalties designated as the writer's share of performance royalties earned by any of the works in any foreign territory, Publisher shall promptly pay such royalties to the writer or writers of the works involved. If Publisher is unable for any reason to locate and make payment to any of the writers involved within six (6) months from the date of receipt, the amounts due such writers shall be returned to BMI.

FIFTEENTH:

A. Publisher agrees that Publisher, its agents, employees, representatives or affiliated companies, will not directly or indirectly during the term of this agreement:

(1) Solicit or accept payment from or on behalf of authors for composing music for lyrics, or from or on behalf of composers for writing lyrics to music.

(2) Solicit or accept manuscripts from composers or authors in consideration of any payments to be made by or on behalf of such composers or authors for reviewing, arranging, promotion, publication, recording or any other services connected with the exploitation of any composition.

(3) Permit Publisher's name, or the fact of its affiliation with BMI, to be used by any other person, firm, corporation or association engaged in any of the practices described in subparagraphs A(1) and A(2) of this paragraph FIFTEENTH.

(4) Submit to BMI, as one of the works to come within this agreement, any musical composition with respect to which any payments described in subparagraphs A(1) and A(2) of this paragraph FIFTEENTH have been made by or on behalf of a composer or author to any person, firm, corporation or association.

B. Publisher agrees that Publisher, its agents, employees or representatives will not directly or indirectly during the term of this agreement make any effort to ascertain from, or offer any inducement or consideration to, anyone, including but not limited to any broadcasting licensee of BMI or to the agents, employees or representatives of BMI or of any such licensee, for information regarding the time or times when any such BMI licensee is to report its performances to BMI, or to attempt in any way to manipulate performances or affect the representative character or accuracy of BMI's system of sampling or logging performances.

C. Publisher agrees to notify BMI promptly in writing (1) of any change of firm name of Publisher, and (2) of any change of twenty percent (20%) or more in the ownership thereof.

D. In the event of the violation of any of the provisions of subparagraphs A, B or C of this paragraph FIFTEENTH, BMI shall have the right, in its sole discretion, to terminate this agreement by giving Publisher at least thirty (30) days' notice by registered or certified mail. In the event of such termination, no payments shall be due to Publisher pursuant to paragraph SEVENTH hereof.

SIXTEENTH: In the event that during the term of this agreement (1) mail addressed to Publisher at the last address furnished by it pursuant to paragraph TWENTIETH hereof shall be returned by the post office, or (2) monies shall not have been earned by Publisher pursuant to paragraph FIFTH hereof for a period of two consecutive years or more, or (3) the proprietor, if Publisher is a sole proprietorship, shall die, BMI shall have the right to terminate this agreement on at least thirty (30) days' notice by registered or certified mail addressed to the last address furnished by Publisher pursuant to paragraph TWENTIETH hereof and, in the case of the death of a sole proprietor, to the representative of said proprietor's estate, if known to BMI. In the event of such termination, no payments shall be due Publisher pursuant to paragraph SEVENTH hereof.

SEVENTEENTH: Publisher acknowledges that the rights obtained by it pursuant to this agreement constitute rights to payment of money and that during the term BMI shall hold absolute title to the performing rights granted to BMI hereunder. In the event that during the term Publisher shall file a petition in bankruptcy, such a petition shall be filed against Publisher, Publisher shall make an assignment for the benefit of creditors, Publisher shall consent to the appointment of a receiver or trustee for all or part of its property, Publisher shall file a petition for corporate reorganization or arrangement under the United States bankruptcy laws, Publisher shall institute or shall have instituted against it any other insolvency proceeding under the United States bankruptcy laws or any other applicable law, or, in the event Publisher is a partnership, all of the general partners of said partnership shall be adjudged bankrupts, BMI shall retain title to the performing rights in all works for which clearance sheets shall have heretofore been submitted to BMI and shall subrogate Publisher's trustee in bankruptcy or receiver and any subsequent purchasers from them to Publisher's right to payment of money for said works in accordance with the terms and conditions of this agreement.

EIGHTEENTH: Any controversy or claim arising out of, or relating to, this agreement or the breach thereof, shall be settled by arbitration in the City of New York, in accordance with the Rules of the American Arbitration Association, and judgment upon the award of the arbitrator may be entered in any court having jurisdiction thereof. Such award shall include the fixing of the expenses of the arbitration, including reasonable attorney's fees, which shall be borne by the unsuccessful party.

NINETEENTH: Publisher agrees that it shall not, without the written consent of BMI, assign any of its rights hereunder. No rights of any kind against BMI will be acquired by the assignee if any such purported assignment is made by Publisher without such written consent.

TWENTIETH: Publisher agrees to notify BMI's Department of Performing Rights Administration promptly in writing of any change in its address. Any notice sent to Publisher pursuant to the terms of this agreement shall be valid if addressed to Publisher at the last address so furnished by Publisher.

TWENTY-FIRST: This agreement cannot be changed orally and shall be governed and construed pursuant to the laws of the State of New York.

TWENTY-SECOND: In the event that any part or parts of this agreement are found to be void by a court of competent jurisdiction, the remaining part or parts shall nevertheless be binding with the same force and effect as if the void part or parts were deleted from this agreement.

IN WITNESS WHEREOF, the parties hereto have caused this agreement to be duly executed as of the day and year first above written.

BROADCAST MUSIC, INC.

By ....
              Assistant Vice President

....

By ....
             (Title of Signer)

5/81

250 ■

FORM PA
UNITED STATES COPYRIGHT OFFICE

REGISTRATION NUMBER

PA   PAU

EFFECTIVE DATE OF REGISTRATION

Month   Day   Year

DO NOT WRITE ABOVE THIS LINE. IF YOU NEED MORE SPACE, USE A SEPARATE CONTINUATION SHEET.

1

TITLE OF THIS WORK ▼

PREVIOUS OR ALTERNATIVE TITLES ▼

NATURE OF THIS WORK ▼ See instructions

2 **a**

NAME OF AUTHOR ▼

DATES OF BIRTH AND DEATH
Year Born ▼   Year Died ▼

Was this contribution to the work a "work made for hire"?
☐ Yes
☐ No

AUTHOR'S NATIONALITY OR DOMICILE
Name of Country
OR { Citizen of ▶_____
Domiciled in ▶_____

WAS THIS AUTHOR'S CONTRIBUTION TO THE WORK
Anonymous? ☐ Yes ☐ No
Pseudonymous? ☐ Yes ☐ No

If the answer to either of these questions is "Yes," see detailed instructions.

NATURE OF AUTHORSHIP Briefly describe nature of the material created by this author in which copyright is claimed. ▼

NOTE

Under the law, the "author" of a "work made for hire" is generally the employer, not the employee (see instructions). For any part of this work that was "made for hire" check "Yes" in the space provided, give the employer (or other person for whom the work was prepared) as "Author" of that part, and leave the space for dates of birth and death blank.

b

NAME OF AUTHOR ▼

DATES OF BIRTH AND DEATH
Year Born ▼   Year Died ▼

Was this contribution to the work a "work made for hire"?
☐ Yes
☐ No

AUTHOR'S NATIONALITY OR DOMICILE
Name of country
OR { Citizen of ▶_____
Domiciled in ▶_____

WAS THIS AUTHOR'S CONTRIBUTION TO THE WORK
Anonymous? ☐ Yes ☐ No
Pseudonymous? ☐ Yes ☐ No

If the answer to either of these questions is "Yes," see detailed instructions.

NATURE OF AUTHORSHIP Briefly describe nature of the material created by this author in which copyright is claimed. ▼

c

NAME OF AUTHOR ▼

DATES OF BIRTH AND DEATH
Year Born ▼   Year Died ▼

Was this contribution to the work a "work made for hire"?
☐ Yes
☐ No

AUTHOR'S NATIONALITY OR DOMICILE
Name of Country
OR { Citizen of ▶_____
Domiciled in ▶_____

WAS THIS AUTHOR'S CONTRIBUTION TO THE WORK
Anonymous? ☐ Yes ☐ No
Pseudonymous? ☐ Yes ☐ No

If the answer to either of these questions is "Yes," see detailed instructions.

NATURE OF AUTHORSHIP Briefly describe nature of the material created by this author in which copyright is claimed. ▼

3

YEAR IN WHICH CREATION OF THIS WORK WAS COMPLETED This information must be given in all cases.
◄ Year

DATE AND NATION OF FIRST PUBLICATION OF THIS PARTICULAR WORK
Complete this information ONLY if this work has been published.
Month ▶_____ Day ▶_____ Year ▶_____
◄ Natio

4

COPYRIGHT CLAIMANT(S) Name and address must be given even if the claimant is the same as the author given in space 2.▼

See instructions before completing this space.

APPLICATION RECEIVED

ONE DEPOSIT RECEIVED

TWO DEPOSITS RECEIVED

REMITTANCE NUMBER AND DATE

DO NOT WRITE HERE
OFFICE USE ONLY

TRANSFER If the claimant(s) named here in space 4 are different from the author(s) named in space 2, give a brief statement of how the claimant(s) obtained ownership of the copyright.▼

MORE ON BACK ▶ • Complete all applicable spaces (numbers 5-9) on the reverse side of this page.
• See detailed instructions.   • Sign the form at line 8.

DO NOT WRITE HERE

Page 1 of_____page

EXAMINED BY

CHECKED BY

CORRESPONDENCE
Yes ☐

DEPOSIT ACCOUNT
FUNDS USED ☐

FORM PA

FOR
COPYRIGHT
OFFICE
USE
ONLY

DO NOT WRITE ABOVE THIS LINE. IF YOU NEED MORE SPACE, USE A SEPARATE CONTINUATION SHEET.

PREVIOUS REGISTRATION Has registration for this work, or for an earlier version of this work, already been made in the Copyright Office?

☐ **Yes** ☐ **No** If your answer is "Yes," why is another registration being sought? (Check appropriate box) ▼

☐ This is the first published edition of a work previously registered in unpublished form.

☐ This is the first application submitted by this author as copyright claimant.

☐ This is a changed version of the work, as shown by space 6 on this application.

If your answer is "Yes," give: **Previous Registration Number** ▼   **Year of Registration** ▼

5

DERIVATIVE WORK OR COMPILATION Complete both space 6a & 6b for a derivative work; complete only 6b for a compilation.

Preexisting Material Identify any preexisting work or works that this work is based on or incorporates. ▼

Material Added to This Work Give a brief, general statement of the material that has been added to this work and in which copyright is claimed. ▼

See instructions
before completing
this space.

6

DEPOSIT ACCOUNT If the registration fee is to be charged to a Deposit Account established in the Copyright Office, give name and number of Account.

Name ▼   **Account Number** ▼

7

CORRESPONDENCE Give name and address to which correspondence about this application should be sent.   Name/Address/Apt/City/State/Zip ▼

Area Code & Telephone Number ▶

Be sure to
give your
daytime phone
◀ number.

CERTIFICATION* I, the undersigned, hereby certify that I am the

Check only one ▼

☐ author

☐ other copyright claimant

☐ owner of exclusive right(s)

☐ authorized agent of _____
Name of author or other copyright claimant, or owner of exclusive right(s) ▲

8

of the work identified in this application and that the statements made
by me in this application are correct to the best of my knowledge.

Typed or printed name and date ▼ If this is a published work, this date must be the same as or later than the date of publication given in space 3.

_____ date ▶ _____

Handwritten signature (X) ▼

**MAIL
CERTIFI-
CATE TO**

Name ▼

Number/Street/Apartment Number ▼

City/State/ZIP ▼

**Certificate
will be
mailed in
window
envelope**

Have you:
● Completed all necessary
  spaces?
● Signed your application in space
  8?
● Enclosed check or money order
  for $10 payable to *Register of
  Copyrights*?
● Enclosed your deposit material
  with the application and fee?

MAIL TO: Register of Copyrights,
Library of Congress, Washington,
D.C. 20559.

9

A&R Person—Artist and repertoire person. He or she helps select songs for company's artists as well as coordinating artists' activities with the label.

ASCAP—American Society of Composers, Authors and Publishers: a performing rights organization.

AF of M—American Federation of Musicians.

A Side—The side of a single record that the record company promotes in hopes it will be a hit.

A/C—A/K/A Adult Contemporary–Basic pop music; the softer side of R&B and Country. Much of the past MOR music would now be considered A/C.

Advance—Money given to a writer or publisher in anticipation of royalties to be paid at a future date.

Album Cut—A song included in an album.

Arranger—A person who takes the original song and adds embellishments to it to compliment the song.

BMI—Broadcast Music, Inc.: a performing rights organization.

B Side—The flip side of the A side.

Bootlegging—The unauthorized selling of records and tapes reproduced from original records.

Bullet—A term used to describe a song that is quickly moving up the charts.

Casting—An evaluation of songs for placement with specific artists.

Catalog—A collection of songs to which a publishing company owns the rights.

Charts—Weekly list of top songs by popularity and sales.

CHR— **Contemporary Hit Radio**-Long term for radio stations that play current hits.

Copyright—The exclusive legal right to the publication and sale of a song.

Copyright Infringment—The use of a copyright or copyrights without adherence to the copyright laws (i.e. the sale of bootleg records or tapes).

Cover Record—A recording of a song after the original recording has been released.

Crossover Record—A record that has appeal in several markets, such as black charts and pop charts. Normally a record that begins receiving enough airplay and sales on one chart (such as black) to justify its gaining airplay and sales on another chart (possibly pop).

Cue Sheets—BMI and ASCAP lists from TV stations of songs used on shows. Also a list of all songs, publishers, writers, time of the use of song and type of use (i.e., visual, vocal, background, etc.) in films.

Demo—A tape or record which can be played to demonstrate a song to a publisher, artist, record company or producer.

Dubs—Demo records made of metal with a coating of oil-based resin for the imbedding of grooves.

Dying Single—A record having reached a peak and now falling.

Engineer—A highly skilled person who operates recording studio equipment during a recording session.

Final Mix—A final combination of music from numerous tracks into 2-track stereo or mono tape.

Folio—A book of assorted sheet music, often a compilation of an artist's songs from an album.

Gold Album—An album whose sales reach half million units as certified by R.I.A.A.

Gold Record—A single record whose sales reach one million units as certified by R.I.A.A.

Label Copy—The information that appears on record labels such as the producer, publishers, writer, correct song title, and artist name.

Lead Sheet—Written music which usually contains the lyric, chords, and melody of a song.

Leader Tape—Tape used to separate songs on a reel; also used at beginning and end of the reel.

Logging—A listing of music played by a radio station to determine performance royalties for the performing rights organizations.

Master—A finished tape recording used to make a plate to press records.

Material—Term used to describe a group of songs.

Mechanical License—A license given to a record company upon release to the public of a recording containing a composition owned or controlled by a copyright holder.

Mechanical Royalty—A per unit payment by a record company to a publisher for the right to reproduce the song mechanically.

Mechanicals—Term used in publishing specifically as "song on a record" but generally as a song reproduced through equipment (mechanical).

Miking—Refers to the connecting or lining up of microphones from instruments to recording console.

Mix—The electronic balancing of many different instruments and voices.

MOR—Middle of the Road: term for easy listening music.

Music Monitors—Employees in performing rights societies who listen to tapes of songs from various radio stations to identify the titles for logging.

Outside Songs—A song recorded by an artist who normally records few if any songs written by writers other than himself or herself.

Overdub—Anything added to a recording, such as a lead guitar or background vocals.

Platinum—A single record or album whose sales reach two million dollars at the manufacturer's level.

Professional Manager—The individual in a publishing company who plays songs from company catalog for producers in hopes of having his/her company's songs recorded.

Producer—A person who is responsible for the selection and recording of a song by an artist.

Program Director—The person who determines the format of a radio station and which records are to be played.

Publishers—Companies active in acquiring, administering, and exploiting songs.

Quiet Storm Format—Easy Listening music of the '80s, usually instrumental, often jazz or jazz flavored.

RIAA—Record Industry Association of America: audits record sales and certifies gold records.

R&B—Rhythm and Blues.

Rate—The "per copy" income paid by record companies to writers and publishers. Sometimes requested to be lower than the statutory income.

Recoup—To take back (i.e., monies that are deducted from royalty income before payment is made to the writer who had received an advance).

Repertoire—List of songs.

Royalties—Legal share of money that artist, writer, publisher, etc., has earned from sale of product.

Screening—Evaluation of material for recording.

Self-Contained Groups—Groups who normally write songs and play and sing at their own recording session.

Session—Term used to describe a period of time spent in recording some material.

Single Face—A dub with a song on only one side.

Spec. Session—The production of a record that is paid for *after* the record is sold to a record company.

Staff Writer—A writer signed exclusively to one publishing company.

Tracks—The different sections of a recording machine in which separate recordings can be made at the same or different times. Most studios have 8, 16, or 48-track machines.

Trade Papers—These are weekly magazines containing information on the music business such as Cashbox and Billboard.

Urban Contemporary—Black radio format.

Wired Music—Systems that provide background music in restaurants, hotels, reception areas of companies, etc. A major system is Musak.